COLUM McCANN AND THE AESTHETICS OF REDEMPTION

COLUM McCANN AND THE AESTHETICS OF REDEMPTION

EÓIN FLANNERY

IRISH ACADEMIC PRESS
DUBLIN • PORTLAND, OR

First published in 2011 by Irish Academic Press

2 Brookside,	920 NE 58th Avenue, Suite 300
Dundrum Road,	Portland, Oregon,
Dublin 14,	97213-3786
Ireland	USA

www.iap.ie

Copyright © 2011 Eóin Flannery

British Library Cataloguing in Publication Data
An entry can be found on request

ISBN 978 0 7165 3049 7 (cloth)
ISBN 978 0 7165 3050 3 (paper)

Library of Congress Cataloging-in-Publication Data
An entry can be found on request

Printed by Antony Rowe Ltd, Chippenham, Wiltshire

Art is an attempt to create a world in which we can live: if not for long or forever, still a world of the imagination over which we can reign, and by reign I mean to reflect purely our situation through this created world of ours, this Medusa's mirror, allowing us to see and to celebrate even the totally intolerable.

John McGahern, 'The Image'

For Ruth and for Derval

Contents

Acknowledgements

In completing this study I would like to acknowledge the help of librarians at the University of Limerick; the National University of Ireland, Galway; Oxford Brookes University; and the Bodleian Library, University of Oxford. I am grateful to Oxford Brookes University for granting me Research Leave to complete this work and to my colleagues in the Department of English and Drama at Oxford Brookes University for facilitating a period of Research Leave also. Acknowledgements are due to *The Irish Review* and *Irish Studies Review* where earlier versions of some of the chapters were published. Thanks are due to Susan Cahill, Michael Griffin, Aaron Kelly, Simon Kovesi, Joseph Lennon, Eamon Maher, and David O'Shaughnessy, who contributed in various ways to the production of the final product. Lisa Hyde, my editor at Irish Academic Press, has been of immense support throughout the writing process.

I am indebted to my family – my parents, John and Mary; and my brothers, Conor and Darragh. In particular, I am deeply thankful for the love and support I have received from my wife, Ruth, and for the inspiration and laughter provided by my daughter, Derval.

Abbreviations

Introduction
Colum McCann and the Aesthetics of Redemption

IRELAND – HOME AND AWAY

At the beginning of the RTÉ Arts Lives documentary, 'Colum McCann – Becoming a New Yorker' (2009), Colum McCann asks, self-consciously, why anyone would want to follow him around with a camera and make a film about his life as a resident of Manhattan's Upper East Side. The newly inaugurated winner of the prestigious National Book Award, 2009, is unsure as to why a permanent and public televisual narrative record, with him as the central topic, would be of interest to a broad audience. Yet, this is only true if we consider McCann's National Book Award triumph as a kind of departure point and if we treat of McCann as a bolting ingénuc to the world of contemporary literary fiction. When, in fact, it is the culmination, thus far, of a virtuoso writing career, which has garnered widespread acclaim, a generous haul of literary prizes, and secured a faculty position on the creative writing programme at CUNY's Hunter College, alongside Peter Carey and Nathan Englander. The weight of McCann's 2009 award cannot be underestimated, given the pedigree of previous recipients such as: Cormac McCarthy, Susan Sontag, Don DeLillo, Philip Roth, E. Annie Proulx, John Barth, and E.L. Doctorow. The National Book Award can be added to a host of achievements by McCann, numbered among which are: the Rooney Prize for Irish Literature (1994), for *Fishing the Sloe-Black River*; two *Sunday Tribune* Hennessy Literary Awards (1995), for his story, 'Tresses'; a Pushcart Prize (1997), for his story 'As Kingfishers Catch Fire'; the Princess Grace Memorial Literary Prize (2000); a nomination in 1995 and a short-listing in 2000 for the IMPAC Dublin Literary Prize for *Songdogs* and *This Side of Brightness* respectively; and in 2003 he was *Esquire*'s 'Writer of the Year'. More recently, McCann has been inducted into the Hennessy Literary Hall of Fame and, in 2009, he became a member of Aosdána and was granted a French *Chevalier des arts et lettres* by the French government. In light of these and other distinctions, McCann's querying of his selection as a subject for an RTÉ Arts Lives feature seems excessively modest.

Winning the National Book Award at the relatively young age of forty-four, then, is a major staging post on a career trajectory that has been international and eclectic and that, perhaps not without coincidence, has its origins in journalism, as well as a family history steeped in writing of all kinds. McCann's father is the well-known Irish journalist and fiction writer, Sean McCann, who was the long-time features editor of the *Evening Press* in Dublin. And despite his father's reservations about pursuing a career in the same field, McCann trained and graduated from the Rathmines School of Journalism between 1982 and 1984. McCann was named 'Young Journalist of the Year' in 1983, during his time at Rathmines, and took this journalistic talent to work as he contributed to a variety of news publications in the years immediately following his education. He worked for various newspapers including: the *Connaught Telegraph* during the summer of 1984, the *Irish Independent* and the *Irish Press* as a freelance, *the Evening Press* as 'youth correspondent' from 1984–1985, and the *Universal Press Syndicate* in New York for six months. And this journalistic output continues, in more global outlets, including: *The New York Times, Paris Match, The Guardian, The Irish Times, Die Zeit*, and *La Repubblica*. But in 1986, McCann returned to the US with the intention of devoting himself to writing literary fiction; as he admitted to Marjorie Kaufman: 'There was a whole enchantment of travelling to America, a wanderlust, with no real intention to stay, but to become a writer. I landed in Boston and got my first job driving a taxi in Cape Cod, bought a typewriter and had the same empty page in it for six months. I had nothing to write about.'[1] A major part of McCann's literary apprenticeship, then, was taken up with locating materials that would animate his future fiction. Having taken eighteen months to travel across forty American states on a bicycle, worked as a wilderness instructor at a youth correctional facility in Texas, and taught English as a Foreign Language in Japan, McCann had accumulated much of the direct inspiration behind his early works.[2] Equally, McCann's concern for ideas such as migration, displacement, the durable currency of private stories, and racial politics resonate in much of the more recent fictions, though based in radically diverse geographies.

While it may seem legitimate to stable McCann's emigrant experience, and that of many of his contemporaries, with previous generations of expatriate Irish artists, such a neat correspondence is limited. In effect, a process of cultural and artistic commuting has largely replaced the qualitative experience of early to mid-twentieth-century artistic exile. That is to say that a writer such as McCann might reside in New York, but he maintains an active participation in Irish social and cultural debate, largely through readings and regular journalistic opinion pieces. In a sense, McCann is a writer in constant flow – his fictions and his other writings are channels through which the mobility of modern Irish identity is trafficked. This is not just a consequence of McCann's biographical history of emigration and migration, but it is also part of 'a new cartography of thought, a new landscape of desires, among the Irish today. Our mental maps are no longer necessarily located in twenty-six and thirty-two counties.'[3] As we have noted, mobility is a constant of Irish political and economic life – whether under duress or by conscious choice. But, perhaps, McCann is alluding to the changing textures of mobility over time: the proliferation of international economic opportunities, the contraction of global spatial and temporal coordinates, the fevered pursuit of multicultural exchanges, and the newly forged, and often disorienting, vectors of movement under postcolonial conditions. Naturally, then, such mobility offers dilated imaginative geographies for the modern writer with which to negotiate the vagaries and tensions of individual identity, and those of his or her communities of departure and those of arrival. McCann's initial foray into literary fiction, the collection of short stories *Fishing the Sloe-Black River*, drew heavily on the author's personal experiences of traversing the North American continent by bicycle.[4] The stories are variously located in Ireland and in the United States, broaching such themes as familial estrangement, regret, emigration, and personal exile – themes that are resurrected in much of McCann's subsequent writing. His fictional works are both reflective of and 'modulated by the physical and literary landscapes'[5] through which McCann has travelled. The impetus towards movement is not just a thematic constant in McCann's literary fictions, but is, he has admitted, an enduring facet of both his personal lifestyle and his *modus operandi* as a writer. McCann underscored this element of both his personal lifestyle and his artistic process early in his writing career in a 1994 interview with *The Irish Times*, admitting that: 'travel is really central to what I do. Travel pushes within me and pushes within these characters. I don't know when, but I suppose I'm going to have to stop and take stock some time soon. But I can't see myself as a writer coming to terms with a single place.'[6] Underlying McCann's novels and short stories, then, is his preoccupation with the historical mobility of successive generations of the Irish population, and the attendant traumas and reliefs of dislocated human interaction.

McCann is seen as a writer who expands and challenges the geographical borders of Irish writing with his eclectic cast list of characters and communities across his fictional narratives. This study will consider the ways in which he navigates and negotiates between Ireland and the international, and between the past and the contemporary – not as a writer who unquestioningly adheres to the liberation of the global, but as one who, following the lines of inspiration drawn from such figures as John Berger and Michael Ondaatje, mediates historical and contemporary moments of cultural and political transaction across borders and between different national/ethnic communities. His attentiveness to the global is never trained on transcending the baggage of the Irish past. He is not a celebrant of unfettered globalization, but is mindful of the traumas, dislocations and disparities that accrue, and have historically accrued, from forms of economic and political globalization. His Irish heritage is a valuable resource in his engagement with the disenfranchized of Irish-American, African-American, and Eastern European histories during the twentieth century. These indicative thematic foci have implications for McCann's 'location' within contemporary Irish fiction. He is not alone in engaging with the Irish emigrant experience in the US, but the manner in which McCann interblends and historicizes the Irish experience with that of other marginal communities provides an insight into a unique ethical and political vision in his work. In combination, McCann's works allow recognizable patterns of Irish historical experience to converse with broader global flows of peripheral peoples, yet what permits them to cohere as ethical rebukes to the indignities of global capital is the creative space of McCann's fictional art. Thus, it is in these ways that his writing re-imagines the possibilities of contemporary Irish fiction; he places Irish history, Irish writing, and Irish culture into productive artistic and ethical dialogue with other marginal cultures. All of the foregoing emphasis on narration and storytelling segues into a discussion of the utopian impulses that are prevalent in McCann's work, and will underscore his belief in the redemptive power of narrative and storytelling as a utopian resource – his stated conviction that stories are the ultimate democracy. In other words, much of McCann's work aggregates form and content in its representation of historically peripheral populations and individuals. He recovers and redeems in furnishing utopian narrative spaces and forms in which these people can articulate their own stories. He is keen to stress the utopian liberation of the creative act as resistance and as agency. In tune with the international thematic sweep of his work, McCann exhibits this broad embrace of international influence in the formal and linguistic features of his fiction. Besides the evidence of the Irish oral tradition, we also note his employment of Roma oral storytelling, the language of ballet dance, and an attention to the cadences of jazz music.

There have been a number of survey and single-author publications within this field in recent years, but none has produced entirely convincing and/or comprehensive perspectives on McCann's fiction. Indicative publications in the survey-mould include: John Wilson Foster (ed.), *The Cambridge Companion to the Irish Novel* (2006); Linden Peach, *The Contemporary Irish Novel* (2004); Rudiger Imhof, *The Modern Irish Novel* (2002); and Liam Harte and Michael Parker (eds), *Contemporary Irish Fiction: Themes, Tropes, Theories* (2000). In addition, recent thematized survey readings of contemporary Irish fiction have not even cited McCann's writings. Elmer Kennedy-Andrews has published a valuable survey of Irish fictions of the Northern Irish 'Troubles' – a topic that McCann has fictionalized. But Kennedy-Andrews' *(De-)constructing the North* (2003) makes no reference to McCann's work. Elsewhere, in her book *The Irish Novel at the End of the Twentieth Century* (2002), Jennifer M. Jeffers makes no reference at all to McCann's fiction. Finally, a range of single-author publications have also appeared which address writers that constitute a 'canon' of Irish prose fiction in the late twentieth century. We have seen studies of John Banville, John McGahern, Edna O'Brien, and William Trevor; it now seems timely to produce an equivalent study of a younger but no less significant writer as McCann.

Joe Cleary offers a neo-Marxist study of modern Irish culture in his book *Outrageous Fortune: Capital and Culture in Modern Ireland* (2006), and he alights upon the topic of Irish literary fiction as part of his analysis. Cleary's focus is principally on what he diagnoses as the 'naturalist' strain in modern Irish fiction, including such writers as: John McGahern, Edna O'Brien, Brian Moore, Seán O'Faoláin, and John Broderick. For Cleary, this tradition is engaged in social and cultural criticism but, crucially, harbours an unrelenting 'scepticism towards all forms of idealism and utopianism'.[7] While these writers are exemplary in their critical stance towards the conservative, repressive elements of Irish society up to the 1980s, in his view they are more interested in 'the awfulness of the actual'[8] than in offering glimpses of subversive hope in the face of such mechanisms of social stagnation. Yet this is as far as Cleary's analysis goes in terms of divining for engagements with the utopian in modern Irish literary fiction. He betrays a critical nostalgia for the energies of Irish modernist literature, but there is no real effort to source utopian impulses, international conscious-ness', or politically progressive voices in contemporary Irish literary fiction. Likewise, the critical and theoretical methodologies employed have largely been confined to issues pertaining to the 'Irish nation', the 'Irish family', Catholic morality, the effects of emigration within Ireland, repression of sexuality, the Northern 'Troubles', and the dispar-ities and tensions of rural life versus urban living. While these thematic foci cannot be gainsaid as relevant prisms through which to read Irish fiction since the 1960s, it seems timely to consider new imaginative thematic horizons of recent Irish prose writing. McCann's work draws on his own biographical experience as an emigrant writer and is concerned with issues such as: contemporary diasporic cultures and communities, the global histories of emigration and diaspora, racial politics in the USA and in Europe, the legacies of the Northern Irish 'Troubles', historical and contemporary global identities, historical injustice and violence, and gender and sexual politics.

As we have stated, McCann is widely considered one of the most accomplished of Ireland's 'international' writers of literary fiction. But the terms on which McCann's work is deemed worthy of celebration are up for debate. Much critical commentary on recent Irish fiction orbits around the dichotomy of the traditional and the modern, on how Irish writers confront and/or overcome the hoary burdens of Irish cultural and social histories. Principal among the imaginative straitjackets is the Irish nation and its facility to dominate cultural discussions and outputs in Ireland in the twentieth century. But McCann, in Eve Patten's view, offers a potential corrective to this trend; for Patten, McCann's 'writing as a whole marks a turning point at which the horizons of literary Irishness are being radically redrawn and expanded'.[9] There is nothing controversial about Patten's argument that McCann's works are remarkable, even pioneering, within his peer group of Irish novelists. His biography and intellectual interests have fostered a body of work that is generously international in its array of characters and narrative contexts. But what are crucial to extrapolate from Patten's contention are the terms on which 'literary Irishness' are being defined. It is important that this not be construed as another 'triumph' for modernity over tradition, for the global over the local, or for the international over the national, because these are not the easy dichotomous terms on which McCann's work and thinking are founded. His renovation of 'literary Irishness' has more to do with an openness to foreign 'others', to a celebration of empathy as a political and cultural force, and to a tendency that permits dialogue between Ireland and the world, the local and the global, and not the supersession of one by the other. Irish histories and locations punctuate McCann's works; they are less dominant in later works than the earlier publications, but nationality is not something that can be readily jettisoned or diminished when we read his work.

In her recent essay, 'Contemporary Irish Fiction and the Transnational Imaginary', Anne Fogarty argues for a more equivocal attitude to the cultural boons of globalization in Ireland. Fogarty's case centres on her conviction that globalization cannot, and should not, be accepted as a cultural given, and that its impacts are entirely open-ended and ripe for mediation and negotiation. Contrary to much political and cultural commentary, Fogarty impresses the enduring relevance of the 'national' as a context that can furnish sites of cultural debate between the local and the global. Fogarty is keen to underscore the fact that many Irish people, writers included, do not view the apparent accruals of globalization as unproblematic. Despite an enthusiastic embrace of the opportunities afforded by globalization within Ireland, and by many Irish artists, this engagement with the global is often a matter of anxious negotiation rather than an abandonment of the anchorage of the local or the national. Ireland's protracted implication in the global flows of people and ideas does not necessarily make us ready-made and unquestioning citizens of the global marketplace. Such embedded historical experiences may also render Irish people all the more alert to and suspicious of the promises and the effects of contemporary globalization. In terms of an Irish literary response to globalization, McCann's novel, *Zoli*, is enumerated among Fogarty's novelistic narratives, together with Roddy Doyle's *The Deportees* and Anne Enright's *The Gathering*. And, in Fogarty's view, these novels 'are cognizant of the impact of globalization on Irish society. They grapple with the effects of such change by probing the ethical responsibilities that this altered milieu brings with it.'[10] Each of these literary interventions, then, is sensitive to the moral questions that accompany accelerated social change in Ireland. In their very different forms and plot-lines, these novels recognize that the relative responsibilities of Irish people and of Irish communities are altered by more concerted implication in contemporary capitalistic globalization. Fogarty continues by suggesting that these novels interrogate 'notions of distance and intimacy, the meaning of locality and…the problematic dimensions of difference', and in so doing, 'they broach many of the ontological problems of global communities as they have been enunciated by recent social theorists…Globalisation in these fictions is less a fait accompli than, as Irigaray says, a shared world which has always still to be elaborated and imagined.'[11]

There are two points to extract from Fogarty's overall argument, which seem to be of acute significance when we broach McCann's oeuvre. First of all, as mentioned, Fogarty underlines 'the ethical responsibilities' adherent to newly globalized topographies of culture, politics, and economics. And in the process she assigns both political and moral responsibilities to the writer. This is not conceived of as a responsibility to pursue a prescribed moral consensus, but, rather, to engage with and to deliberate upon these ethical questions within the literary sphere. Issues such as racial, gendered, class-based inequalities can be enlisted as indicative of the kinds of matters both Fogarty has in mind and that McCann addresses in his writing. Thus, Fogarty's invocation of the ethical in relation to the Irish writer's representations of globalization seems appropriate when we consider the vagaries of McCann's career. He is a writer that navigates between the local and the global, between the national and the international in his work, and he is willing to learn from these combined experiences. McCann is open to assimilating the global in his work, and permits it to illuminate his relationship with the local. In addition, he often diagnoses subtle and keen correspondences between local lives and communities and those that traverse the globe. Yet all along, as Fogarty attests, he cleaves to an egalitarian and inclusive ethics in his aesthetic creations. The second point that seems to resonate with McCann's literary outlook is Fogarty's contention, via Irigaray, that ours is a 'shared world which has always still to be elaborated and imagined'. Certainly there are postmodernist strains within the theoretical animus of Fogarty's concluding point, but of more relevance is the profoundly resistant hopefulness that is implied in its futurity. Such an attachment to process and becoming has deconstructive roots, but, equally, is magnanimous in its ethical tone. One of the key features of McCann's writing is that its expansive range of characters, histories, and geographies are, at least, partly inspired by the author's own appetite for knowledge. In essence, as we outline below, McCann writes towards discovery and knowledge. The breadth of his authorial focus chimes with the kernel of Fogarty's and Irigaray's assertions: part of the response to the ethical responsibilities cited above is precisely to embrace 'otherness'. In other terms, the response is to seek out one's ignorance proactively and to remedy that through aesthetic acts of imaginative empathy. Ultimately, this combination of the theoretical and the aesthetic underwrites the inclusive utopian politics of McCann's entire literary project.

McCann's work has been consistently championed as offering an illuminating corrective to the dark night of literary insularity within recent Irish fiction. Rather than focalize his stories through burdened rural Irish protagonists, who battle daily with the baleful constants of religion, nationalism and the family, McCann's literary foci are lauded as emergent rather than residual; his fictional geographies literally fly by these oppressive topographical nets to embrace the global dimensions of Irish and, more importantly, human experience. Representative of just such commendations for McCann's writing is Dermot Bolger's contention that: 'more than ever it is clear that future editors will not just be turning to the banks of the Liffey, the Lee and the Lagan, but to McCann's "the Thames, the Darling or the Hudson or the Loire or even the Rhine itself" to search out the new heart of Irish writing.'.[12]

The final phrase in Bolger's summation, rather symmetrically, is redolent of Francis Stuart's 1976 essay 'The Soft Centre of Irish Writing', which appeared in *The Irish Times*.[13] But to return to Bolger, it seems as if his intent is to establish a more modernized (but not modernist) and international breed of Irish writing. A genus of writing that dilutes the nationality or national specificity, of both the writing and the writer. Distance, anonymity and foreignness become the privileged terms and conditions of this critical orthodoxy – while the local and the national are now outworn artistic currencies. Yet there is something profoundly misguided about Bolger's ambitions to transcend the dailiness of the national in favour of the modernity of the international, and in a recent essay Derek Hand persuasively contradicts Bolger's co-option of McCann for such a literary programme.

Bolger's appropriation of McCann's writing can be legitimately stabled with the Irish revisionist school of literary critical and historical writing – for Bolger, nothing better will do than to rouse Irish culture from its nostalgic narcosis. As Hand suggests in his rebuttal of Bolger's assessment:

> The implication [of Bolger's argument] is clear: to be able to write about anywhere but Ireland is good, and why? Because, simply, the place of Ireland is itself restrictive and associated with all that is supposedly negative about the Irish past, about Irish history and Irish tradition. The future, therefore, is elsewhere – or, to put it another way, anywhere else but here.[14]

Under such a judgement, Ireland becomes a staunch to genuinely modern creative expression; Bolger, then, articulates a well-stated critical position vis-à-vis national identity: it constricts and distorts the vision of the literary artist with its dependence on the local and on the past. The future lies beyond these restricted horizons, and to embrace the international requires a definitive break with the gravities of the past. And while it is fair to claim that McCann's works document the travails of newly configured and accelerated transnational experiences, to suggest that the Irish dimensions are in some way alien to such debates is plainly incorrect. As many recent postcolonial scholars within Irish cultural studies argue, Ireland's imperial interface with Britain meant that during the eighteenth and nineteenth centuries it experienced a process of modernization without industrialization; in other words,

Ireland was fast-tracked into global modernity without the mediating periods of protracted industrial development and attendant cultural adjustment. Put simply, Ireland has always been implicated in global flows of commodities, people and ideas, and for Bolger to imply that these long and differentiated histories are signs of a deeply insular society are a gross historical injustice.

But equally Bolger's insistence on the added value of the global belies the potential perils of homogenous globalized identities. Forsaking the local for the sake of the global is not an inherently positive step; making a fetish of the global over the local is, potentially, replacing one delimiting cultural economy for another. And finally, such a critical trajectory rather presumptuously and prematurely renders redundant the possibility that Ireland as a national place/space might play some, even fragmentary, role in this freshly hewn global aesthetic market. Again, Hand's response to Bolger is instructive in countering such one-sided argumentation. Rather than portraying McCann's fiction as a body of work that actively strives to escape national entrapment, Hand maintains that: 'McCann's fiction moves easily between boundaries, especially Ireland and America. Yet, his writing still documents the psychic uneasiness of this movement between places. Even his American work possesses traces of Irish concerns, highlighting how difficult it is to shed the past and the places of the past.'[15] The basic point remains that McCann's fictions are thematically mobile and they display an authorial, and biographically-informed, sensitivity to cultural polyphony. This is not some form of postmodern pageantry that revels in relativism, but a body of fiction that acknowledges such diversities in all of their positive and negative impacts and legacies. Contrary to Bolger, one cannot wish away national histories and one's investments in those histories in pursuit of apparently less contestable, progressive presents and futures. Again Hand, at length, firmly locates the Irish experience within historical and contemporary versions of the global, countering the willed historical amnesia of Bolger's argument. As we have seen, Ireland has always played a central role, for instance, in the globalizing Atlantic world and continues to be deeply implicated in all contemporary networks of global communications and cultural exchange. Hand's argument, and that of McCann's fictions, acknowledges these facts but neither sees them as unproblematic causes of celebration. Hand suggests:

He [McCann] realises how the contemporary postmodern world demands people live in new ways. No longer do the certainties of rigid and real boundaries – national, personal or spatial – operate as they once did, as people exist imaginatively in many places simultaneously. Yet, the specific Irish experience – as outlined above – would seem to throw that general experience into sharp relief. The Irish have always resided in a problematic world or space: in terms of physical space within Ireland and in relation to the vexed problem of emigration, of being Irish in Berlin or Boston; in terms of culturally belonging because physically in Berlin or Boston. These difficulties registered also for those left behind in a depopulated Ireland; where space carries traces and echoes of those who have gone away.[16]

THE STORYTELLER

In an op-ed contribution to *The New York Times* on Bloomsday, 16 June 2009, Colum McCann invokes James Joyce, Vladimir Nabokov and his own [McCann's] grandfather as he distils the essence of humanity's narrative impulse. Referencing the Russian modernist, McCann writes:

> Vladimir Nabokov once said that the purpose of storytelling is 'to portray ordinary objects as they will be reflected in the kindly mirrors of future times, to find in the objects around us the fragrant tenderness that only posterity will discern and appreciate in far-off times when every trifle of our plain everyday life will become exquisite and festive in its own right: the times when a man who might put on the most ordinary jacket of today will be dressed up for an elegant masquerade'.[17]

Nabokov's précis cuts to the wick of storytelling – its precious and, often, prophetic fictionality. There is substantive futurity nested within the narrative act; its creative essence is transfused with a progressive orientation. In a sense, there is a muted utopian energy palpable in Nabokov's anticipatory aesthetic. And it is these aesthetic tenets that McCann candidly endorses later in the same article: 'This is the function of books – we learn how to live even if we weren't there. Fiction gives us access to a very real history. Stories are the best democracy we have.

We are allowed to become the other we never dreamed we could be.'[18] McCann's aesthetic and ethical alignment with the tenor of Nabokov's earlier conclusions betray a deeply empathetic artistic vision, and this will be the guiding critical perspective from which his literary fictions will be broached. As the previous authorial quotation elucidates, 'books' are educational spaces in which author and reader convene in differential imaginative solidarities. Storytelling facilitates imaginative access to narratives, lives and geographies beyond the ken of our imme- diate rote of lives and places. For McCann, storytelling is a singular utopian process, and in the art of storytelling one accrues the capacity to imagine and to empathize. These features of literary narrative, then, lend McCann's works distinct political inclinations. Indeed, elsewhere McCann takes the author's fictional interface with the 'other' down to the level of rudimentary techniques of creative writing. In an interview with *Poets & Writers* magazine, McCann was prompted to respond to the idiosyncrasy of his thematic focus in *Dancer*. The selection of Rudolf Nureyev as a subject for a novel struck many critics as an unusual decision, as it apparently strayed from one of the principles of creative writing pedagogy: 'write what you know'. But tersely refuting this principle, McCann responded by offering the counter-principle: 'I've always believed that you [should] write about what you supposedly don't know about, or you write towards what you supposedly don't know. This sounds strange, of course. But in making these imaginative leaps you can sometimes find out what you know, but weren't aware that you knew.'[19] Again there is a discernible futurity inherent to such an authorial process of investigation and production, one that, while directly mechanical in this instance, is fundamentally present in Nabokov's more abstracted ideas on the ethics of storytelling above. There is an affinity between the authorial impulse towards the 'other' as a subject of literature and the egalitarian politics of narration as a democratic space. McCann's *modus operandi* enables an engagement with the unknown, but also with the limits of writing: his decision to enter the unknown is a self-conscious and reflexive act of interrogation with the act of narration *per se*. In combination, we see a deliberate attentiveness to the questions of literary form and content, and a cognizance of their implication in the 'living stream' of cultural and political histories. McCann does not indulge in a breed of literary catholicism merely for its own sake, but is sensitive to the political motivations for and implications of narrative representation. What is equally important to emphasize is that his fictions are not didactic spaces either, and they are not ministering polemics. Whether we approach McCann's narratives that deal with the Northern Irish 'Troubles', the mole people of the New York City subway system, Roma gypsies in Slovakia, or Irish emigrants of the 1980s, the kernel of McCann's authorial intent is that these stories are told and that they deserve to be listened to by others. His works are narrative spaces of grace and redemption, and not didacticism or relativism. Put simply:

> The thing is, we all have a deep need to tell a story – that's the thing. Everybody needs to tell a story, whether it be to your shrink, whether it be to your publisher…that's the vast democracy – the only democracy, in fact, that we have that goes across every geography, every age group…But at heart, everybody wants somebody to talk to and to be listened to. That's the function of literature. This is why we do get charged up about talking about books, because it's somehow how we have our finger on a pulse that's alive.[20]

HOPE AND REDEMPTION

The link between art and ethics is succinctly expressed in his recent collection of literary critical essays, *The Curtain*, by the Franco-Czech novelist, Milan Kundera. In a neo-Aristotelian register, Kundera argues: 'The history of art, because it is the history of values, thus of things we need, is always present, always with us.'[21] Kundera's own fiction is a body of work that preserves an acute sense of itself as art that contradicts the centripetal inclinations of authoritarian power, although without ever becoming artless propaganda. More specifically, Kundera views the longer history of the novelistic tradition as part of a genealogy of aesthetic resistance, what has been termed 'a genre of questioning'.[22] And it is in this spirit of novelistic interrogation, or scepticism, that we should broach the fictions of Colum McCann. Though McCann's emigration provides an easy correspondence with Kundera, the nature of their relative travels, and the content of their fiction, decommissions any prospect of further correspondence along these lines. But both seem to speak to each other on the terms outlined in

Kundera's initial quotation; there is a profound concern with the ethical agency of literary art. Ranged across McCann's fictions, then, are highly affective narratives of displacement, impoverishment, vulnerability, exile, grief and disorientation. Yet in each case McCann encourages us to empathize with his abjected protagonists, and, furthermore, he cleaves to the utopian notion that even in these lives and stories there is the prospect of redemption. The simple act of telling one's story to a willing listener might constitute the redemptive act, but for McCann, there is currency in such acts of simple sharing. And in this way we see a modulation of the ethics of the literary from Kundera's argument to McCann's writing. McCann's sense of the literary is encapsulated in his tribute to one of his foremost literary influences, Benedict Kiely. For McCann, 'The true value of literature is that there's always another story to tell. The work of any writer is concerned with the doings of his fellow men and women with whom he shares some territory, some rage, a little loss and maybe even some faith. He doesn't speak for them, but with them.'[23] This qualitative statement on literature partakes of the ideals of a range of contemporary critics and philosophers in its privileging of the democratic space of narrative and with its empathetic relation to 'fellow men and women'. Empathy and redemption are two of the key words that structure McCann's entire literary project. Literary art is disabused of any transcendent formalist exclusivity in this school of thought, and both literary form and content are freighted with extra-literary responsibility. In this view, the metaphorical structure of literary art enables imaginative empathy and, therefore, facilitates a productive ethical engagement with the literary narrative. Indeed, there is an obvious connection between these sentiments and those articulated by Kundera, again, on the intimacy of art and values across human history. In simple terms, as Richard Kearney states, 'stories make possible the ethical sharing of a common world with others in that they are invariably a mode of *discourse* [original italics].'[24] Stories are shared experiences of real or imagined events, worlds and personalities, but all involve the invocation of the figurative as structural features of emplotment, as well as the interface of two or more people in narrative exchange. For critics from Alasdair MacIntyre to Richard Rorty, and Martha Nussbaum to Wayne C. Booth, stories and narratives are elemental to the formulation and the dissemination of human selfhood and to ethics. For both MacIntyre and Rorty, storytelling is a means of inaugurating communal coherence out of which moral consensus can flourish. In another vein, and of more pressing relevance to our discussion, Nussbaum and Booth promulgate the moral virtue of the novel form and the effectiveness of the reading experience as an ethical encounter. The importance of novels to Nussbaum's ethical criticism is revealed in her contention that 'it is not as economic historians but as readers of novels that we should approach the social choices before us, trying, before our death, to consider our fellow citizens, our fellow human beings, with the wonder and generosity that this imagination promotes.'[25] Revoking the licence of the social sciences, and in the same manoeuvre highlighting the intellectual limits of empirical philosophy, Nussbaum extols the social traction of novelistic readership. In her view, other disciplinary fields lack the imaginative resources to inform ethical understanding. It is only in the form of the novel that we can expose ourselves to the true 'enlightenment ideals of the equality and dignity of all human life'.[26] The critical and imaginative excitations of the novel form on its readership far exceed those of other epistemes, which depend upon the imparting of facts or empirical description. Fiction is figuratively provocative and suggestive, and, thereby, equips readers to think 'otherwise' – a process that enables ethical imagination. The full import of literature's effects on the reader is emphatically condensed by Nussbaum in, somewhat ironically, geometrical terms, and her argument here is a close approximation of McCann's authorial philosophy:

> The point is that in the activity of literary imagining we are led to imagine and describe with greater precision, focusing our attention on each word, feeling each event more keenly…So literature is an extension of life not only horizontally, bringing the reader into contact with events or locations or persons or problems he or she has not otherwise met, but, also, so to speak, vertically, giving the reader experience that is deeper, sharper and more precise than much of what takes place in life.[27]

The ethical focus of McCann's fictions, taken together with their international content, are suggestive of, firstly, the author's critical disposition towards the contemporary world, and, secondly, his concern for the possibility of mutually enriching solidarities across ethnicities and nationalities. Thus in foregrounding the ethics of the literary, the ethical within literature, and in placing Irish fiction in conversation with global thematics, McCann's writing displays a critical utopian inclination. Clearly his fictions cannot be filed with those of the utopian literary tradition that project and imagine alternative and holistic literary worlds, following Thomas More's foundational literary utopia. Nevertheless, there is a level of political and social concern evident across McCann's body of work that betrays a definite critical utopian stance. Furthermore, his commitment to the ethical and 'community-creating' potentials of storytelling and/or shared narrative acts reveal equivalent utopian impulses. In these ways McCann's work belongs to a strand of contemporary utopian consciousness elucidated by Fatima Vieira, which is conceived of as 'the desire for a better life, caused by a feeling of discontentment towards the society one lives in'.[28] There is no doubting that such a desire is present in McCann's work as it narrates micro-dramas of trial, hope and redemption. His work does not offer any macrostructural solution or alternative on a grand utopian scale, rather it tracks the displacement and the possibilities of recovery in scattered local lives and cultural networks. McCann's utopianism might be profitably described as 'a matter of attitude, as a kind of reaction to an undesirable present and an aspiration to overcome all difficulties'.[29] Vieira's explication of this utopian orientation diverges from other historically constituted versions of utopianism, which are theoretically monumentalized in systematic, ideological programmes. Indeed, Vieira's approximation of utopian desire reclaims the agency of utopian critique in the contemporary. What is important in Vieira's argument is that is delegitimates the assertions of critics who deny the valence of utopian thought in critiquing the contemporary economic and political conjuncture. Utopian thought does not naturally equate to systematic teleology or singular definitions of perfect social conditions. Following Vieira's first point, it is justifiable and productive to view utopia as an intellectual and political strategy, not as an insoluble goal or indivisible aspiration. In other words: 'Utopianism is not a blueprint for a "perfect society" but may be better conceptualized as a moment of hope. It undermines dominant understandings of what is possible and opens up new conceptual spaces for imagining and practising possible futures…it is about opening up visions of alternatives rather than closing down on "a" vision.'[30]

Key to understanding utopia is the motive force of desire – desire to imagine and desire to change the present array of social conditions.

Utopia occupies a particular space between life as it is lived and our appetites for something different. In Ruth Levitas' view, 'we learn a lot about the experience of living under any set of conditions by reflecting upon the desires which these conditions generate and yet leave unfulfilled.'[31] It is precisely the space between the generation of and absence of fulfilment of our desires that is tenanted by utopia. But, crucially, utopia is not simply a fantasy to be revelled in, but is 'a vision to be pursued'.[32] Again, it is thinking and imagining 'otherwise' that represents the life force of utopianism. McCann's narratives are, evidently, not programmatic assertions of alternative political worlds, but human desire for change; the imagination of redemption, the anticipation of a better life, and the prospects of solidarity being forged with previously 'othered' communities are all tangible utopian foci of his fictions. In another resonant utopian phrase, there are traces of 'social dreaming' in McCann's works, in his fictions that endorse intercommunal connections and interpersonal commonality in a world that circulates atomization as a daily condition. Out of the 'negativity' of alienation and suffering detailed in McCann's narratives, there are consistent and durable moments of hope and recovery. In Blochian fashion, hope emerges out of despair; the positive is present in the negative. As aesthetic artefacts, McCann's novels embody the utopian agency of art, but, equally, in their content, which frequently labours the role of the artist and the power of the aesthetic, these novels accent the redemptive possibilities of literary creation. These are fictions of journeys, of despondencies, of learning, of hidden memories and histories, of national and global politics, and of inter-ethnic and inter-racial meetings. Each and all of these thematics are implicated in broader questions of ethical deliberation and utopian imagining. The coordination of ethical and utopian trajectories in McCann's fictional works, then, roots his art securely within our titular 'aesthetics of redemption'.

For McCann redemption is not an unrefined event but a journey and a testing process undergone by the individual, and this is apparent across his fictional protagonists. Redemption as a literary theme centres on the possibility of a character reaching a level of triumph subsequent to a measure of earlier failure, and in this respect chimes with the general utopian dynamics of McCann's work. There are obvious theological overtones to any discussion of human redemption, but literature can employ the structural features of redemption to its own effects. Differentiating

the theological from the literary, Daniel Boscaljon contends: 'Literature...looks at the process as being more important than the event', a
point alluded to already.[33] But he adds: 'By seeing suffering as more than
a means to the end of salvation and by being able to explore agents of
redemption other than a divine being, literature – which keeps the form
of the theological construct while altering the content – is able to
explore a variety of ways in which human suffering can be redeemed.'[34]
As will become apparent, McCann travels in a variety of directions in his
portraits of how people can process from suffering to redemption. At
this point, Boscaljon places a premium on the content of the literary as
a redemptive form, but he later alludes to a general formal feature
of literature – the novel in particular – which, appropriately, weds his
argument to that expounded upon by Nussbaum and Kearney. According
to Boscaljon: 'One possibility for redemption...is in the telling
of stories...Storytelling thus opens up the possibility of redeeming
others.'[35] This final point brings us back to McCann's repeatedly stated
preoccupation with the ethical currency of the narrative act.

NOTES

1. Marjorie Kaufman, 'An Author Fishing for Souls of Irish Emigres', *Sunday New York Times* (10 November 1996).
2. For a more detailed biographical sketch of McCann see Joseph Lennon, 'Colum McCann', in Michael R. Molino (ed.), *Dictionary of Literary Biography: Twenty-First-Century British and Irish Novelists* (Farmington Hills MI: Thomson Gale Publishers, 2003), vol. 267, pp.181–91.
3. Colum McCann, 'The International Bastards', p.38. Cited in Eamonn Wall, 'Winds Blowing from a Million Directions', in Charles Fanning (ed.), *New Perspectives on the Irish Diaspora* (Carbondale and Edwardsville, IL: Southern Illinois University Press, 2000), p.281.
4. During this time McCann worked a number of temporary jobs including as a journalist, fence-builder, ranch hand, bicycle mechanic, house painter, ditch digger, and dishwasher.
5. Wall, 'Winds Blowing from a Million Directions', p.282.
6. Luke Clancy, 'Writer and Wanderer: Interview with Colum McCann', *Irish Times* (21 June 1994).
7. Joe Cleary, *Outrageous Fortune: Capital and Culture in Modern Ireland* (Dublin: Field Day Books, 2006), p.134.
8. Ibid.
9. Eve Patten, 'Contemporary Irish Fiction', in John Wilson Foster (ed.), *The Cambridge Companion to the Irish Novel* (Cambridge: Cambridge University Press, 2006), p.273.
10. Anne Fogarty, 'Contemporary Irish Fiction and the Transnational Imaginary', in Eamon Maher (ed.), *Cultural Perspectives on Globalisation and Ireland* (Bern: Peter Lang, 2009), p.147.
11. Fogarty, 'Contemporary Irish Fiction and the Transnational Imaginary', p.147.
12. Dermot Bolger, 'Introduction', in Dermot Bolger (ed.), *The New Picador Book of Contemporary Irish Fiction* (London: Picador, 2000), p.xx.
13. Francis Stuart, 'The Soft Centre of Irish Writing', cited in *Paddy No More* (Nantucket, MA: Longship Press, 1977).
14. Derek Hand, 'Living in a Global World: Making Sense of Place in Colum McCann's This Side of Brightness', in Susan Cahill and Eóin Flannery (eds), *This Side of Brightness: Essays on the Fiction of Colum McCann* (Bern: Peter Lang, 2011).

15. Ibid.
16. Ibid.
17. Colum McCann, 'But Always Meeting Ourselves', *New York Times* (16 June 2009). http://www.nytimes.com/2009/06/16/opinion/16mccann.html.
18. Ibid.
19. Joseph Lennon, 'An Interview with Fiction Writer Colum McCann', *Poets & Writers* (2003).
20. Robert Birnbaum, 'Interview with Colum McCann', *Morning News* (2007). http://www.themorningnews.org/archives/birnbaum_v/colum_mccann.php.
21. Milan Kundera, *The Curtain* (London: Faber, 2007), p.16.
22. Hana Pichova, *The Art of Memory in Exile: Vladimir Nabokov and Milan Kundera* (Carbondale and Edwardsville, IL: Southern Illinois University Press, 2002), p.13.
23. Colum McCann, 'The Heavens be his Bed', *Irish University Review – Special Issue – Benedict Kiely*, 38, 1 (2008), p.66.
24. Richard Kearney, *On Stories* (London: Routledge, 2002), p.150.
25. Martha Nussbaum, 'The Literary Imagination in Public Life', in Jane Adamson, Richard Freadman and David Parker (eds), *Renegotiating Ethics in Literature, Philosophy and Theory* (Cambridge: Cambridge University Press, 1998), p.246.
26. Ibid., p.243.
27. Martha Nussbaum, *Love's Knowledge: Essays on Philosophy and Literature* (Oxford and New York: Oxford University Press, 1990), pp.47–8.
28. Fatima Vieira, 'The Concept of Utopia', in Gregory Claeys (ed.), *The Cambridge Companion to Utopian Literature* (Cambridge: Cambridge University Press, 2010), p.6.
29. Ibid., p.7.
30. Valerie Fournier, 'Utopianism and the Cultivation of Possibilities: Grassroots Movements of Hope', in Martin Parker (ed.), *Utopia and Organization* (Oxford: Blackwell, 2002), p.192.
31. Ruth Levitas, *The Concept of Utopia* (Bern: Peter Lang, 2010), p.9.
32. Ibid., p.1.
33. Daniel Boscaljon, 'Possibilities of Redemption through the Novel', in Andrew Hass, David Jasper and Elisabeth Jay (eds), *The Oxford Handbook of English Literature and Theology* (Oxford: Oxford University Press, 2007), p.761.
34. Ibid.
35. Ibid., p.766.

1

Arrival and Departure: *Fishing the Sloe-Black River* (1994)

'Fishing the Sloe-Black River', the title story of McCann's first published collection, appeared in print a year before the complete volume of stories was published by Phoenix House. The quasi-magic realist narrative was included in an edition in 1993 entitled, *Ireland in Exile: Irish Writers Abroad*, edited by Dermot Bolger. This volume gathered Irish writers, some well known and others relatively obscure at the time, who lived outside of Ireland in London, Tokyo, Cambridge, New York, and elsewhere, and included Emma Donoghue, Harry Clifton, Rosita Boland, Joseph O'Connor, Sara Berkeley, and Greg Delanty, among others. At the time, McCann was teaching English in Japan and, as we shall discuss, 'Fishing the Sloe-Black River' is a story that confronts the experience of Irish emigration from the perspective of those that remain resident in Ireland. The story deals, specifically, with the generation of parents whose children have departed the country. The collection, *Ireland in Exile*, strove to capture, in Bolger's editorial words, 'the experience of a new breed of Irish writer abroad – writers who have frequently turned their back on a country which has long since turned its back on them, but whose work is increasingly a central part of Irish literature'.[1] While Bolger's first clause is sound, the remainder of his assertion is characterized by a generalized temper of bitterness, a feeling that one cannot reconcile with the tones and themes of McCann's writings. There is a melodramatic overstatement to Bolger's contention, one that seems rather delayed in its portrait of the Irish writer who has been evicted from an unhomely homeland. The novelist Joseph O'Connor provides a greater level of subtlety in his introductory remarks to the same volume, when he suggests: 'being an emigrant isn't just an address. You realise that it's actually a way of thinking about Ireland.'[2] O'Connor's point contrasts with Bolger's in its tone, but more importantly in its embrace of multiplicity. Responses to emigration are not universal; motivations for emigration were certainly not uniform in the 1980s, and literary representations of these variegated stories are far from homogenous. But what is resonant in O'Connor's argument is the notion of conjoining Irish emigration with critical thought about one's country of origin and what kinds of implications this process might manifest.

This historical juncture, which saw the publication of *Ireland in Exile* in 1993 and *Fishing the Sloe-Black River* in 1994, also saw the appearance of other publications that sought to deliberate on Irish emigration and/or the Irish diaspora. As representative examples from different discursive fields, we can start with the first newsletter published by *The Irish Diaspora Project* in 1993, with the stated objectives: 'to facilitate improved communications between, on the one hand, the Irish in Ireland and, on the other, the Irish and friends of Ireland throughout the world; to encourage networking among the Irish abroad; and to assist organisations, promoters and individuals in arranging events overseas of Irish interest as well as exchanges with Ireland'.[3] While a year later, in 1994, *The Irish Reporter* issued a special number on the topic of 'Ireland – The Global Nation', which included high-quality critical and historical essays on: the economics of the Irish diaspora; gender and Irish emigration; and criminality and Irish emigration, among several other topics. The aggregation of these four differential but implicated publications situates McCann's volume of short stories within a broader intellectual and popular process of reflection on modern Irish emigration. It suggests the urgency of the matter given the breadth and variety of the media and registers evident in those debates, and it gestures to the historical and theoretical context out of which McCann's early fictions of emigration emanate. Finally, these publications remind us that, following O'Connor's salient point above, there actually was a deal of energy expended upon thinking about Ireland and its emigrant population.

By the early to mid-1980s, Ireland faced the prospect of revisiting the dog days of pre-Lemassian impoverishment. Hamstrung by a national debt that by 1986 stood at IR£22 billion and an unemployment figure that stood at 17 per cent, the entire viability of the Irish nation-state was not beyond question. Testimony to this spiralling economic failure was the high level of emigration among Ireland's young adult population. The country was in the throes of being abandoned by a generation that felt let down, if not actually betrayed, by a political system that operated its economic policies with one eye on party political rivalries. Perhaps one of the more cutting, and precise, summations of the early part of this period was by Desmond Fennell in his 1983 *The State of the Nation: Ireland since the Sixties*. Fennell's portrait is of a country that is deeply disoriented and whose grip on the nature of reality is defined by misapprehension and confusion:

> As we passed through the recession of the '70s and early '80s, with the government borrowing wildly to keep the party going somehow, while unemployment grew weekly and the North rumbled on, people seemed dazed, like sleep-walkers, and were afraid to think. Chatter about unemployment, wages and prices, the bankruptcy of the public finances, political scandals, divorce and abortion, and Northern violence filled the air.[4]

Terence Brown portrays a similarly troubled country during this historical period in his *Ireland: A Social and Cultural History, 1922–2002*. It is revealing that Brown entitles the eleventh chapter of his survey 'The Uncertain 1980s'. 'Uncertainty' reflects, on the one hand, the perilous economic condition of the country, as well as the intermittent political turbulence that destabilized government administrations. But equally, in the context of McCann's early emigrant fictions, 'uncertainty' raises questions about the roots of modern Irish identity in the light of renewed mass flight from the country. The 'uncertainty' initially referred to by Brown is, of course, economic, political and social upheaval, and these provide biographical and literary nourishment to McCann's first formal literary output. Not only does Brown refer to 'The *Uncertain* 1980s [my emphasis]', but his assessment is even more apocalyptic. As the 1980s progressed, Ireland's economic conditions degenerated into what he terms 'a full-blown crisis'.[5] And for many reasons, it is difficult to contradict such a chastening analysis of the decade. On foot of the disastrous government White Paper of 1977, 'National Development, 1977–1980', Ireland entered into an inexorable spiral of indebtedness, which, compounded by two oil crises, had catastrophic effects on the abilities of successive administrations to fund the public sector in the form of welfare support and employment creation. As Brown states: 'By December 1984...[unemployment]...would reach 208,000 which represented 16.4 per cent of the workforce (well ahead of the overall EEC figure of 10.3 per cent).'[6] Of pressing relevance to the narratives of McCann's collection is the resurgence of net emigration from Ireland in the 1980s, a phenomenon that had abated in the 1960s and 1970s since the vast haemorrhaging of the 1950s. From 1988 until 1996 there was net emigration from Ireland, and 1989 saw the emigration of 70,000 people.[7] There was a renewed exportation of young people from across the social classes, as the departures became qualitatively different in motivation from earlier periods of Irish emigration.

FISHING THE SLOE-BLACK RIVER

'In the 1990s and beyond,' according to Heather Ingman, 'the Irish short story showed its readiness to tackle current ideas and topics (gender as performance, retrieving women's history, immigration), as well as a willingness to experiment with language and form and embrace complex, non-linear narratives.'[8] Ingman's survey of the contemporary short story, then, underscores the genre's vitality in dealing with social and cultural insecurity through experimental forms. As we shall discuss further in Chapter 4, there has always been a link struck between the fleeting suggestiveness of the short fictional form and social dislocation in Ireland. And McCann's first collection might well be read in terms of this latter point and, to some extent, in the light of Ingman's attention to urgent social ideas and formal innovation. Short story collections, explicitly or implicitly, create a sense of community between the characters across stories. Not necessarily availing of the leanness of the formal short story cycle, collections can suggest an intimacy across narratives; *Dubliners* is an example of this implied implication. And *Fishing the Sloe-Black River* touches upon this idea at the level of theme; so many of its characters are connected by their common experience of emigration. McCann does not, however, collapse these unique life stories of displacement into each other in the collection. Furthermore, the multiplicity of voices and narratives included in the collection is suggestive of dispersal, a polyphony facilitated by the nature of the form. The short story does not bear the cohesive powers of the social novel, and it is this very lack that McCann exploits in his portraits of several Irish lives touched by emigration and globalization. *Fishing the Sloe-Black River* is a literary meditation on travel and displacement, both within Ireland and from Ireland. The collection is a formal admixture of first-person realism and omniscient magic realism, a confection of approaches that captures the anxieties of its thematic foci. Internal and external exile preoccupy the lives of the volume's protagonists, and the combined stories by McCann the emigrant writer bring into view Theodor Adorno's contention that sanctuary from exile can be sought and found in the process of writing. The composition of narratives surrogates as a homeland for the displaced person. This is not, of course, to collapse exile and emigration as identical phenomena, but Adorno's conjunction of writing and physical distance is suggestive in discussing McCann's first volume of fictions. McCann's subsequent works have also anatomized the personal and communal rites and consequences of physical movement, and the upshots of traversing physical and figurative borders.

McCann opens his debut collection in the first-person in 'Sisters', and provides an arresting lyrical passage that congregates many of the preoccupations of the ensuing narratives.[9] In an idiom that overtly invokes Heaney's *North*, McCann's opening paragraph draws in 'the past', personal and family history, geographical separation and the excavation of memory in brute physical terms, as well as cognitively. Invoking the peaty, tactile repository of the Irish landscape, the passage is an immediate companion to the allusive title of the story. Thus in quick succession the author has shouldered his way into the lyrical as well as the socio-political arenas of Irish literary history: 'I have come to think of our lives as the colours of that place – hers a piece of bog cotton, mine as black as the water found when men slash too deep in the soil with a shovel.'[10] The focalizing protagonist is precise in the attribution of relative moral guilt and innocence, but as of yet the specificity of place, time and gender are withheld from the reader. We can, of course, deduce from the title that the narrator is female, but there is an initial sense that McCann's narrative, indeed aspects of much of the collection, assumes parabolic or even mythic qualities. Yet still further, this opening paragraph combines the lyrical, the physical real and resonances of the mythic/symbolic, and it is this admixture of characteristics that is, perhaps, the singular feature of much of McCann's writing. We are witness to characters, objects and places that assume symbolic, cohesive qualities within a given narrative, yet McCann deftly combines such moments of respite, of faith, of unity with oppressive material experiences of isolation, distance and loneliness.

What is of immediate relevance in the light of the discussion above, however, is the manner in which this debut story oscillates from the past to present, and from Ireland to America – none of which the protagonist can escape definitively. As mentioned, the titular detail is a precise literary historical intertextual allusion to the first story of Joyce's *Dubliners*, and yet the material of the story, ostensibly, deviates quite significantly from its Joycean predecessor. Indeed if we concentrate on McCann's title, it offers a helpful wedge with which to expand our previous discussion on McCann's fictional relationship with the country of his birth. 'Sisters' relates the story of two sisters, Brigid and Sheona, siblings of very different temperaments and behavioural patterns. The younger sister, Sheona, is the narrator and, as the extract above implies, her adolescent and young adult behaviour were largely devoid of any sense of moral reference point. In essence she was sexually promiscuous, and garnered a reputation in her home town in the west of Ireland for her wanton sexual mores. By way of contrast, her older sister lived a consummately ascetic life, eventually assuming religious orders as a nun. Both sisters, then, employ their bodies as relative means of self-expression – sexual liberation on the one hand and moral penitence on the other. Eventually having exhausted Ireland's possibilities, Sheona emigrates further west to San Francisco. Now it would be easy to expect that up to this point McCann is patterning a kind of morality tale that is of a piece with the dichotomous imaginary construed for his work by Bolger. However, Sheona's American experience is no arrival in utopia; in the end, after a brutal rape by police officers she is briefly imprisoned and deported back to Ireland. Thus, McCann's story recedes from the facile construction of a liberatory flight from Ireland with its trammelled imagination to the multifaceted possibilities of a global America. Sheona's exit from America and return to Ireland are violent, degrading and bitter.

And while the story's central narrative is founded on the transatlantic axis between Ireland and America, and the traffic of emigration that has traversed that axis, McCann's narrative makes copious use of deliberate Irish references and Irish place names that are crucial to Irish history. The Irish context in terms of space, time and cultural milieu are repeatedly claimed through the author's narrative attention to detail. While Sheona's libertine ways are described in the following terms:

> A man with a walrus moustache gone grey at the tips took me down to the public lavatories. He was a sailor. He smelled of ropes and disuse and seaport harridans. There were bays and coverts, hillsides and heather in that place. Between a statue of Our Lady and a Celtic cross commemorating the dead of Ireland, my hand made out the shape of a question mark as a farm boy furrowed his way inside me. (*FSBR*, 1–2)

Immediately succeeding, Brigid is portrayed thus:

> My older sister, Brigid, succeeded with a spectacular anorexia. After classes she would sidle off into the bog, to a large rock where nobody could see her, her school sandwiches in her pocket, her Bible in her hand. There she would perch like a raked robin, and bit by bit she would tear up the bread, like a sacrament...the rock had a history – in penal times it had been used as a meeting place for mass. (*FSBR*, 2–3)

McCann erects a clear moral dichotomy from the outset – both sisters adrift in the world, both cleaving to somatic rituals for self definition. They are resolutely absent from each other but, still, it seems, fully cognizant of each other's actions. In other words, while Brigid's votive acts can clearly be viewed as redemptive acts for her promiscuous younger sister, Sheona's physical excess, her sexual indulgence can be read as equivalent acts of redemption for Brigid. The sexual engagements are not just bare moral affronts to Catholic Ireland, but are reversions of Brigid's ascetic physical self-immolation; Sheona's bodily excess is a compensation for the atrophied condition of Brigid's body. These particular intimate moral and physical economies are not exclusively Irish, of course, but do strike of specific relevance and familiarity to twentieth-century Irish theocratic authoritarianism. Perhaps what is equally significant are the cultural coordinates alluded to in McCann's descriptions of the sisters' separate but affiliated rituals.

Sheona recalls her sexual coupling between 'a statue of our Lady and a Celtic cross commemorating the dead of Ireland' (*FSBR*, 2) – her prostrate, sexually active body, firstly, contradicts the virginity of the iconic Catholic matriarch. But, furthermore, the cult of the Virgin Mary was a peculiarly intense vocation in Ireland during the 1950s, which saw the construction of Marian shrines throughout the country's Catholic parishes. Physically and figuratively embedded between two intensely Irish forms of Christian worship, Sheona affronts the universal mores of Catholic piety, and, from this Irish perspective, her specific location increases the voltage of the affront. Caught between symbols of chastity and sacrifice, it seems she is capable of neither. In distinction to the formally sanctioned aesthetic kitsch symbology of Catholicism, Brigid's private space resembles Biblical or Irish monastic ascetic retreats. But, we learn, this rock to which she retreats has a very specific history – it too gleans symbolic value from its past associations and uses. The Mass Rock is a potent symbol of Irish national recalcitrance in the face of English penal legislation designed to reform or dissolve Catholic worship in Ireland. Brigid's actions, then, are historically sensitive yet are not mere historical mimicry. While her ritual is based on the actions of the past, it is very much grounded in the present and towards the future. As we have argued, it is at least partly an act of redemption for her younger sibling and in this way it speaks to the ongoing present moment. Importantly, for Brigid, the Irish past and Irish history are not simply voided nostalgia; her actions are not hollow imitation, but are pregnant with agency in the hope of reforming and saving her wayward sister. The histories of Irish punishment symbolized by the Mass Rock are rendered dynamic in the present and transfused with renewed spiritual vigour by this youthful penitent. It is apparent, then, that both sisters possess historical consciousness; they are both aware of the symbolic currency of the respective contexts in which they pursue their somatic rituals. And what we see in the end is not the consignment of one version of the past to oblivion; McCann does not permit one to trump the other. The fact that Sheona and Brigid are sisters intimates that it is, in reality, very difficult to sever the links between the past and the present. Sheona may strive to achieve some form of severance, a form of release from the calcified mores of the past, but as her older sister demonstrates, these ties are surely too ingrained, too anchored in our 'selves' and in our intimate cultural communities to be jettisoned so readily.

Although the story is related in the present tense by the protagonist, it is essentially a narrative about her reconciliation with the past, with her sister, with her own dissolute adolescence, and with her country of origin. McCann punctuates the narrative with a number of significant Irish cultural, social and historical allusions – as we have discussed, the historical symbolism of Irish Catholicism is one noteworthy example. But there are several others that perform a variety of differential functions within the narrative, both confirming and contesting the national limits of the story. We have seen the explicit Joycean and Heaney invocations that frame and initiate the story respectively, but the literary echoes are not limited to these instances. At different stages Patrick Kavanagh and Brendan Behan are also name-checked. Recalling her dismal job on her return to Ireland via deportation, Sheona remarks: 'The day I received that letter I thought of quitting my secretarial job in a glass tower down by Kavanagh's canals...Days in Dublin were derelict and ordinary. A flat on Appian Way, near enough to Raglan Road, where my own dark hair weaved a snare' (*FSBR*, 10). Sheona's employment of Kavanagh to locate her workplace and her home are far from romantic invocations of Kavanagh's love song or his poetry of attachment to the Grand Canal. Firstly, the rather obvious manner in which Kavanagh is summoned captures Sheona's voice as a character, as it were; it suggests that she is familiar with the popular facets of Kavanagh's canon. Yet for McCann it situates him as an author within the sphere of Irish letters. Invoking Kavanagh is a means of attachment for McCann, but the fleeting reference does not bestow any degree of intimacy or solidity to this link. The use of Kavanagh is an allusive fragment of the history of Irish writing to which McCann, as debut author, stakes a claim and which, *pace* Bolger, he clearly does not disown. The combination of authorial and textual allusions might even be interpreted as the watermarks of McCann's early uncertainty as an Irish writer. In fact, such a view is only corroborated by the further allusion to Behan later, again by Sheona: 'It seems appropriate that there is no room for us in the Chelsea hotel, no more Dylan, no more Behan, nor more Cohen remembering us well' (*FSBR*, 14–15). Joyce, Kavanagh, Behan all represent misfit Irish writers across twentieth-century Irish letters – each spent time living outside Ireland, some were more committed to Irish nationality than others, but they all cohere at the level of being Irish writers for McCann, and in this sense each is a fraction of a larger story that McCann is highly conscious of and indebted to as a creative artist. While 'The Chelsea Hotel... Dylan ...Cohen' are grandstand popular cultural references that shoulder into the Irish consciousness, they are, in fact, global brands of popular cultural chic. And in McCann's view this is not entirely exclusive from the Irish artistic genealogy discussed above.

Granted, then, we can pinpoint Irish affiliations within the story, but what of their connections to the global, the international and/or the modern. If we return to the Kavanagh allusion mentioned above, we are witness to the gradual modernization of Dublin (and by implication, Ireland). In this extract Sheona references the sprouting of 'glass towers' of business and finance as part of Dublin's cityscape; she also mentions the underside of such urban development, and she 'began to notice cranes leapfrogging across the skyline. Dublin was cosmopolitan. A drug addict in a doorway in Leeson Street ferreted in his bowels for a small bag of cocaine' (*FSBR*, 10). The sylvan charm of Kavanagh's poetry belies its infiltration, if not supersession, by the scaffolding and the depravities of urban modernity. Emphatically, Ireland is not an anachronistic, traditional society but is as equally traduced by the architecture, physical and cultural, of modernity as any other First-World country.

This trend to locate his collection within both Irish and international contexts characterizes the self-consciousness of the collection as a whole, yet, equally, this tactic coheres with the presiding thematic cores of displacement, globality, locality, and cultural exchange. McCann's broadly intertextual and allusive style can be adjudged to perform several functions at once: as we have noted, it betrays the self-consciousness of a debut collection of stories; it is part of the sophisticated self-reflexivity of the text as both form and as content; it coalesces with the thematic foci of the range of stories; and it re-asserts McCann's interest in the richness and fecundity of cultural flows across borders and boundaries – flows that do not of necessity, however, extinguish the energies of the local or the national. These intertextual and allusive fragments are stylistic sound bites that imply the larger whole of global interaction and cultural commerce. McCann's style, then, is broadly dialogic – these fragments are assimilated into his stories yet they gesture outward to their external textual, authorial and cultural origins. And, as we shall see, it is a strategy that one can track right across *Fishing the Sloe-Black River*.

As a combined work, *Fishing the Sloe-Black River* is replete with explicit and implicit intertextual allusions, quotations and resonances, to the extent that it has, at times, a fractured, even a derivative, character. In a sense, at various points the collection resembles nothing less than T.S. Eliot's 'heap of broken images' from 'The Wasteland'. Allusions and quotations are, in their own way, bits of broken text and imagery; they are fragments from other texts, broken off bits of an original whole, and, seemingly, taken out of their present context, they are of necessity incomplete. Yet, even if the allusion or the quotation is a broken off piece of another whole text, it does work to suggest that other text. So what we see is an effort to construct a potential connection, a suggestion of *this* text as one of many other texts. In other words, it establishes affinity or linkage, while at the same time accepting difference and separateness. Furthermore, this stylistic feature establishes McCann's 'awareness' of and articulation among a large history of Irish prose and poetic writing, but also positions the collection as a textual intervention in a wider contemporary cultural continuum. It acknowledges the antecedent, established world of Irish writing and lyricism but also the historical gap between those texts and the modern/post-modern texts of post-industrial America and contemporary Ireland. The textual fragments, then, are deployed as partial content in tandem with the 'partial' form of the short story genre. They intimate the passage of history/time – yet they equally stake a claim within a national context too. In the end, it would be incorrect to construe these fragments as imbued with the same degree of deconstructive play as might befit a poststructuralist reading; rather, they intimate the contemporary experience of combined belonging and displacement. Throughout the collection, then, we see particular Irish and international cultural signs and referents jostling for position within the narratives. Indeed, as we have argued, they become central to, if not even part of, the formal architecture of the stories themselves.

'Step We Gaily, On We Go' is set in New Orleans on 9 July 1992, but takes its title from an altogether less urban Scottish folk ballad. So, and not for the only time in the collection, McCann juxtaposes a titular European anterior folk culture with a narrative that is set in the white heat (quite literally in this story) of emigrant, urban America.

These occasions point, of course, to the deliberation engaged in by the author in his efforts to navigate, to mediate and to understand the complexities of the emigrant experiences within Irish America. His titular selection in this case comes from a Scottish wedding song entitled 'Mairi's Wedding', and the line extracted by McCann is originally in the chorus of Hugh Robertson's version. Thus it immediately signals one of the presiding themes of the story – marriage; yet there are numerous other unions, communities and close relationships alluded to in the story, and none, including marriage, bring any degree of individual contentment and respite. What is equally apparent, and what can be further extrapolated, from McCann's lyrical title is the title's symmetry with the remainder of the story – 'Step We Gaily, On We Go' is dense with lyrical extracts and allusions; these quotations, in fact, provide much of the narrative content of the story, and are revealing of the nuances of the elderly and mentally unstable protagonist.

The story borders on the fantastic and it retains a deeply disturbing character when we consider the deviant behaviour of the protagonist, Danny Flaherty. Flaherty is an elderly Irish emigrant living alone in New Orleans, and he has been long abandoned by his wife Juanita. The intervening years have seen him tortured by the memories of her departure, which he cannot entirely come to terms with, and by the lingering memories of his youthful promise as a boxing prize-fighter. We are introduced to the sharp decline in Flaherty's fortunes by McCann's opening description of the working-class tenement in which he resides. And one of the striking features of Flaherty's surroundings is the presence of copious graffiti on the interior spaces of the building. As he descends the staircase he is met with a visual medley of vulgarity, humour and racism in the forms of these guerrilla texts. On the third floor he reads: '*When did the black man learn to walk? Beneath it: When the white man invented the wheelbarrow. Beneath that: Eat shit, honky motherfucker*' (FSBR, 58). Continuing to the second floor he encounters his favourite piece of graffiti: '*Women of the world rise up out of the bed of your oppressors…and go make breakfast*' (FSBR, 59). Still further, he descends to the ground floor: 'through all the words. *Eat the homeless. Johnny X is hung like a horse. Leroy is sprunger than a mofo*' (FSBR, 60).

While graffiti can certainly be read as a form of political assertion or utopian cultural articulation, the artefacts that adorn Flaherty's building are not of this order. Yet at the same time their presence does allow McCann to make a political point: the very presence of the graffiti suggests that Flaherty is living in a relatively disadvantaged complex; the presence of the form and not necessarily the content, then, raises the issue of class within the story. Flaherty is neither an economic success story of Irish emigration nor indeed a personal triumph either – his departure from Lisdoonvarna via Dublin and onto the United States is littered with perceived and actual betrayals, hardships and abandonment. Thus McCann's engagement with the issue of Diaspora (the Irish Diaspora) is further nuanced in 'Step We Gaily, On We Go'. Flaherty is not living among an expatriate Irish community in America; he is not a part of a stable, and perhaps stabilizing, network of Irish or Irish-Americans. Instead, his lot is that of an isolated and impoverished Irish emigrant living in a racially heated tenement and city. In a sense, then, the buoyant lyrical momentum of the title stands in stark contrast to the abjection of the narrative content. Flaherty's citation of graffiti, firstly, underscores his own personal hardship; it permits McCann to delve into the heterogeneity of the Irish emigrant experience; and, thirdly, locates the narrative within a particular kind of American urban milieu. In addition, the plain textuality of these graphic expressions is surely significant when we consider this story's and the collection's broader textual allusiveness. The details of the graffiti may resort to crude racism or sexism, or bawdy humour, devoid of any obvious, serious aesthetic merit, but within the formal mechanics of McCann's collection, these intrusions by a subcultural or popular cultural textual archive do interface with the more orthodox literary references that punctuate the stories. In this way, then, they increase the sense of fragmentation within the text; they are even less cohesive and coherent than the literary allusions, and, likewise, they remain authorially anonymous. They are usually ephemeral, but it is clear that in this case Flaherty is acquainted with at least one of the pieces and favours it. So while the fragmentary contributes to the combined whole, it also always signals its own partial nature – the sub-cultural and the transient text speaks back to the canonical and the culturally endowed text. In each of these ways, and quite explicitly in this story, McCann establishes an intertextual and cross-cultural exchange, all within the context of the working-class Irish emigrant experience in the United States. Flaherty himself is a source of the lyrical and of grace in more ways than one within the story. During his erstwhile career as a prize-fighter, which was, he laments, destined for greatness, his trademark was to sing a song in the ring after each successful bout. Flaherty was the consummate performer with his noted grace and deft boxing acumen added to his renowned singing voice. Yet within the contemporary narrative, both of these personal accomplishments have now become elements of Flaherty's threnody of nostalgia. Firstly, his defeat, in controversial circumstances, in a decisive bout is a persistent source of pained regret, and, secondly, the catalogue of his singing days is evident in the disjointed quotations that pock-mark the central narrative, or in uncertain allusions to songs and their composers. Thus the poise of Flaherty's pugilistic pomp and his lyrical stride are both dissolving, and are only present in their increasing absence.

The crux of the story centres on his unrealized ambition of becoming a boxing champion; it is a failed aspiration that haunts Danny Flaherty. Like many of McCann's stories, 'Step We Gaily, On We Go' is concerned with a painful confrontation with the past, but in Flaherty's case he seems to have become interred in the past and cannot reconcile himself to the strained actuality of the present. The decisive moments, and movements, in his life came when he departed Ireland driven with this overriding conviction that he was destined for greatness. And it is this time of his life that is forever filled with promise in Flaherty's nostalgic narcosis; at one point Flaherty engages in an extended reverie on that lost promise, that still-born utopian moment:

> Those were the days. Indeed. He left for America on the Washington cruiser, swearing to Ireland that he would come home Heavyweight Champion of the World. Days of cowlicks and curls. It was the Great Depression, he remembers, and unemployed men hung around warming their hands over hot barrels on the dockside in Cobh, eating pigeon sandwiches. Some among them had mouths festered from eating nettles. Hard times and, even back then, America was the place to go. Lachrymose young girls sold daffodils so they could buy tickets. Boys stood up high on the back of dung carts, looking out to sea, dreaming. Bilious crowds watched the white of the waves while the ships foghorned a song of exile. Getting on the boat, standing on the deck, he sang *Ireland, I love you, a Chusla Mo Chroi.* (FSBR, 64–5)

Flaherty's departure is again one of high lyrical performance; his exit from Ireland is one loaded with prospects of sporting achievement and financial success. In this sense it is akin to many emigrant departures, a crossing of borders with the possibility of hope. His departure, though apparently materially discrepant from the millions of Irish who made the same journey before and after him, is linked to the realities of those that emigrated because of extreme economic poverty. The historical and geographical contexts of his departure on the Washington cruiser from Cobh gesture to the dire economic circumstances endured during the 1930s across the globe on foot of the Great Depression. While Flaherty's emigration is motored by idealistic dreams of authentic accomplishment, McCann embraces more mundane and traumatic instances of enforced exile in America. And in a sense, the wretched poverty and demoralization alluded to in this extract actually anticipate, implicitly, the disappointed future that awaits Flaherty in the United States. The inflated dreams of Flaherty the young athletic boxer are leavened in this extract by the portraits of Irish desperation for food and/or for escape – little did he realize they were glimpses of poverty that is not confined to Ireland but that can be the emigrant's lot too.

Flaherty's life in the present, then, has signally failed to meet the expectations he harboured on leaving Cobh in the 1930s. And the action of the narrative reveals a character that has, it seems, been deeply psychologically scarred by the ensuing years of failure and bitterness. His once satiated marriage has long since collapsed under the pressure of his private disappointments and he now occupies himself with a ritual that is both criminal and votive at the same time. Flaherty habitually thieves clothes from the local launderette, ostensibly as gifts for his wife Juanita – stolen tokens that concretize his delusion that his wife is still a part of his daily life. On this sweltering day in New Orleans, Flaherty is on his way to the launderette, and on arriving, in mid-song, he wonders: 'What will Juanita like? A flowery skirt? A pink blouse with tassels? Another flowery number like Miss Jackson was wearing? No. What's in order, he thinks, is something that will fit her like the sky fits the earth. That much she least deserves. Today is a very special anniversary – July 9th 1992. Juanita is still as beautiful as ever and she deserves something special' (*FSBR*, 64). As we soon learn, the special anniversary is the date on which Juanita abandoned her marriage to Flaherty, and yet he remains ensnared in a delusional fantasy that his past life persists in the present. His commitment to his former wife is mediated through his symbolic criminal act of devotion, yet there is something undeniably pathetic about his actions. There is also the suggestion that Flaherty's thieving is a perverse form of redemption for him – these clothes act as a kind of salve to his private guilt, his sense that he was responsible for his wife's intense unhappiness and eventual flight. Equally, we learn that he occasionally leaves items of clothing on doorknobs of other apartments in his complex, donating to the poor teenage girls of his neighbourhood. Thus Flaherty becomes a latter-day Robin Hood-type figure, in his own mind, and his donations too act as some form of redemptive absolution for him. His minor acts of robbery and donation actually create a sense of community or solidarity for him, and not only ease his personal guilt but appease the loneliness of his life. The robbery becomes a necessary facet of his life – a curious dependence on criminality to alleviate guilt and isolation.

'Step We Gaily, On We Go' is, as we have seen, a remarkably inter-textual narrative, and, like several of the other stories in the collection, it explicitly anticipates McCann's subsequent novel *Songdogs*. In many ways, then, *Fishing the Sloe-Black River* is an anticipatory collection of stories, a testing ground for McCann of many of the themes, landscapes, character-types and figurations that populate the later novel. And Flaherty's narrative bears striking resemblances to the situation of Michael Lyons, the father, in *Songdogs*. The 'intertextuality', which is clearly only discernible in hindsight, is perhaps, firstly, a signal of McCann's relative youth as an author in maturation. McCann displays an overriding concern with human loneliness and with the coping mechanisms that people develop in such circumstances – and this is a feature of several of his fictional works. He is also preoccupied with the symbolic import of the mechanisms through which people live on and live through parental or marital abandonment or exile. So that on many occasions in McCann's fictions, apparently mundane, material actions or habits or objects assume symbolic or spiritually sustaining capacities. And this seems to be the case in the lives of Danny Flaherty and Michael Lyons, both of whom have been abandoned by their wives. Indeed, at a basic level the intertextual symmetry begins with the fact that both Irishmen were married to Mexican women named

Juanita; both adopt rituals in later life that possess qualitative differences but that seem aimed at common goals. It is arguable, in fact, that both Flaherty and Lyons are culpable for the breakdowns of their respective marriages, and that they spend the intervening years partially atoning for their guilt. As we have seen, Flaherty's redemption is tied to his ritual robbery from the local launderette – petty thievery that assumes life-sustaining significance. In a similar vein, but different register, Lyons devotes himself to a votive ritual of fishing for an elusive prize salmon in his local river. Symbolically, the contemporary river has become polluted and stagnant with the arrival of a modern factory in the area, but Lyons is insistent in his commitment to pursuing the salmon. Lyons is habituated to a necessary consoling fiction that helps to soothe the hurt of the past and the present with the prospect of a redemptive symbolic harvest in the future. While the devotion to a symbolic act unites the two elderly men, not only are the particulars of their actions discrepant, but it seems that while Flaherty remains materially deluded that his wife is still present in his life, Michael Lyons is fully aware that he will never see his wife again. We are never told definitively what might have become of either Flaherty's or Lyons' 'Juanita', but it is suggested that the latter committed suicide in that very river. Both men, then, are blighted by the aggregated burdens of guilt and ignorance in relation to their marital abandonment.

'Stolen Child' is a second story that takes its title from what can be termed a traditional lyrical source: W.B. Yeats' 'The Stolen Child', published in his 1889 volume of poems, *Crossways*. The titular selection again acts as a self-reflexive authorial gesture on McCann's part and can be read in a number of ways. The choice clearly invokes the idea of a national literary and cultural identity; in fact it invokes a specific kind of national characterization associated with the late nineteenth and early twentieth-century Irish Literary Revival. An identity, of course, that Irish culture has variously been trying to eschew, to modify or commercially exploit in subsequent decades. And given the urban setting of this story in New York City, it would seem that McCann is, in some ways, ironizing or critiquing the Yeatsian version of Irish national identity – certainly if we were to follow the logic of Bolger's argument above. Yet it seems equally unlikely that McCann is actually forwarding an explicit critique, but rather he is teasing out the necessary interaction of different strains within national and communal identities within the narrative; in fact, within the narrative we see the appearance of instances of peculiar cultural hybridity. Essentially, 'Stolen Child' is a story about idealism: McCann explores a range of personal and communal visions of idealized identities or patterns of behaviour. Ranging across literary history to morality and personal ambition, and embracing the mythic as well as the materials of recent political history, 'Stolen Child' interrogates the ideals of a raft of characters and communities. And it is in this vein that we should interpret McCann's titular selection of Yeats' poem. Yeats' 'The Stolen Child' is replete with images and sounds that invoke the esoteric aspects of Irish myth, which proved so attractive and useful to Yeats in his contrary view of the empiricism of British urban modernity. This 'traditional' lyricism and the mysticism on which it was founded were, in Yeats' view, the truly progressive and the modern.

What we see, then, from the outset of this story is a direct engagement with idealism – in Yeats' case a species of national cultural utopianism. The titular reference lends itself not to a sceptical or cynical latter-day critique of Yeatsian mythmaking, but suggests a more universal concern with the need for, but also the limits of, idealistic expectations. And McCann captures the tension between hope and disappointment in the opening paragraph; from the connotations of Yeats' verse in the title, McCann swiftly relocates us to early-morning Brooklyn:

> Padraic closes the heavy oak door of the children's home and steps out into the Brooklyn morning light. He looks across the river to where the sun is coming up like a small red tranquiliser, leaving smudges of dirty light on the New York City skyline, galloping in and out of the skyscrapers. He pulls the hood of his coat and steps across the road. In the background he hears one of the boys kicking at the wooden door, a dull rhythmic thud. A young girl screams from the third floor window. In the distance a police siren flares. *Christ*, he thinks, *no day for a wedding*. (FSBR, 95)

This is a highly sensory passage, with a dissonant interplay of light and sound – all of which is overseen by McCann's startling pharmaceutical simile of the early-morning sun. A new day may be breaking but the light is 'dirty' and obscured, while the soundscape of the city is undertoned with violence and trauma. Again the 'stolen child' of the title is thrown into sharp relief as we learn that Padraic, our protagonist, is employed at a home for blind children – children who have been abandoned, or whose parents are incapable of administering their care. Thus McCann pitches his idealistic title against the stark institutional backdrop of the children's home as well as the imagescape and soundscape of the awakening city.

The early-morning description of Brooklyn dispels any sense of imminent hope, and, in fact, might be profitably compared to Whitman's enthused and protracted response to the same milieu in 'Brooklyn Ferry'. And even in this brief, perhaps oblique, cross reference, we are again confronted with a text, and an author, who was at the heart of a version of national and cultural idealism. Whitman's 'Manifest Destiny' constitutes another breed of resolute idealism that is, perhaps, marginal to McCann's story in real contemporary terms, but is a latent presence in the emigrant situation of the protagonist Padraic Keegan. In another way the invocations of Yeats and Whitman by McCann alert us to two different species of national identity – both infused with high levels of utopian idealism – and it allows us to consider the contemporary narrative of an Irish emigrant couple in the US with the hopes envisaged by those respective nations' foremost cultural architects. This triangulation of authorship, then, raises a number of questions: How does the contemporary reflect the aspirations of Yeats and Whitman as cultural visionaries? What forms of idealism persist into the contemporary? Do breeds of historical idealism burden the present? Is there evidence that idealism itself can become a national or personal burden? Can it become oppressive when projected onto the needs and expectations of others? And each of these issues can be profitably mapped within McCann's story. But for the time being it is sufficient to inquire as to where idealism surfaces in the specifics of 'Stolen Child'. Padraic Keegan, our protagonist, is a social worker in the children's home in Brooklyn; he is recently arrived from Ireland with his wife, Orla, and they are a young couple who have set up home in the outskirts of New York, in Brighton Beach. The dramatic tension of the story centres around Padraic's professional and personal relationship with one of the blind children: a black teenage girl named Dana. The bond that develops between Padraic and Dana is immediate on his arrival at the children's home:

She ran up to him, scouring her fingers through his wiry hair, fingering the side of his acne-creviced face, lifting his glasses and trying to touch his eyes...She was sixteen, well into the awkward throes of adolescence, and she wore dresses with patterns of furious flowers flinging themselves around her waist. Her hair was the colour of burnt grass. She had dyed it that way so that it would flare against her black skin. (*FSBR*, 98)

For Padraic it is the unique energy and luminescence of Dana's personality, as well as her latent intelligence, that sparks and maintains his concern for her as a patient and as a friend. They develop an intimate, quasi-paternal relationship, as, for instance, Padraic teaches Dana about the origins of her name: 'The Irish goddess who was believed to have come from North Africa in ancient times. Dana was in charge of a tribe of druids, the Tuatha de Danann, who landed on a fair May morning and conquered the country by ousting the Firbolgs, the men with the paunchy stomachs' (99). What we see, then, in this example is a strategic utilization of Irish myth by Padraic for his professional purposes – we witness the mobilization of the mythic/traditional to modern medicinal ends. Of course, his employment of ancient Irish myth recalls Yeats' work, particularly in the early stages of his career, and simultaneously summons up a particular strain of Irish national identity. But what we see is the accommodation of a peculiar suite of national myths with the demands of the modern; McCann shows us the productive interaction of the archaic local with the alien international. In a sense, the professional idealism of the young emigrant social worker, confronted with an acutely tragic case, meets the esoteric cultural national idealism of the Yeatsian variety.

As his professional treatment of Dana continues, Padraic develops a personal investment in the teenage girl, especially when she finds an older boyfriend, Will, on one of her walks outside the confines of the home. This is the point at which Padraic's professional idealism mutates into an unhealthy personal idealism, that in a way becomes autocratic, however grounded his reservations about this burgeoning relationship may appear. Padraic's transition from professional to intense personal investment in Dana is initiated by her blossoming relationship with the older Vietnam veteran. She 'met Will in the park. He sat in his wheelchair, wearing a long roll of grey beard that went down to his stomach as if growing it to cover the place where he had no legs. He was more than twice her age. Paperback books about Vietnam curled dog-eared in his overcoat pockets' (*FSBR*, 103). Dana's relationship with Will is, initially, clandestine and this ignorance allows Padraic to continue his tutelage and professional commitments to Dana. And through his dedication to her case, Padraic provides Dana with copious intellectual education to the extent that he harbours the ambition that she may achieve a scholarship to Art College. But it is the intrusion of this destitute and disabled war veteran that tests, and it seems, irreparably breaks Padraic's expectations for Dana. The fervent idealism of the young health professional founders on the arrival of Will, himself a victim of another form of misguided political idealism. This episode, which closes the narrative with Will and Dana's wedding, dramatizes another instance in the story in which two differential forms of idealism cross paths. Again, Padraic's professional idealism, so successful and keen in the first half of the narrative, encounters Will's defeated and deformed frame, which represents the detritus of the idealistic contest conducted in the crucible of Vietnam. The hollow idealism that infuses war-time rhetoric returns to haunt the professional and personal idealism of Padraic Keegan. And yet, we could argue that Padraic is simply exhibiting gross self interest in his prescriptive treatment of Dana and her future; he is accruing benefit from the reflected glory of Dana's overachievement. It is here, then, that his didactic idealism, centred on her intellectual attainments, is trumped and frustrated by her perhaps naïve, but apparently genuine, pursuit of emotional sustenance. Perhaps her romantic idealism is unrealistic or ill-judged, as Padraic maintains, but is it any less legitimate than his urge to exert a different form of control over her? What we see in 'Stolen Child' is McCann's non-judgemental and lyrically rendered exploration of an international blend of communal and individual, intellectual and emotional forms of idealism – some of which enable levels of self-confidence and self-liberation and others that eventually accrue oppressive characteristics.

In both 'Sisters' and 'Stolen Child', as well as in a less successful story, 'Through the Field', McCann chooses an institutional setting as the central or partial context for his narrative. In each of these stories we are confronted with a second-hand, yet equally intimate, portrait of a damaged individual confined to a corrective institutional space. In 'Sisters', we are not certain if Brigid will recover, or indeed if she has the will, desire or capacity to regain her full physical and mental health. In 'Stolen Child', Padraic takes his beloved patient, Dana, as far as he can to rehabilitation – despite his paternalistic frustrations at the limits imposed on his efficacy. But the most extended treatment of the internal dynamics of a secure institution for the mentally infirm is the longest story in the collection, 'Around the Bend and Back Again', a title that captures the maniacal unreason and delusion of much of the narrative. Numbered among the story's concerns are, obviously, its Irish institutional context, but equally given its first-person narration, the story's focalization raises issues such as fantasy, naïveté, sexual exploitation, language and reason, and the psychological pressures of social entrapment in a frustrated and frustrating rural Irish town.

Perhaps the most distinctive feature of this story actually returns us to the idea of intertextuality – but in the case of 'Around the Bend and Back Again' we are exposed to a layered intertextual effect. The range of explicit cross-cultural references veers from the high cultural such as Sean O'Casey, Edna O'Brien, the Bible, and Shakespeare to a mass of popular cultural references including Hollywood in the shape of Steve McQueen, the 1988 Michael Keaton film *Beetlejuice*, the Wild West genre, and the Daniel Day Lewis vehicle *Last of the Mohicans*. Adjacent to these international indices of popular culture, the narrative references more parochial Irish icons, including Paul McGrath, Johnny Logan, Chris de Burgh, and The Sawdoctors. The frequency and range of international and Irish cultural allusion gives the narrative a decidedly fractured form, and an almost manic energy; the narrator is constantly referring beyond the text to other cultural referents for comparison or legitimacy. His mind is a maelstrom of popular culture and in a sense it becomes one of the principal ways in which he mediates his sense of reality. These cultural reference points saturate his consciousness and provide solid coordinates on which to found his frustrated personal identity. He becomes a second-hand composite of his cultural accumulations. Yet from a meta-critical perspective, this is precisely the point at which we can divine that second layer of McCann's intertextual effect. The intertextual references combine in their apparent disparity and randomness, and point us to one text to which this one story seems irrevocably linked. The narrative voice, the geographical setting, and the thematic content

align this story with Patrick McCabe's *The Butcher Boy*.[11] The consonance between these two narratives is solidified precisely by the
inventory of cultural references – they are wedded at the levels of
content and form through this employment of cultural allusion.

The action of McCann's story unfolds, primarily, within the
confines of an asylum in Castlebar in County Mayo, where our narrator and protagonist is a cleaner. From the outset, we gather that he has
become infatuated with one of the female in-patients, a young woman
whose parents were both recently killed in a car crash. The girl has
an enigmatic family background, and the fact that they resided in a
disused but renovated rail-car singled them out within the local
community. Nevertheless, our narrator is intrigued and gradually
becomes emotionally involved with the girl, and her plan to re-visit
her erstwhile home, if they can engineer a temporary escape from the
asylum. As we have said, the evidence of the narrator's infatuation
with her is immediate:

> Strange bloody cuckoo, that one. Couple of rhododendrons
> hanging in her hair. Chewing on her fingernails like she's starv-
> ing. Spent yesterday afternoon circling one of the puddles out by
> the greenhouse, just walking round and round like there's no
> tomorrow...But she's not half bad all the same. Dressing gown
> giving a bit of a peep there, right down to the brown of the
> nipple. (*FSBR*, 117)

Her inscrutable, feminine beauty charges the narrator's frustrated
sexual urges, and the description emphasizes the intellectual and
sexual adolescence of this character. McCann, then, sketches a narrator
who is, firstly, palpably immature, even naïve – yet this opening admir-
ing description is not consistently repeated through the course of the
story. What we also get, through his opinions and descriptions of
'Ofeelia' is an insight into his uneven temperament – a glimpse of his
immature volatility. So while the opening portrait of 'Ofeelia' is relatively positive, subsequent reports vary: 'And she's a wild one too. Had
to grab a hold of her feet when they brought her here. Strong as an ox.
Wonder Woman how are ya' (*FSBR*, 120); 'Two weeks now she's been
here and she's awful nice. I don't think she's as mad as half the bloody
people in the country' (*FSBR*, 129); to 'Another fucking delay. It was
pissing rain tonight. Ofeelia went barmy with the sugar. Christ that

girl's definitely off her rocker' (*FSBR*, 136); and finally, 'Christ, I'm thinking, she's off her rocker and beyond, Doctor Garlic should have kept her in solitary' (*FSBR*, 142). The danger that 'Ofeelia' represents and the relative immaturity of the narrator's sexual experience combine as he is unable to fashion a clear or distinct judgement on the female object of his adolescent desire. And this incapacity to exercise a definitive judgement is not only a signal of his intellectual limitations and emotional youth, but carries through to other areas of his engagement with his colleagues and friends. As a starting point, the narrative's formal presentation is not uniform; rather it appears as an episodic reportage of the narrator's shifts at the asylum. The discrete entries are fitful and discrepant in their relative lengths and in the focus of the information furnished. Thus the story is rendered as a subjective account of this narrator's fevered emotions and actions – a tactic which intensifies the volatility of the narrative content and of our sense of the protagonist's mindset. Equally, in his dealings with other peripheral characters in the story, or in his interior reflections on these characters, the narrator revels in bawdy humour, vulgarity and, often, violent rage towards these colleagues. There is an uncensored directness to the narrative voice, an unguarded innocence that nevertheless pulses with seething frustration and disoriented passion – all of which adds to the tenor of the piece as a form of personal confession. The unselfconscious immediacy of the storytelling at the same time revisits the linguistic and emotional intensity of McCabe's Francie Brady. Yet, Francie Brady's influence is equally palpable in our narrator's insistence that the abject present in which he is mired is temporary; that a potential future of hope and happiness is eminently possible. These dreams of escape from his menial employment in the asylum are paired with those of his colleague Barney; typical of these aspirations, he resolves that: 'One of these days me and Barney are going to get new jobs. No doubt about it. We'll be up there with the mining boys wearing three-piece suits and colourful ties and the doctors at the bin can lick the piss off the floors themselves' (*FSBR*, 124). Born out of a withering social immobility and dislocation, these banal yet seismic dreams recall Francie's recurring plans for future familial happiness and renewed friendship with Joe in *The Butcher Boy*. Moments such as these are signs of sustaining hope for the narrator, but perhaps what is most tragic is the tone of innocent sincerity that infuses his fantastical everyday dreams.

'A Basket Full of Wallpaper' is a reflective narrative, relayed in the past tense by our first-person narrator and protagonist, Sean Donnelly. In many respects the story is a fragment of a coming-of-age narrative; it recounts one memorable summer that Sean spent apprenticed to a Japanese emigrant, who specialized in wallpaper decoration. Sean narrates his story from his present situation: as an Irish emigrant living in London, a fact that we do not uncover until the conclusion of the story. Sean and Osobe, the Japanese wallpaper merchant, are finally united at the end of the story – joined by their shared, and for a time co-terminous, experiences of distance from their homelands. But the majority of the narrative focuses upon the reception and gradual acceptance of Osobe and his curious ways by Sean, and by the larger body of his local Irish community. In locating a Japanese migrant at the dramatic core of 'A Basket Full of Wallpaper', McCann, in fact, continues the trend of the two preceding stories, in which we get variations on the theme of the development and the course of international relationships. But, perhaps most explicitly, by placing Osobe the exile at the centre of his narrative and locating him geographically in a small town in Ireland, McCann suggests that exile is not exclusively felt by those who actually depart the island. As we shall see in the next, and titular, story, 'Fishing the Sloe-Black River', McCann is also concerned with the effects of emigration on those that remain behind in Ireland. They are not immune from the traumas (or benefits) of emigration and they are equally beholden to the vertiginous networks of global movement of people and capital as those that emigrate. Osobe, then, can be read as a literal figure of exile, a man whose past is unclear but whose present is defined by his distance from home and his cultural distance from those he now dwells among. But we can just as easily read Osobe as a figurative or symbolic character; he represents the universal experience of exile – and he also stands in for the history of Irish emigration. From this figurative perspective, Osobe is the ever-presence of history in Ireland; he is the inescapable history of emigration that constitutes the Irish diaspora in the present. Equally he is the storehouse of narratives and micro-histories that animate the genealogies of Ireland's emigrant pedigree.

One of the most striking features of 'A Basket Full of Wallpaper' is that narrative itself is one of the primary thematic strands in the story. As we see elsewhere in the collection, McCann has authored a suite of stories that reach high levels of authorial and narrative self-consciousness, and this story is no different. Osobe's ambiguous past is, naturally, the catalyst and the justification for a wild economy of rumour and gossip. His personal diffidence on the topic, of course, is adequate nourishment for the imaginative and the preposterously groundless to thrive: 'Some people said that he'd been a chicken-sexer during the forties, a pale and narrow man who had spent his days interned in a camp for the Japanese near the mountains of Idaho. Endless months spent determining whether chickens were male or female. He had come to Ireland to forget it all' (*FSBR*, 37). Osobe's alleged incarcerated past obviously refers to the Second World War, and this lends him a degree of further exoticism, supplementing his difference with an additional layer of past and potential menace. The scope of rumours about his origins and his prior actions are differentiated across divergent groups in the local community. So that: 'the older men, elbows on the bar counter, invented heinous crimes for him. In Japan, they said, he had attached electrical cords to the testicles of airmen, ritually sliced prisoners with swords, operated slow drip torture on young Marines' (*FSBR*, 37). While in another crucible of rumour, 'even the women created a fantastic history for him. He was fourth son of an emperor, or a poet, or a general, carrying baggage of unrequited love' (*FSBR*, 37). And finally, to the narrator's peer-group: 'To us boys at school he was a kamikaze pilot who had gotten cold feet, barrelling out in a parachute and somehow drifting to our town, carried by some ferocious, magical wave' (*FSBR*, 37). Implicit in each of these speculations on Osobe is a degree of exoticization; one might even suggest orientalizing racial profiling. To these rumour-mongers, Osobe is the accumulation of cultural stereotypes that have, historically, been traded in the West about Japan. The narrator and his neighbours merely default to accepted, but no less damaging and insular, clichés about the Japanese settler. A further commonality to each of these speculative narratives is that each searches for a root cause as to why a Japanese man would wash up on Irish shores; precisely what is the reason for his presence in Ireland and his absence from Japan? These narratives, then, try to give a form to Osobe and to his past; he does not belong to the collective memories that constitute this local community, and, consequently, narratives of his past are invented and fabricated out of necessity. This is done in order to appease the minatory sense of cultural difference that he imports into the locale. The community cannot tolerate silence about his past, so they step in to speak for him so as to alleviate the disconcerting ambiguity of this silence. The community's urge to 'narrate' the stranger is the obvious point of narrative self-reflection. So while the story's explicit self-consciousness is made manifest, in one respect, in the plethora of narratives invented to explain and to domesticate Osobe, what we actually witness is a community in the throes of re-inventing itself in order to accommodate the presence of this exotic outsider. Despite the overt parochialism of some of the default stereotypes employed, one might suggest that this community does prove itself flexible in its imaginative embrace of the Japanese exile. McCann dramatizes a process of cultural negotiation, wherein national identities are not forsaken or diluted; respective pasts are not abandoned but re-imagined in contemporary moments of encountering the 'other'.

In emphasizing the centrality of McCann's focus on cultural flexi-bility and exchange, this narrative is not confined to detailing how the local community responds to Osobe's presence. It is here that the adolescent experiences of Sean Donnelly are utilized as further self-conscious reflections on the nature and the functions of narrative at the level of the personal, but with implications for the macro-structural in terms of the communal or the national. The narrator's adolescence coincides with a period of economic hardship in Ireland; and he recalls, in blackly humorous fashion, that: 'my father would moan at the dinner table about the huge toll that emigration was hav-ing on his undertaking business. "Everyone's gone somewhere else to die," he'd say' (*FSBR*, 40). In the shadow of these social conditions his mother encourages Sean to seek out work with Osobe, a prompt which initiates a quixotic but enduring emotional attachment between the pair. The proximity that working with Osobe affords the narrator lends him a degree of authority on the Japanese man's character, his origins, and his enigmatic ways. And this is an advantage that is recognized and yearned for by the teenager, as he wills Osobe to have a past worthy of the rumours that have congealed around him over time: '…I wanted Osobe to tell me a fabulous story about his past. I suppose I wanted to own something of him, to make his history belong to me' (*FSBR*, 42). But Sean's appropriative narrative urge is continu-ally frustrated by Osobe's reticence – Osobe never divulges arresting

details about his homeland or the motives that occasioned his departure, nor does he mention Hiroshima (an obvious cause of his flight?).
Indeed the appetite for dramatic revelations such as those demanded
of Osobe is a signal of the narrow horizon of the Irish townland in
which the narrator resides; equally it borrows from the narrative
frames of American cinema, to which the narrator is likely to have
been exposed. But Sean's queries and imaginative speculations also
evidence the seedlings of his imaginative, and eventually physical,
desire to experience the foreign, and to live and to think beyond his
homeland. In other words, one cannot disaggregate the local and the
international – they are always already implicated in each other – they
are never mutually exclusive in the same way that the past and the
present are never quarantined from each other. Sean exhibits a desire
to take Osobe out of the ordinary mill of life in his hometown; to
remove Osobe from the grimness of historical banality and to create a
figure who is elusive, fantastic and heroic, and who truly symbolizes
the idea of escape. In a sense, Osobe must act as a screen onto which
Sean projects his own fantasies of tragedy in Osobe's past life and
future flight in his own life.

Working with Osobe, then, does not further the apparent 'factual'
store of information about the Japanese emigrant for the narrator or
for his community. But the financial gain grants Sean a degree of
independence that coincides with his first steps into adolescent behaviour such as smoking and drinking illicitly with his peers in a remote
location 'under the bridge' (*FSBR*, 44). In addition to this slightly
rebellious behaviour, the fact that the location is removed from the
public spaces of the town is made even more significant by the fact
that on these clandestine evenings with his friends, Sean begins to
regale them with stories about his Japanese employer. 'Under the
bridge', then – a transitional space – becomes a site of initiation and
imagination for Sean and his teenage peers. He assumes the privileged
role of creator or author of Osobe's past. Recalling the dynamics of the
Irish oral storytelling tradition, the already exotic (and exoticized)
stranger and foreigner is further tethered to this function within the
community by Sean's narrative accounts:

> I read books about World War Two and created fabulous lies
> about how he had been in that southern Japanese city when the
> bomb had been dropped, how his family had been left as shadows

on the Town Hall, all of them vaporised, disappeared...He had never found his family. They were scattered around the centre, dark patches of people left on broken concrete. He reeled away from the pain of it all, travelling the world, ending up eventually in the West of Ireland. (*FSBR*, 45)

Osobe is figured as a tragic, vagrant hero, a wandering exile whose familial roots have been scorched irreparably. He carries a dark and insuperable burden of grief with him across the globe, as he bears the weight of a tragic political history. Yet just as in Sean's version of his life here, in which his family are rendered as 'shadows', Osobe assumes this kind of quality in the Irish town itself. It is as if part of Osobe has been vaporized in the eyes of the local community – he is elusive, intangible and ghostly. There is symmetry, then, to Sean's imaginative account linking Osobe to the devastation of Hiroshima and Osobe's existence in the west of Ireland. And Sean's commitment to framing Osobe's life-story in terms of historical tragedy comes to dominate his storytelling sessions with his friends: 'Every evening I continued with Osobe stories for them, their faces lit up by a small fire we kept going. We all nodded and slurped at bottles, fascinated by the horror and brilliance of it all' (*FSBR*, 46). The younger, next generation of the town commune in a primitive fashion to hear Sean author, and authorize, the consented to version of Osobe. At these evening meetings there is an admixture of innocence, curiosity, and a desire for the exotic, all of which are nourished and exploited by Sean's narration: 'Fireballs had raged throughout the city as he fled, I told them. People ran with sacks of rice in their melted hands. A Shinto monk said prayers over the dead. Strange weeds grew in places where the plum trees once flowered and Osobe wandered away from the city, half-naked, his throat and eyes burning' (*FSBR*, 46). Osobe's past and that of his country are patently alien to these young listeners, and yet Sean's narration of this exotic actually serves to accommodate Osobe within the local Irish community. He may be portrayed as the 'other', but the establishment of narrative, the articulation of a narrative, offers a degree of anchorage to the Japanese emigrant – he is made knowable and is produced from within the community at the level of narrative.

Despite his willingness to expound upon the tragic intimacies of Osobe's personal history to his friends, Sean is aware, privately, that Osobe is not the personality that he constructs on a nightly basis under the bridge. Osobe's silence, and Sean's particular proximity to that silence, as they work together from day to day over the summer months foments an intense feeling of anger in Sean. Osobe's reticence at such close quarters and with such regularity only serves to repel Sean: 'For a moment I felt a vicious hatred for him and his quiet ways, his mundane stroll through summer, his ordinariness, the banality of everything he had become for me. He should have been a hero, or a seer. He should have told me some incredible story that I could carry with me forever' (*FSBR*, 47). McCann juxtaposes this private admission by Sean with the previously cited examples of his storytelling fictions on Osobe's past for a specific reason. While Sean fulfils the expectations of his peer group – he allows them the facility of viewing history as exotic, as nostalgic, as heroic and as thrilling – he is not afforded the same by Osobe. Osobe may not reveal the mysteries of his Oriental past to Sean, but he does help the young man to realize that history and histories – personal and communal – are not always heroic or monumental. Osobe's example: the likelihood that his arrival in Ireland was occasioned not by the stories that attach themselves to him but by altogether more banal and human reasons. The histories of diaspora and emigration, in McCann's terms – and this is the acute point that Sean eventually learns – are overpopulated with narratives of banality and ordinariness rather than alluring and enigmatic strangers. They are histories of hardship, isolation and distance; Osobe becomes an historical symbol within the story and the collection of the unadorned commonplaceness of emigration and its historical subjects.

'A Basket Full of Wallpaper' is an Irish emigrant's reminiscence on one summer of adolescence, recalling the impact an ambiguous stranger had on a small Irish town. The end of the story moves us briskly forward in time, and demonstrates the symmetry between Osobe's and Sean's lives as emigrants. At this juncture we learn that Osobe died a number of years subsequent to Sean's emigration, and that the healthy circuit of speculation about his origins did not cease with his passing. Sean receives a letter from his father, relating the latest wave of emigration, but, more importantly, the details of Osobe's death and burial. As is often the case, it is only with their absence that an individual's centrality to or impact upon a community is fully appreciated, and Osobe is no different. Just as he animated a communal network of rumour and gossip during his life, his death is met with expressions and gestures of genuine sympathy and generosity, as well as widespread agreement that his roots were, after all, to be found in the tragedy of Hiroshima. And in the same way in which his family had been vaporized by the nuclear bomb, Osobe's death reveals nothing that might confirm or contradict the town's versions of his life. It is as if, in the end, he too disappeared without any physical trace remaining: 'There had been no clue in the house, no letters, no medical papers, nothing to indicate that he had come from that most horrific of our century's moments' (*FSBR*, 50). There may have been no documentary or factual explanation of Osobe's history, but this is no obstacle to the demands of communal memory. Ultimately, Osobe represents a triumph of imaginative memory and authorship over factual recollection and narration. His life in the town, its scripting by his neighbours, problematizes the bases of individual and communal memory and highlights the contingency of historical authorship. Yet out of this apparent fragmentation, a culture of communal identity emerges; Osobe is the exotic 'other' of this locale, who is domesticated to a degree by rumour, but always remains aloof from the privacies of his 'creation' among the townspeople.

'Fishing the Sloe-Black River', the title story, is one of two in the collection that assumes magic realist qualities – the other is 'Cathal's Lake', dealt with below in Chapter 4. The narrative is brief yet highly effective as it captures the after-effects of emigration on a 'small Westmeath town' (*FSBR*, 53). Quite simply, it describes the mothers of the town casting their fishing rods into the local river as they fish for their emigrated sons while, simultaneously, the men of the town play a Gaelic football match against a neighbouring parish. Belying the sense of abandonment that underlies the thematic core of the story, McCann's narrative is a lyrical portrait of the remainders of emigration. Though the ritual of fishing for absent children is tragic, McCann's descriptions seem to counter this with their grace. Thus it seems that form and content are, at times, working productively in counterpoint:

> Low shouts drifted like lazy swallows over the river, interrupting the silence of the women. They were casting with ferocious hope, twenty-six of them in unison, in a straight line along the muddy side of the low-slung river wall, whipping back the rods over their shoulders. They had pieces of fresh bread mashed onto the hooks so that when they cast their lines the bread volleyed out over the

river and hung for a moment, making curious contours in the air, cartwheels and tumbles and plunges. (*FSBR*, 53)

The 'ferocious hope' of these mothers is not verbally articulated, but is expressed in a gestural mode, in violent symbolic acts of devotion to their absent children. And it is striking that the river takes such a central role in McCann's symbolic economy, as it is a figuration that he returns to in later works such as *Songdogs* and *This Side of Brightness*. The river is a dynamic symbol of change yet also of re-birth, renewal, and regeneration. For these women the river may, on the one hand, be a symbol of the movement attached to emigration, but it is, equally, an element of life's natural cycle, capable of returning lost or absent loved ones. Their ritual may well be in vain, but it is a sustaining rite, which is at once somatic and emotional without need for verbal mediation. McCann presents a litany of lonely mothers, giving them specific names and, occasionally, some personal details about their children. Thus, while the ritual lends the narrative a mythic or magically real air, the identification of the individual women returns to the realms of realism: 'Mrs King was there with her graphite rod. Mrs McDaid had come up with the idea of putting currants in the bread...Mrs Kelly was sipping from her little silver flask of the finest Jameson's, Mrs Hogan was casting with fire-fly flicks of the wrist...' (*FSBR*, 55).

The ripple effects of a population denuded of its younger generation are not only mediated through the mothers' dedication to their fishing ritual, but are also made explicit in the form of the physical decline of the male population. A Gaelic football match provides the aural backdrop to the story; the sounds of the ebb and flow of the game resonate across the townscape, providing a stilted soundtrack to the mothers' actions. McCann references one of the dominant indices of traditional, and modern, Irish identity in alluding to the lapsed physicality of the male population: the GAA. References to the match are inserted at irregular intervals in the story, but when they are, they are not affirmations of a blossoming future in physical terms. As she casts her line, Mrs Conheeny worries 'that her husband, at right half back, might be feeling the ache in his knee from ligaments torn long ago' (*FSBR*, 54). And when the game ends in inevitable defeat: 'Their husbands arrived with their amber jerseys splattered with mud, their faces long in another defeat, cursing under taggles of pipes, their old bones creaking at the joints' *(FSBR, 56)*. The brute physicality of the husbands' Gaelic football match aches in their ageing bodies; the grace of their sporting youths has atrophied and is as insubstantial a memory as the catch their wives quarry for in the local river. Likewise, the inevitability of their defeat on account of an ageing team is matched by the inevitable futility of their wives' fishing ritual. Both will end, and do end, without a productive result: 'Another useless day fishing' *(FSBR, 56)*. Whether it is the graceful arcs of the mothers' fishing rods or the diminished athleticism of the football team, the marks of emigration are deeply felt in this small Westmeath town. The realities of physical mortality and the surreal ritual of fishing combine as an odd coupling in McCann's narrative to produce a sense of the unsettling repercussions of emigration. The twin narrative strategy deployed by McCann, then, evokes an ambiguous, almost insubstantial, and ill-defined society. We are, at moments, located resolutely in Ireland, with geographical coordinates: the GAA, Brennan's bread, and a further lyrical intertextual reference, this time to the traditional Irish 'Rose of Mooncoin'. But we finish this story with a deeply unsettling feeling, a sense of disorientation and uncertainty as to what we have just read, where we have read about, and who these people actually are. 'Fishing the Sloe-Black River' oscillates between this typically Irish town, with its recognizable cultural coordinates, and international elsewheres: 'like the Thames or the Darling or the Hudson or the Loire or even the Rhine itself' *(FSBR, 56)*. This geographical and cultural oscillation between home and away does not, however, privilege one over the other, but retains an authorial sensitivity to the human stories involved in the histories of Irish emigration.

NOTES

1 Dermot Bolger, 'Foreword', in Dermot Bolger (ed.), *Ireland in Exile: Irish Writers Abroad* (Dublin: New Island Books, 1993), p.9.
2 Joseph O'Connor, 'Introduction', in Dermot Bolger (ed.), *Ireland in Exile: Irish Writers Abroad* (Dublin: New Island Books, 1993), p.14.
3. Carmel Heaney (ed.), *Ireland Worldwide: The Newsletter of The Irish Diaspora* (November 1993) volume 1, pp.1–8.
4. Desmond Fennell, *The State of the Nation: Ireland since the Sixties* (Dublin: Ward River Press, 1983), pp.15–16.
5 Terence Brown, *Ireland: A Social and Cultural History, 1922–2002* (London: HarperCollins, 2002), p.316.

6   Ibid.
7   Mary P. Corcoran, 'The Process of Migration and the Reinvention of Self: The Experiences of Returning Irish Emigrants', *Éire-Ireland*, 37, 1 and 2 (2002), p.176.
8. Heather Ingman, *A History of the Irish Short Story* (Cambridge: Cambridge University Press, 2009), p.255.
9. See Miriam Mara, 'The Geography of Bodies: Borders in Edna O'Brien's *Down by the River* and Colum McCann's "Sisters"', in Helen Thompson (ed.), *The Current Debate about the Irish Literary Canon: Essays Reassessing the Field Day Anthology of Irish Writing* (Lewiston, NY and Lampeter: Mellen Press, 2006), pp.311–30.
10. Colum McCann, *Fishing the Sloe-Black River* (London: Phoenix House, 1994), p.1. All further references to *Fishing the Sloe-Black River* will appear in parenthesis as (*FSBR*).
11. Patrick McCabe, *The Butcher Boy* (London: Picador, 1992).

2

Rites of Passage: *Songdogs* (1995)

The communities of separation that populate *Fishing the Sloe-Black River* give way in McCann's next fictional work, *Songdogs*, to a family history that is equally marked by migration, but that also embraces multiculturalism and references the heterogeneity of the Irish diaspora. In its exploration of the Lyons' family narrative of international mobility and local dissolution, the novel draws our attention to the intergenerational tensions within a diasporic family. Though Michael, the father, has resettled in Ireland, the memories and consequences of his emigration resonate in the present. While his son, Conor, born in Ireland of Irish and Mexican parentage, remains an emigrant on a return visit home, ostensibly, to renew his visa. The narrative is suggestive of the fact that 'diasporas are historical formations in process', as Pnina Werbner argues.[1] In other words, the Lyons family are part of the historical genealogy of the Irish Diaspora, but the traumas that are structural to their family history reveal the internal complexity of any emigrant family or community. The father/son tension is indexical of the very 'process' alluded to by Werbner, and it is one of the factors that fuels the dramatic tension of the novel. *Songdogs* is also a painful confrontation with the past, and McCann probes the unavoidable stress involved in the ceaseless search for origins, for causes and ultimately for answers. McCann charts the individual's progress through a strangely familiar liminal landscape in search of a more complete personal narrative. In the novel, Conor Lyons' narrative indices are his mother's own childhood stories, his father's photography, their beatnik friend Cici's half-invented, half-remembered narratives; and his own imaginative fusion of all three. His transition is a conscious retracing of his parent's travels and is ostensibly a journey to locate his estranged mother. Indeed the most continuous feature of the Lyons family unit is the desire for 'elsewheres' that manifests in all of the members – as Eamonn Wall suggests, '[*Songdogs* presents] a critique of settled life: in McCann's vision, people are more content as nomads because the more settled the Lyonses are, the more they are confined and unhappy.'[2] Conor has inherited a discontinuous family history. Not only has he been separated from his mother and was too young to realize the forces that precipitated her estrangement, but at the beginning of the novel we learn that his father, Michael, was orphaned as an infant. Michael Lyons was actually raised as Gordon Peters by two benevolent Protestant ladies, who were, in turn, drowned when he was a teenager. Subsequent to their death and the receipt of his inheritance from their estate, Michael departed on several years' travel, taking in the Spanish Civil War, Mexico and North America, before returning with his Mexican wife to County Mayo. Thus, Conor Lyons' immediate genealogical lineage is profoundly ambiguous, a condition that is not unravelled in any constructive way by his father, with whom he maintains a limited relationship. And it is the maternal absence that has most acutely fostered a profoundly distanced relationship with his father. His father is an unwilling source of information regarding his mother, and her potential whereabouts. The novel charts both Conor's physical pursuit of his mother and his imaginative rendition of his parents' marriage on the American continent before he was born and resolving ultimately in the cultivation of a final détente between father and son.

Conor has returned to Ireland, and to his home in Mayo, for the first time in five years. But he has returned temporarily in order to address his visa requirements for residency in the United States – he now lives a semi-hermetic life, reminiscent of his father's own youth in Wyoming. Thus the dramatic catalyst of the story is centred on the ideas of movement, of emigration and of the adoption of new physical homelands. On one of his first nights at home, Conor reflects on his restless nature and on the ambiguous emotions his return has engendered:

> I sat up in the bedroom tonight and looked out the window to the bible-dark of the Mayo night, the stars rioting away. In a strange way it's nice to be back – it's always nice to be back anywhere, anywhere at all, safe in the knowledge that you're getting away again. The law of the river, like he used to say. Bound to move things on.[3]

In many ways, then, this return to Mayo does not represent a homecoming at all; Conor's attachment to his roots in the west of Ireland is, as his sentiments reveal, quite shallow. Indeed, as Wall further argues, this is likely to do with the fact that Ireland is not really his motherland at all – that role belongs to Mexico and to the western seaboard of the United States. The foundations of identity, as McCann's fluid metaphor embodies, are dissolute in an increasingly hybridized global community. With his orphaned father and Mexican mother, Conor is, perhaps of necessity, more than willing to subject himself to the fluctuating patterns of 'the law of the river'. Conor's movement is an ambiguous undertaking – the very act of mobility rejects the stasis of containment and contentment, and in so doing, the action of his investigative travel scrutinizes the narrative authority of his father. If Conor had ignored his urge to move, to escape the constricted emotional and physical bonds of his Mayo home, his father would have retained an autocratic proprietorship of the narratives of remembrance of the Lyons family. But in his inquisitive migrancy, Conor produces a challenge to the rememorative tyranny of Michael.

SONGDOGS AND BILDUNGSROMAN

In his seminal text on the genealogy of the *bildungsroman* in European literary history, *The Way of the World*, Franco Moretti refers to the Bakhtinian view of the genre's synchronization of the temporal plain of 'world history', and that of the 'temporal emergence' of the individual men. Emerging from the closeted sphere of the private, the individual in formation enters the public realm of 'world history'. As Moretti argues, citing Bakhtin's formulation of the *bildungsroman*:

> It's the same 'elevation' of the everyday that we encounter in Bakhtin's view of the *Bildungsroman* as a 'mastering of historical time': in these novels, he writes, 'man emerges along with the world and he reflects the historical emergence of the world itself...the image of the emerging man begins to surmount its private nature (within certain limits, of course) and enters into a completely new spatial sphere of historical existence.[4]

Bakhtin's schematic version of the genre's narrative trajectories is suggestive of the transitional and processional character of the *bildungsroman*. In many ways it adheres to a linear conceptualization of the historical time; a competitive progression towards maturation away from the blindness of youth to the full vision of maturity. And such a consistency of narrative momentum across the genre bears distinctively conservative overtones – there is a sense in which the *bildungsroman* does not contest society's received machinations, but, alternatively, serves as a minor superstructural agent of continuity and consensus. As Moretti later suggests: 'the *Bildungsroman* seemed to have its own private ideology…they were not trying to shape consistent worldviews, but rather compromises among distinct worldviews.'[5] The form is, then, reflective of the primary consciousness within these novels; the *bildungsroman* showcases the contradictory, chafing intellectual, political and personal possibilities on offer to their protagonists. And yet, typically in the classical *bildungsroman*, these options are settled, or resolved, into a productive bourgeois individuality. The process of *bildung* is co-extensive with the form of the novel; it has limits, and therefore a form of comfortable conclusion or resolution must be alighted upon, within the space/time of the narrative at least. Naturally this does not preclude the inclusion of stock narrative indices of mobility, transformation, or insecurity – these are all integral to the formative staging of the genre. These apparent structural tensions within the genre are vital, again in Moretti's terms: 'dynamism and limits, restlessness and the "sense of an ending": built as it is on such sharp contrasts, the structure of the *Bildungsroman* will of necessity be *intrinsically contradictory* [original emphasis].'[6] Despite these contradictory impulses, there is little doubt that the classical varieties of the genre are ideologically predisposed to harmony, while we witness the dramatization of 'the conflict between the ideal of *self-determination* and the equally imperious demands of socialization'.[7] This existential agon cannot continue without any punctuation (as narrative demands), and consequently, a functioning, recognizably bourgeois self must be birthed.

Over the course of the nineteenth century, according to Moretti, the *bildungsroman* had performed three great symbolic functions. It had:

> contained the unpredictability of social change, representing it through the fiction of youth; a turbulent segment of life, no doubt, but with a clear beginning and an unmistakeable end. At a micro-narrative level, furthermore, the structure of the novelistic episode had established the flexible anti-tragic modality of modern experience. Finally, the novel's many-sided, unheroic hero had embodied a new kind of subjectivity: everyday, worldly, pliant –

'normal': a smaller, more peaceful history; within it, a fuller experience; and a weaker, but more versatile Ego: a perfect compound for the Great Socialization of the European middle classes.[8]

Moretti's summative comments on the genre reflect his belief in the ideological functions of its narrative features. Specifically, his final assertion of its linkage to both the sociological and the socio-economic signals the political nature of the *bildungsroman* form. It is implicated in the superstructural summoning and pacification of the literate middle classes. The *bildungsroman* is not simply reflective of a worldview, but is productive of that worldview. In affording privilege to youth, the genre establishes itself as the literary outrider of modernity; in other words, it is the genre of the future, of potential and of progress. But, as always, it is a cultural agent that sets limits to the range of life's possibilities. It may be dynamic and oriented towards the future, but it is not revolutionary nor is it subversive. And under these philosophical and political guises, the *bildungsroman* is the quintessential European literary genre, as it fetishizes its own progress, confirming its own convictions and reflecting upon its own self-crafted images. What is, perhaps, most interesting in relation to our discussion is the question of how and where McCann's novel coalesces with and/or chafes against the classical tropes and teleologies of the *bildungsroman*. Or do we have to reconsider the genre when we approach McCann's fiction, or Irish variants of the genre? What can we extract from the history of the genre towards our discussion of the lives that animate *Songdogs*?

Moretti's treatise on the *bildungsroman* clearly privileges the 'classics' of the genre as they arose in England, France and Germany, which begs the question as to the relevance of such a discussion to our reading of McCann's debut novel, *Songdogs*. And before we can adequately map the longer histories of the *bildungsroman* into McCann's narrative, it is worth, cursorily, considering the pre-history of the Irish influence on the genre, particularly in the twentieth century. In addition, this preamble will permit us to foreground both the continuities and the discontinuities that pertain between the 'classical' and the 'Irish' variations on the *bildungsroman*. In any discussion that brings *bildungsroman* into contact with modern Irish fiction, Joyce's *A Portrait of the Artist as a Young Man* is summoned as the *locus classicus* of an 'Irish' modernist variant of the form. But not only is Joyce's novel more closely allied, arguably, to the adjacent novelistic form, the *kunstlerroman*, it is frequently read either as a 'failed' *bildungsroman* or as one that performs a modernist critique of the form. *A Portrait of the Artist* bears superficial resemblances to the classical tropes of the *bildungsroman*, but this retention of formal indices is not, Gregory Castle argues, evidential of a passive inheritance by Joyce. Castle's contention is that modernist and, indeed, postcolonial strains of the classical *bildungsroman* retain the familiar narratological features of the genre precisely to conduct the destabilizing critique of its literary and political assumptions. In his view, such an operation is a 'double gesture of recuperation of critique', under which the 'generic rudiments are not only retained but embraced with a new vigour'.[9] Castle's case, then, is founded on the adjacency of modernist and postcolonial appropriations of a conservative, bourgeois European literary form, which, as Moretti maintains, was a recognizable superstructural agent of western capitalist modernity. What is suggestive about Castle's proposition is that the *bildungsroman* cannot be seamlessly imported into Ireland, and its narrative faculties are not viewed without scepticism or as unproblematic by Irish authors. Beginning with Joyce, but stretching across twentieth-century Irish literature, we can point to consistent re-inventions of the formal indices of the classic *bildungsroman*. Contradictorily, this historically conservative novelistic form gains in elasticity as it crosses borders, as it is compelled to narrate and to mediate lives and histories that are outside the central crucibles of European modernity. And in testing the limits of the *bildungsroman*, one can also see an implicit critique of the political and cultural foundations on which it is based and which it fosters and propagates. In addition, this is the case with the multicultural mobility of Conor Lyons' and Michael Lyons' *bildung* in *Songdogs*.

Following on from Castle's alignment of modernist and postcolonial declension of the classical *bildungsroman*, we might well read McCann's *Songdogs* in terms of the postcolonial *bildungsroman*. As we range across McCann's fictions it is clear that he is exercised by many of the most urgent issues animating critical debate within contemporary postcolonial studies. Equally, *Songdogs* loosely appropriates the structure and central drama of the *bildungsroman*, and its Irish context warrants its inclusion within discussions of the postcolonial *bildungsroman*. Contemporary postcolonial *bildungsromane* include: Tsitsi Dangarembga's *Nervous Conditions*, Ben Okri's *The Famished Road*, and Chimananda Ngozi Adichie's *Purple Hibiscus*, and each of these plays their own dissonant melody on the classical *bildungsroman*. Naturally, there have been efforts to diagnose dominant generic characteristics of the postcolonial *bildungsroman*, attempting to generate a formal typology of the genre. One such effort details at length the conceivable attractions the *bildungsroman* might have for postcolonial novelists:

> As possible ground for the extraordinary success of childhood narratives, we could speculate on the large number of children who live in the postcolonial world or refer to the feelings of nostalgia experienced by writers living in exile. We could mention as well the possibilities that the *Bildungsroman* offers to those writers who wish to situate their stories in the first years following independence, in order to draw parallels between the experience of the new nations and their young characters. From a different angle, the interest that *Bildungsromane* take in the construction of subjectivity, and the didactic potentiality of the genre, appeal to the postcolonial agenda, with its emphasis on *questions of identity*, pedagogy and power. Finally…one of the reasons why postcolonial writers turn to the *Bildungsroman* is the desire to incorporate the master codes of imperialism into the text, in order to sabotage them more effectively [my emphasis].[10]

It is a given that this inventoried snapshot of the genre by Vázquez is excessively instrumental, but it is equally true that all such rigid typologies are grounded in some degree of critical accuracy. Vázquez's catalogue is prompted by his reading of Okri's *The Famished Road*, but it is worth bearing in mind when we approach *Songdogs*. Specifically, we can draw from this list as preliminary points of departure: McCann's novel reflects the author's biographical experiences of travel and distance from his native country, so there may well be an infusion of authorial nostalgia in *Songdogs*, as it charts the youthful wanderings of an exiled Irishman across the North American continent and his troubled return to his home place in Ireland. Similarly, while the ostensible central *bildung* of Conor Lyons is a generation removed from the period covering Ireland's postcolonial independence, we get a parallel *bildung* narrative of his father, Michael Lyons, which is coterminous with this period. Furthermore, and as we mentioned above, McCann's fictions, including *Songdogs*, are preoccupied with issues of national and ethnic identity, international cultural exchanges, migrancy, and the dynamics of global political power, which are foci of what Vázquez calls 'the postcolonial agenda'. Aligning McCann's novel, tentatively then, with the postcolonial *bildungsroman* also suggests that *Songdogs* performs a formal and thematic critique of the classical modes of the genre. And this is evident in the hybridized internationalism of the narrative, and in the multi-temporal structure of the presentation of the plot.

Of the points of correlation between *Songdogs* and Vázquez's typology of the postcolonial *bildungsroman*, it is the second dealt with above that is the most intriguing. Rather than solely chart the *bildung* of our focalizing protagonist, *Songdogs*, in fact, delivers what might be termed a dual *bildung*. We are witness to elements of both the father's and the son's journeys of international maturation. In this sense, when we read McCann's epigraph to the novel, we might easily be reading Michael's reflections as those of his son Conor. Despite the fact that we can say with some certainty that these are Conor's words, they are haunted by the presence of his father. The feelings and the events described therein would not be entirely alien to Michael's own life experience: 'Just before I came home to Ireland I saw my first coyotes. They were strung on a fencepost near Jackson Hole, Wyoming…The hanging was a rancher's warning to other coyotes to stay away from the field…But coyotes aren't as foolish as us – they don't trespass where the dead have been. They move on and sing elsewhere' (*SD*). What is most significant about this brief epigraphic passage is the traction that Ireland still retains for Conor despite the extensive international travel he has undertaken, and the depth of the discord that fomented his departure from Ireland in the first place. For both father and son, Ireland remains the locus of their emotional and cultural peregrinations across the globe. McCann may appeal to the exotic in his figurative encounter with the consequences of re-visiting the past, but there is a stubborn locality retained and problematized by the novel's contemporary location in Ireland. And finally, the epigraph obliquely gestures to the consequences of unfettered motion; it notes the violence that is consequent upon trespassing. In this particular figuration, the past assumes a vital and physical form – the coyotes – which is precisely how it materializes in the novel.

It is never specified as to when precisely this narrative is being narrated; we can assume that our narrator, Conor, is slightly older than when the events in the novel ensued, but we are not certain if he has remained in Ireland or departed again. Formally, the reflective form of the novel, its predominantly historical viewpoint, allows us access to the personal histories and developments of both Conor and his father and, in this way, to approach the realms of the *bildungsroman*. To return to the epigraph, because it is written in the past tense, we register that this is the 'mature' self narrating an emergence out of youthful innocence or ignorance. In addition, the epigraph's references to music, travel, violence, the natural world and the past signal some of the primary thematics that resound across the narrative. The violence prefigures the variously tense and intimate relationship that exists between father and son. However, the suggestion that both lives actually bear remarkable resemblances, as revealed by the developmental structure of many parts of the narrative, takes us back to the notion of *bildung*. In an oblique echo of the 'Law of the Father', which is a principal narrative agent in the classical *bildungsroman*, the first chapter of *Songdogs* is entitled 'the law of the river'. This title has the supplementary effect of alluding to one of the recurrent symbolic tropes in the novel, as well as locating the subsequent narrative within the generic territory of the *bildungsroman*. But what is more acute in establishing the father/son relation as the dominant narrative axis is McCann's opening description of Conor's stealthy return to his father's, and his own childhood, home. Unlike the epigraphic coyotes, Conor is now, physically and emotionally, trespassing where the dead have been: 'I sat on my backpack, behind the hedge, where the old man couldn't see me, and watched the slowness of the river and him' (*SD*, 3). McCann herein establishes the physical and emotional remoteness that obtains between father and son. And at the same time flags, in symbolic terms, the affective bond that persists between Michael Lyons and the local river. Notwithstanding the tensile nature of this relationship, McCann initiates the novel with a deliberate co-location of father and son – in proximity but still distant. Conor's stealthy vigil observing his father continues:

> Yet still the old man was fishing away. The line rolled out, catching the light, and the fly landed softly. He flicked around with his wrist for a minute, slumped his head when he finished each cast, reeled in the slack and rubbed at his forearm. After a while he went and sat in a red and white striped lawn chair under the branches of the old poplar tree. He turned his head in the direction of the hedge, didn't see me. (*SD*, 3)

In purely symbolic terms, Michael's fishing ritual harkens back to the abandoned ageing parents of 'Fishing the Sloe-Black River'; uniting the two is the insistence of redemptive ritual in the face of the departure of children. Yet there are clear distinctions to be made between the two figurative uses of fishing as ritual act by McCann. Tellingly, Michael does not see Conor when he looks in his direction, but of more significance is the profusion of detail in Conor's descriptions of his father and of the homestead during his brief week-long stay. Such precision is important given the context of the narrative drama; Conor has returned after a lengthy period away from home, having left in an ill-tempered break with his father. The next day, having reunited with his father, Conor is, again, surreptitiously watching the old man burn rubbish, and once more his description is painstaking in its accuracy:

> I dragged a chair to the window, propped my elbows on the big high armrests, watching him in the farmyard. When he was done with the burning he turned to come back from the pit, and still the whole of his body was leaning over, walking at an angle, paying some sort of homage to the ground. He shuffled back along the muddy trail, stopped and scratched at his head, then moved his fingers curiously along his right cheek as if trying to ruddy it, walked over to the wheelbarrow. (*SD*, 41)

The physical and emotional gaps that have festered for a number of years are, it seems, being filled by a dense accumulation of detail. It is almost as if in light of the previous years of separation and in preparation for those that may well follow, Conor is husbanding memorial details of his father. In another sense, his deep concentration on his father may be conditioned by the tension that exists between them both, and that, in fact, he is looking for moments of weakness, searching out for evidence, however minute, to stoke his longer-term anger towards Michael. Perhaps what is most convincing is that Conor's laboured descriptions, here and elsewhere, are superficial physical portraits, and that the mass of details actually masks the extent to which their emotional links have become emaciated by years of separation. The waves of detail, the telescopic eye for minutiae, betrays an enduring absence of genuine intimacy and mutual familiarity.

The contemporary guiding narrative arc of *Songdogs* mobilizes stark, microscopic detail in its narrative technique but this litany of present-day detail is punctuated by Conor's delivery of impressionistic descriptions of his father's formative years, of his years spent travelling the Americas and, crucially, of the ramifications of Michael's return to Ireland with his Mexican wife, Juanita. Thus, while McCann dramatizes the struggle between father and son in the present, we are also given a longer, genealogical narrative, which provides a narration of Michael's own earlier *bildung*. The overall effect is that of a subtly double-voiced *bildungsroman*. Conor's is the focalizing consciousness, but the extent to which his life, his *bildung*, materially intersects with that of his father generates this sense of doubling within the narrative. The respective motivations for both young men to depart Ireland and to travel westward are discrepant, but not unrelated. Both leave because they become convinced that all measure of emotional attachment within Ireland has disappeared. In fact, Conor's journeying through Mexico, San Francisco and Wyoming is a mix of first-hand experience and encounters with personalities and places from his parents' former life. Although he is, putatively, seeking to reconcile with his absent mother, Juanita, the more he travels through the coordinates of his father's youth, the more his first-hand experiences seem derivative of his estranged father's life. Thus this first-hand adventure is constantly shadowed by its paternal predecessor.

If the logic of the classical *bildungsroman* was centred on the inauguration of a coherent and rational selfhood, then McCann's novel seems to test the limits of that underlying logic. In *Songdogs*, both father and son are, at various times and in different ways, cast adrift from the familiar anchoring referents of familial and communal identity. The Lyons family history across the twentieth century is founded on absence, illegitimacy and rootlessness. Recalling his father's parentage, Conor reveals: 'A russet-haired woman who only wore one sleeve on her dress gave birth to my father on a clifftop overlooking the Atlantic, in the summer of 1918. She was known in town as a madwoman' (*SD*, 5). In addition to this compromised maternity, Michael's father was killed before his birth: 'She had just received a letter saying that her lover had been fed to the guns of the Great War' (*SD*, 6). And just as Michael's father never sees his son, the mother, it is implied, abandons him almost immediately after his birth too. Thus, Michael is born of separation and death, and, prophetically, born overlooking the ocean that will become a defining presence in his own and his son's lives. Michael is rescued from his orphaned condition by two Protestant ladies, who endow him with a life of relative comfort. Far removed from the precarious exposure of his birth:

> The Protestant ladies raised him in a house of fine china tea cups, radio broadcasts, scones privileged with spoonfuls of clotted cream…His were ordered all the way from Dublin, beautiful white shirts that he destroyed running through the bogs…They baptized him in the Protestant Church with the name Gordon Peters, and years later – beaten up in school for the name – he repaid them by urinating on their toothbrushes. (*SD*, 6)

His urination is not his only reaction to his name, when, at the age of eleven, when he learns about his natural mother, he renames himself Michael Lyons. The Lyons family 'name', then, is an adolescent fiction – a wildly postmodern gesture by the youth that establishes a family narrative. In another way, it further complicates the apparent 'law of the father' dynamic of McCann's *bildungsroman*, as paternity is now doubly undermined in death and in name. To add to Michael's dislocation, his two adoptive parents are drowned when he is sixteen; and this further parental loss foregrounds the family as a thematic hinge of the novel. Both of Michael's 'families' are deeply unconventional in their historical context, and in a sense, they challenge the heteronormativity of the nuclear family in Ireland during this period. The stabilizing agency of the family unit is troubled in *Songdogs*, which has clear repercussions for the development of the individual, in this case both Michael and Conor.

'THE LAW OF THE FATHER' – ARTIST AND PHOTOGRAPHER

Prior to the catalytic family breakup of the contemporary narrative, we learn, through Conor, of his father's peripatetic youth. His rootlessness is at least partly a consequence of his displacement within his home town in Ireland, and his lack of any tangible family connections. But such itinerancy facilitates artistic freedom for Michael, latitude to pursue his newly formed passion for photography. On inheriting the estate of his Protestant benefactors, Michael discovers a camera among their possessions. The camera, photography and the photographic image become recurrent fertile motifs in the novel, assuming a figurative significance equivalent to that of the river.[11] This becomes the single most lasting legacy of the inheritance that he is bequeathed by his Protestant mothers; it is an enlivening discovery for the young Michael:

> It was the camera that woke him. He found it in a large red box

under one of the beds, forgotten. It had belonged to Loyola, but she had never mentioned it to him. Opening the silver snaps, a Pandora of dust arose around him, and he lifted the parts out onto the bed. It was an old model with a dickybird hood, glass plates in perfect order, wooden legs sturdy, lens unscratched. (*SD*, 8–9)

The camera is an historical artefact, a quaint antique that will, nevertheless, prove a medium of liberation and creativity for Michael. McCann's mise-en-scène of this discovery has echoes of a mythical unearthing of an enigmatic object, which can endow unimagined powers on the bearer. And akin to many of these mythic gifts of endowment, the camera exacts retribution for misuse or perceived misuse of its gifts. Michael is consumed by the object and its creative possibilities, as well as by the mechanical intricacies of its operation. He devotes considerable time and money in operating and maintaining the camera, while aiming its lens at his local natural surroundings and, more provocatively, at many of his neighbours. Yet behind all of this relatively innocent photography, as Conor notes: 'He didn't know it then, but the camera would burst him out onto the world, give him something to cling to, fulminate a belief in him in the power of light, the necessity of image, the possibility of freezing time' (*SD*, 9). Just as we all remember in images rather than in words, *Songdogs* is an aggregation of a verbal narrative, and an historical narrative that is heavily dependent on the testimony of visual imagery. In a sense, McCann presents us with another narrative doubling – interwoven and speculative registers of textual and visual representation. As Conor notes, Michael's and, subsequently, Juanita's lives are measured out in the visual record of their photographic archive. Michael's immersion in the bare mechanics of photography soon matures into a steady flow of income from the vocation and, finally, emerges as a desire to achieve a level of aesthetic mastery and critical acclaim. In these ways, not only does *Songdogs* bear affinities to a curiously doubled *bildungsroman*, but the novel also approaches a photographic *kunstlerroman*.[12] The thematic and geographic sweep of Michael's photographic archive is immense – from humble beginnings, his Mayo photography develops into more risqué portraits, as we see the first intrusion of erotic photography, which will violate his future domestic space. Almost as an affront to the ossified moral climate of Ireland in the 1930s, Michael's photographs are testimonies to the presence of desire and sensuality. The voluntary eroticism of his photographic subjects is at once a benign exploration of sexuality, but also a misrecognition, on their part, of the nature of photographic representation. The photographic exposure might appear a momentary, transient enactment of bodily sensuality, but it harnesses the image and can disempower the object of its gaze, as eventuates later in the novel. Nevertheless, Michael's role as photographer enables him to chronicle briefly the public and private impulses of Irish rural youth culture in the 1930s: 'The owner of the dancehall…wouldn't allow any cameras inside. Still, my father was quite content to hang around, smoking, waiting for Manley [his friend] to emerge, looking for opportunities to use Loyola [his camera]…Outside the dancehall he sometimes took pictures of young women smoking for the first time, new hats cocked sideways, daring lipstick smudged upwards to thicken lips' (*SD*, 10–11). And in tandem with the minor lasciviousness of these public displays of sensuousness, Michael's photography captures more discrete moments: 'My father had rescued an old *chaise* with three legs. When the women reclined on it, their hair swooped towards the floor, Manley, giving politics a rest, let a licentious tongue hang out as he peeped in through the barn slats' (*SD*, 12). The contrast between Michael and his friend Manley in these two extracts is telling; Manley is portrayed as engaged in the social networks of his peers, whereas Michael remains removed and disinterested. This distinction, then, presages Michael's imminent and decades-long travel outside of Ireland, and it exposes his attitude to his photographic vocation. Manley's 'licentious tongue', perversely, is attuned to the ethical content and nature of photography, and explicitly of such erotically charged images. The very licentiousness of his disposition betrays his acknowledgement of the moral code under which he lives. By way of contrast, Michael's guiding principle is not the morality or immorality of his work, or how it might offend. Rather, he is primarily focused on the objective aesthetic merits of the images. In a larger sense, the ethical responsibility that Michael as an artist has to his photographic subjects is ignored or subordinated to the need of the artistic process and the artistic product. Michael does not always jettison the ethics of photographic representation, but does so at crucial times, and such regular neglect, ultimately, sunders his marriage and his family. Having resolved to leave Ireland, Michael invests in two new Leica cameras and follows Manley to civil war Spain. Indoctrinated into Marxism, Manley enlists for combat and Michael pursues as a war photographer. Even here at the vanguard of global ideological warfare, in the most visceral and public spaces of his photographic career, Michael retreats behind his art: 'he had no politics...he was only a photographer' (*SD*, 20). From Spain and onto Mexico, both in public and in private, Michael chases an aesthetic ideal determined to attain critical recognition for his photographic output. At first it is the public output that Michael retails as his creative portfolio; his work documents the hardships of Mexican copper miners, the summer forest fires of Wyoming, and the multi-ethnic communality of mid-century New York City. But Michael's festering desire for artistic acclaim remains frustrated; the public photography is ignored and is only resurrected and given narrative form years later by Conor. However, contrary to his expectations, Michael's discrete, private images are, in the end, far more explosive. In particular, photography becomes an intimate and sensual theatre within his marriage to Juanita. But it is also the medium through which that marital bond is severed.

Emerging from the Mexican desert, Michael alights upon an isolated hamlet and, while resting briefly, Juanita ganders into his view. He is immediately entranced by the primal erotic physicality that she exudes and, naturally, he reaches for his camera. Less predictably, Juanita responds: 'She pursed her lips provocatively for the camera, her blouse open flirtatiously, her head thrown sideways like a film actress' (*SD*, 36). The minor flirtation is abruptly, and violently, ended in a hail of threats from Juanita's mother. Yet Juanita's derivative erotic performance anticipates the mutual pleasure derived from the medium by the couple in later years. But even within the bond that is struck between Michael and Juanita, a sense of misrecognition persists. As Conor reveals: 'She wasn't performing for the camera – she was performing for him. She never asked to see the prints. There wasn't an ounce of vanity in her poses' (*SD*, 38). The theatre of photographic representation is the crucible in which the erotic drama of their relationship unfolds, but there is a sense in which they are speaking past each other. The camera is the unifying catalyst, but is also, strangely, absent and defunct at the same time. In other words, it seems as if their individual desire bypasses the other – hers for him, and his for the aesthetics of photography. We might suggest that in posing for Michael, and not for the camera, Juanita escapes objectification, that she retains her sensual agency in her deliberate carnal posturing for her husband. She is not reduced to or confined to the de-eroticized machinery of visual reproduction.

The twin foci of Michael's photographic vocation are his ambition to publish a collection of his images and the private realm of erotic photography with his wife. The two vectors are, for the most part, mutually exclusive, as Michael's attentions are given to securing recognition either through a book-length publication or employed in full-time print journalism. Their journeying along the western seaboard of the United States culminates in their sojourn in rural Wyoming and it is here that Michael is presented with his most electrifying spectacles of natural destruction. The unrelenting summer fires offer propitious material for dramatic visual representations, and in McCann's opening description of that 'summer of fires', the pyrotechnic sublimity of the flames imitate the nubile beauty of Juanita's somatic exertions in Michael's private images: 'A summer of fires, that summer of 1956. They licked their way salaciously through the trees. Ran like lizards alongside ridges. Leaped their way over brown streambeds, languished for a while by new ditches and blackened the yellow hardhats that were left hanging on the branches of trees, tongued their way out towards northern corners of the forest' (*SD*, 102). The scenes in Wyoming are characterized by immolation on a grand scale as well as heroism on a very local scale. And reeling and revelling in their midst is Michael Lyons, quarrying visual art from the ashes of the burning landscape. The surging intensity of the summer fires, their fevered pitch of immolation, runs in symphony with the vocational dedication of Michael as he relays around the blazing mountain-sides. The more severely the landscape burns and the greater the scope of its destruction, the more Michael becomes convinced of his imminent professional success. But, inevitably, the imagined publication never materializes, and Michael is faced with another professional and public diminution. And as his prospects of meaningful professional ratification diminish with increasing haste, the worlds of public and private photography become more proximate.

By the time she abandoned her family in Ireland, Juanita may have become physically and emotionally weathered by her exile from Mexico, but as Conor's revelations about the contents of his father's private photographic archive suggest, she was once a woman of extraordinary physical presence and beauty. Despite the potential to be overwhelmed by the medium, it seems to Conor that his mother retains her volition, even as Michael's photographic process attempts to seize her as an aesthetic object. Detailing the content of these images, Conor notes that his mother's body 'was nude, not flagrantly so, but her stomach was smooth and dark, it held no creases, her legs curved softly, white sheets exposed small tufts of hair' (*SD*, 59). The collection of photographs 'took on a Victorian attitude of lounge and lust, as if being peeped at through a curtain' (*SD*, 59) – a description that evinces the managed aesthetic postures of Michael's images, and equally that foreshadows their calamitous public exposure years later.

As Michael and Juanita travel further, leaving Mexico behind, the improved technical proficiency of Michael's photography is evident in these private erotic stills: 'Some photos were taken when the sun came up, my mother unclothed once more, but more subtle, more precise around the edges than the ones from Mexico' (*SD*, 108). One is left to speculate whether the increasing professional disappointment and the apparent attainment of photographic skill are in proportion to Juanita's 'disappearance' from the artistic process in Michael's eyes. As she strives to retain a vibrant subjectivity, his appetite for egotistical recognition is incrementally evacuating her of such as photographic object. This tension between Michael's objectification of Juanita and her resistant vibrancy is played out in the photographs of their time spent living in New York. At one moment we witness further evidence of the redundancy of her subjectivity – she is sacrificing herself to the needs of her aspirant and discontented husband, to the extent that: 'the only time that her husband seems to be truly at peace is when he's taking those photos...They make him content. It's a small enough price for Mam to pay, and it's an attention of sorts. He is still in love with her. He still makes a temple from her body – even though it's much like a minaret now' (*SD*, 140–1). Yet in another image from the same period, Conor remarks that: 'the shot is loaded with more sexuality than almost any of the others – something to do with its casualness' (*SD*, 143). These two scenes enact the central contest at the core of the Lyons' marital discord, and they are symptomatic of the manner in which the medium siphons away the authenticity of the emotional and sexual energy of the marriage. Michael's artistic ambition, and his *bildung* as a photographic artist, begins to take precedence within the marriage and the family; family and love are sacrificed for aesthetic achievement.

But Michael's ultimate reckoning with his professional inadequacies is quickened by his return to Ireland; he secures a post as a freelance photographer for some agricultural magazines. From the grand public spectacles of his Spanish, Mexican, Wyoming and New York photographs, Michael's beat now comprises 'fields of barley, gleaming red combine harvesters, cows with splatterings of shit on their tails, formal committee meetings, product launches' (*SD*, 163). His physical and photographic horizons have been foreshortened, and the mesmerizing topographies that energized photographer and his photography are now tapered to the domains of the banal and the beastly. For Michael, photography as a validation and as a redemption seems to have escaped his grasp, but the final death throes of his vocation now occasion that of his family too. Michael's pursuit of an artistic legacy leads him to self-publish a compilation of his life's work, and he ransacks the images of his marital intimacy in a cheap and desperate attempt to secure this legacy. In so doing, he betrays the integrity of his wife's body and her subjectivity, prostituting their sexual past, their combined erotic narrative, for the satiety of his own artistic ego. And it is this final act that propels Juanita's psychological and physical disengagement from her Irish environment and from her family. The privacy and the specificity of her desire is exposed as a public commodity by Michael, as it is reproduced and circulated beyond her control at the behest of her husband. It seems that Michael's artistic pride supersedes the carnal intimacy offered by his wife. In this way, we see the manifold frustrations of Michael's artistic failures traducing the trust and faith of his marriage, and fracturing his entire family irreparably.

PHOTOGRAPHY AND/AS INHERITANCE

Returning to the formative moments of his parents' relationship, Conor retells the story of how his father redeemed himself in the eyes of his Mexican mother-in-law. Several days after her violent warning to him, Michael is permitted entry to the household on foot of an innocent, yet outrageous, fiction concocted by Juanita. In his new guise Michael 'was related to John Riley, an Irishman who had commanded the San Patricio Battalion in the Mexican War' (*SD*, 37). With his revolutionary Irish pedigree established, Michael's courtship of Juanita and her family can begin in earnest. But what is most significant is the necessity for a fiction to enable the consummation of a burgeoning romance. Just like Michael's own insubstantial family and nominal origins, his new life in Mexico is ushered into life on further fictional premises. The requirement for such enabling and sustaining inventions, then, is not only a recurring, but a dominant, feature of *Songdogs*; in this way the novel highlights the notion of the invention and re-invention of the self and selves over the course of a life. In another vein, and as we shall see, it is the ability to acknowledge and to recognize the need for such consoling fictions that becomes one of the central lessons of the novel and of Conor's *bildung*. The novel throws into relief the urgency and the ubiquity of such enabling personal, familial and communal fictions. Indeed, the persistence of this theme in the novel is, effectively, the link between Michael's and Conor's engagements with photography. Beginning as empirical representations, these images become, differentially, resources of fictional sustenance for both Michael and Conor – Michael, to the extent that the continued productions suggest the vitality of his professional aspirations, and Conor, in the manner in which these images become a restorative imaginative geography that he can share with his absent mother. Resident in Wyoming, Conor developed the habit of perusing his parents' photographs, and in the evening: 'I would rise from my chair, step out the door, look at the Wyoming sky, the thump of creation, and then I'd take another step forward on to the edge of the porch, and I would walk my way slowly into old photographs' (*SD*, 135).

While the public photography of Mexico and Wyoming might be counted as remnants of Michael's professional failure, it is Conor's protracted reveries in the 'Saturday' chapter over a series of photographic images of New York City that reveal most about the son's relationship with the visual record of his parents' American life together. The sequence of four images range from 'the end of the 1950s' (*SD*, 135), to 1964; three of the images are taken by Michael and one by their companion, Cici. Prefiguring the New York streetscapes of *This Side of Brightness* and *Let the Great World Spin*, these pictorial renditions of the blossoming metropolis capture the diversity of emigrant populations, particularly the Irish emigrant community. The Bronx, Queens, and Fifth Avenue form the urban backdrop, and Marilyn Monroe, JFK, and Elvis furnish the cultural scenery experienced by men and women from 'Galway and Dublin and Leitrim and Donegal' (*SD*, 136). The portrait provided by Conor of the interior life of his father's images permits a glimpse of the international cultural networks occasioned by [Irish] emigration. But of more urgency are the ways in which Conor telescopes his mother's appearance in the photographs. The images deliver what are, essentially, over-familiar coordinates of New York City, but their real currency is the speculative narrative Conor weaves from their representations. Willing his mother to emerge from the stasis of the images, Conor's narrative tense begins to mould new possibilities from the frozen moments. And it is his repeated employment of the conditional tense that draws our attention to his use of the photography as a source of affective consolation. His conditional speculations may be born of ignorance but they are not tainted by frustration, rather they are moments of imagined attachment to the banalities of his absent mother's life before he was born:

> Mam is just about smiling as she looks down at her hands. It is not an unhappy smile, just a little lost on her face. Maybe she's wondering what she's doing here. Wondering what has led her to this. Wondering if life is manufactured by a sense of place, if happiness is dependent on soil…Wondering if there is a contagion to sadness. Or an entropy to love. Or maybe Mam isn't thinking this way at all. Maybe she is wondering about the sheer banalities of her day. (*SD*, 138)

Not only is Juanita physically absent and elusive to her son, but her thoughts and motivations remain unreachable to him also. Conor's speculative meandering through the photographic narrative of his parents' lives yields as many questions as it does answers. And his conditional register signals the ambiguous feelings of attachment and distance that are engendered by his photographic reveries. Equally, it is significant that he imagines the likelihood of his mother dwelling on the strains of migration and displacement, perhaps displacing his own feelings of alienation onto his mother's life. The questions he implants in his mother's mind about her sense of belonging are, then, just as germane to his life and reflect his own emotional equilibrium. In these instances the photographic image, the erstwhile index of veracity, becomes an enigmatic referent for Conor – one that confounds through silence, but thrills through the possibility of imaginative suggestion. At the same time, there are moments of fantasy catalyzed by the images. An image from 1960 of his mother dancing on the streets of the Bronx to an Elvis Presley song transports Conor directly into that euphoric scene: 'I walk out there to go dancing. I twirl my hips, too. I move with abandon. She says to me: When are you going to get rid of that stupid earring, Conor? I take it out and give it to her, and she smiles' (*SD*, 142). Sensual, somatic abandon are twinned with good-humoured tutelage of parenthood here, and the image enacts Conor's desire for intimacy with his mother's past and, also, the presence of a guiding maternal figure in the present. The present-day narrative delivered by Conor represents the continuing difficulty he has in forging some degree of intimacy with his father, Michael. His photographic fantasies demonstrate the extent to which Conor is caught between the living and the dead; his absent (deceased?) mother is a proximate presence in his life, and for much of the novel Conor prefers to dwell in the landscape of the dead and the geography of the past. Its imaginative memorial respite relieves the frigid realities of his relationship with his father: 'Mam has a bead of sweat on her brow. Maybe she will wait for it to negotiate its way down her face to where she can tongue it. Or maybe not. Maybe she will wipe it off with a quick flick of the hand. Or maybe it will stay there eternally' (*SD*, 142). The conditional narrative tense is not a feature of his representation of his father's life, and this suggests that the conditional and the possible are not appropriate to the sedentary life led by Michael, or, it seems, to the father/son relationship.

From a formal perspective, then, it seems that hope, invention and imagination are attached to his relationship with his absent mother, whereas there appears to be a more functional idiom attached to his father. It is only when this functionalism is leavened does Conor begin to empathize with the tragedies of his father's life and with the private contrition of Michael's memories. And the insistence on the conditional tense in the novel returns us to the end of the narrative. As we have argued above, there are utopian impulses embedded across McCann's fictions, which are centred on the idea of redemption. Although there is no final rapprochement dramatized by the close of the novel, we can recognize that a thawed mutual understanding has displaced rigid austerity in the father/son relationship. At the root of this utopian prospect in *Songdogs*, where the central relationship moves towards recovery, are the evident imaginative capacities of both men. Conor's conditional idiom in his imaginative plotting of the photography, coupled with the frustrated artistry exhibited by Michael in producing the images in the first place, are signs of their individual creativity. In addition, we see Michael's deft production of fishing flies and his graceful fishing technique, and all of these aggregated creative skills are indicative of the possibility of an imaginative empathetic resolution to this fractured relationship. Having emerged from his hunkered position behind the hedge at the opening of the novel, Conor has matured, to some extent, into a position where he can share in the sustaining symbolic and ritual economy of his father's life. Conor is both willing and able to subscribe to the necessary fictions that underpin any loving relationship. This is not to confirm that the novel ends on a definitive note; Conor's magnanimous gesture is a signal, not an end in itself. As we shall see below, McCann's novel deviates, again, from the denouement of the classical *bildungsroman*. By the end, there is the possibility of hope towards the future, of a potential peace between two exiled people.

MOVING BEYOND THE IMAGE

In his late 1974 novel, *Lazare*, André Malraux reflects that: 'images do not make up a life story; nor do events. It is the narrative illusion, the biographical work, that creates the life story.'[13] Malraux's point consummately expresses the fabricated nature of verbal and visual meanings that are attached to, or are extracted from, literary and imagistic texts. Open-endedness and contingency, then, intrude on the easy patterning of meanings and identities from the raw materials of visual or verbal testimonies. Photographic portraits may superficially impose narrative structure, or perhaps endow identities and personal histories a sense of anchorage, but as Malraux, among many others, indicates, such identitarian assurances are shallow and unsustainable. In an Irish context, photographic images of 'home' have historically been employed to retail nostalgized versions of 'Ireland' and 'Irishness' to diasporic Irish communities, or to advertise the incorruptible, and alluring, fabric of the Irish nation. In other words, such visual texts fall victim to the conviction that photography imposes a narrative truth to the objects represented within its contours – the photographic image is unquestioningly seen as complete and 'truthful'. As we have seen, in *Songdogs*, Michael Lyons has catalogued his own, and his wife's, life of international migration in a range of photographic registers: informal snapshots, individual and group portraits, as well as more intimate and erotic artistic images. But just as these visual texts confound Conor's yearning for clarity and revelation, so too do the physical landscapes through which he travels in imitation of his parents' journeys.

Photography provides an effective symbolic and representative device for McCann, but is not the primary mode through which Conor reconstructs his disjointed identity. Michael Lyons' frozen memories are distilled in Conor's interpretation or re-imagination of their contexts, their tone and their violent stillness. Conor must populate the 'frozen time' of photographic stasis with his own catalogue of incongruous memories and imaginative remembrance. The photographs represent monumental spaces in which his parents' lives are held in stasis and it is part of Conor's task to re-imagine these images. He is charged with transcending the frozen lens through the physical experience of liminality. The stasis of photography embodied in the smiles and the seductive gazes are interrogated in spatial terms as Conor looks beyond the representation. He attempts to identify the interpersonal dynamics and relations, with their motives, betrayals and choices that contextually frame the still representation. He cannot know his mother or the genealogy of his constitution through simple photographic representation but must seek for it in the liminal spaces of Mexico, San Francisco and Wyoming. Conor negotiates a 'threshold, a no-man's-land betwixt and between the structural past and the structural future as anticipated by society's normative control of development'.[14] The dominant images of his father's photography are portraits of his mother, in which she is represented as an object. And we appreciate the incompleteness of photographic representation with its static, mute limitations as Conor's mother is portrayed as a body turned 'temple' (*SD*, 141). Thus, photography performs as an imaginative and ultimately physical catalyst, and Conor consciously pursues the realities within and behind the photographic images.

Conor must go beyond such representations in order to immerse himself in the heterotrophic physicality of these liminal spaces. A process of cataloguing characterizes his sojourn in Mexico, as he digests the kaleidoscopic physicality of the Mexican town: 'graffiti rolled in red on the courthouse walls. Policemen, chameleons in the shadows, flicked in and out between the scrawls. Old men sat outside in cartinas, gesturing. A labyrinth of laneways...a young man sat on the hotel steps' (*SD*, 67). There is a sense of colour, of light and darkness, in McCann's description, combined with the contradictory feelings of hope, threat or revelation in the town. Initially it assumes a menacing and an ambiguous aspect, seemingly populated by figures of potential threat, and even the forces of order are portrayed in an ambivalent manner. The fructile chaos of a Mexican village manifests itself in both the visceral technicolour of the rural landscape and concurrently in the hapless linguistic incommensurability that obtains between Conor and the indigenous population. Conor's labours in the native tongue are met 'with loud guffaws' or alternatively by a woman who 'simply shrugged, a little perplexed, a little amused' (*SD*, 69–71). He soon realizes that the mediated memories of his parents' recollections of Mexican life do not correspond to the ambiguous milieu that he now confronts:

> The town was bigger than I had imagined. I wandered for days, through bars and cafés, bills coming crisply from my pockets, ordered up shots of tequila, tried to picture myself here forty years before, in a stetson and boots. But the simple truth of it was that I was leaning drunkenly against a bar counter, wearing a gold earring, red Doc Martens and a baseball hat turned backwards, in a town where I could barely understand what the people were saying. It was only with enough tequila in my system that I could make sense of the stories my parents had told me, their endless incantation of memories. (*SD*, 68)

McCann's panoramic description accentuates the defamiliarizing physicality of the transitional experience, as Conor traverses the nocturnal Mexican desert-scape aboard a bus that 'rattles along in darkness, through desert and small towns on the edge of spectacular canyons, and into vast city suburbs' (*SD*, 71). However, the town slowly emerges as simply a place of colour, of contrasts and of unsophisticated contentment, as Conor muses: 'nobody disturbed me...the town was quiet among strangers and sunsets' (*SD*, 71).

In San Francisco, Cici's testimonies to Conor are framed within her own belief in the imaginative fabric of memory. Her recollections are the most intimate anecdotes that he has or is likely to encounter, but her significance within the narrative goes beyond this simple acquaintance. Cici consistently alludes to the promiscuity of identity and of memory; not only is memory three quarters invented and the rest a pack of lies, but even people themselves 'just ain't what they seem, sometimes you dream them up for yourself' (*SD*, 88). Conor's reconciliation is dependent upon his appreciation of the fictive elements of narrative and identity as well as the characteristic uncertainty and discontinuity of personal remembrance. Conor's North American experience is coloured by his mother's stories concerning Cici and his parents' journey to San Francisco. Cici's hyper-accentuated powers of description, indicated by her incarnation as a pseudo-beatnik poet, thrill his imaginative recollections of his mother. However, her world is perhaps the most elusive, and it is populated by the detritus of a bygone era. Her home is a refuge of bohemian bric-a-brac, a graveyard of defunct beatnik culture. Like her memory, her apartment is cluttered and indistinct: 'the shelves lined with amulets, a strange footlong marijuana bong on the coffee table, the mantle-piece full of candles, a few paintings on the wall, a Warhol imitation' (*SD*, 110). Nonetheless, Cici's stories retain a valency for Conor with her 'startlingly lucid memories and threnody of nostalgia' (*SD*, 112). Latter-day hippies, vagrants, wanderers, and 'people searching for someone' (*SD*, 116) inhabit Cici's San Francisco. The middle-aged men who lounge on the pavement are conducting a silent vigil of remembrance for the passing of their youths. Their desire is indistinguishable from their despair; they are figures of uncertainty lodged in the present but perpetually divining for some trace of the past.

'THE LAW OF THE RIVER' – HOPE AND GRIEF

The most prominent symbol in *Songdogs* is the river, specifically the river that flows adjacent to the Lyons' house in County Mayo. And its flow and gradual stagnation are woven into the emotional fabric of the family over the course of several decades. But by the close of the novel, the river is all but lifeless – a polluted, turgid body of water that has been asphyxiated by discharge from a meat-rendering factory. Slaughter and its offal seep into the natural lifecycle of the river and this incremental suffocation is appropriated by McCann in his tragic narrative. The image of the river, with its incessant flow and latent violence, stalks the narrative. Michael Lyons and the river are intimately connected, as Conor reflects: 'the old man and the water are together in all of this – they have lived out their lives disguised as one another (*SD*, 5). He has grown old with the votive obsession of landing a prize salmon, and he understands the 'law of water' with its remorseless onward flow that is 'bound to move things on', (*SD*, 5). Conor initially misdiagnoses the contrite ritual as inertia and his lingering misapprehension of his father is evident as he expectorates: '[he led a] life of half-emergence. A consistency of acceptance' (*SD*, 101). Conor's reading of his father's life is confined to a literal perception during his initial period at home; he does not appreciate the totemic aspect to the old man's routine. The catch is a symbolic act. It is an emotional displacement with which he combats the emptiness of solitude. Michael grasps that his abandonment cannot be redressed by any amount of travelling or retrospective questioning. Thus, the incongruity of his father's routine coupled with a recrudescence of their emotional distance militates against reconciliation upon Conor's immediate return. The absence of discourse between father and son enjoins Conor to pursue his answers elsewhere.

Michael's sedulous fishing signals his prevailing love for his absent wife, but the penitent act is framed within the stark understanding that nothing will bring her back. The narrative or sequence of events that led to his marital abandonment cannot and will not be reversed. Mexico, Cici, and his photography are forsaken as tethers to an immutable past, and just like the coyotes of McCann's epigraphic extract, Michael has moved on and learned to sing in a different place and in a different way. The votive fishing ritual is an act of love. Michael has taken the very real love that existed between his now absent wife and himself in the past as the structural locus of his daily routine. While the malignant elements of the past remain, the vital element of love is his guiding principle, and the narrative's conclusion works towards reconciliation. Michael, in two abrupt responses, summarily dismisses Conor's expansive transcontinental experience, and the motives for such a journey. But the journey furnishes Conor with the necessary knowledge or experience to speak tentatively upon his homecoming with his father. It prompts him to 'accept that the past cannot be changed' and finally to understand 'that there can be no peace if certain cherished illusions are not nurtured'.[15]

As the novel nears it conclusion, Michael rises and sets about his daily routine of fishing the river for its equally symbolic bounty: a salmon. On this occasion, Conor accompanies him: 'We went out beyond the yard. Clouds were out, swifts following them. A breeze blew over our heads. It was too early for the factory smell. He negotiated his way over the stile and through the gap in the bushes down towards the water. The river was as dead as ever' (*SD*, 210–11). Within this passage McCann moves from the explosive energy of the swifts in flight and their fragile transcendence on the currents of a light breeze, to the morbid gravity of the corpse-like river. As if stumbling through the overgrown hedging of County Mayo to a scene from Eliot's 'The Wasteland', McCann's image promises the grave and the terminal. Yet even in the final few passages of the novel that succeed this grim spectacle, there is still time for resurrection and for redemption. McCann's narrative sees Conor finally apprehending the necessity for fictions of consolation and imaginative acts of generosity, which can repair and redeem his fractured relationship with his father. Almost as soon as he commences his ritual of fishing, Michael exclaims: 'Look at that!...Look!' (*SD*, 211). Sitting nearby on the riverbank, Conor says to himself: 'I looked around and there was nothing, absolutely nothing, not even a ripple' (*SD*, 211). But what is remarkable at this late stage, so soon before Conor's intended departure, is that he does not dismiss his father's sighting as delusional. The previous cynicism, fuelled by anger, which Conor exhibited towards his father's life now yields to a more mature temperament of generosity. Not wanting to foment any further discord between them and, finally, learning *how* to love his father, Conor admits:

> I know what he saw. Caught in mid-twist in the air, the flash of belly shining, contorted and unchoreographed in its spin, reaching out over the surface so the skips were alight in the air around it, fins tucked in, tail in a whisk throwing off droplets, making a massive zigzag of itself, three feet over the surface, mouth open to gulp air, eyes huge and bulbous, a fringe of water around it – place and motion caught together, as if in one of those old photos. (*SD*, 211)

Again Conor exercises his imagination to commune with his parent, this time his father, and in that imagining he feels: 'joy there, I felt it, marvellous, unyielding, and he leaned his shoulder against me and said: "Fucking hell, amazing, wasn't it?"' (*SD*, 211). The symbolic fish breaks the surface of the polluted river as a token of the dissolution of the tension that obtains between Michael and Conor. McCann's elongated single sentence, which is replete with figuration, natural athleticism, and sensuousness, is the vehicle for a brief but dense moment of reve-lation. His lyrical prose may stretch to a protracted paragraph, but it bears the poetic gravity of a haiku. Likewise, the final, almost epiphanic, moment aggregates the principal symbolic reference points of the novel. This is a culminating action that convenes the diverse symbolism of the narrative; the river, the salmon, movement, and photography are condensed into Conor and Michael's complicit 'sighting' of the salmon. Crucially, this passage expresses a spirit of hope and redemption, as the salmon's imagined leap suggests a rebirth of the father/son relationship. At the very close of the novel the heavily figured hope of the previous extract is translated into a concrete gesture of solidarity and into a will to believe for the sake of reconciliation. Conor approaches his father having retrieved the fishing rod and equipment from the house, and he reflects: 'Let this joy last itself into the night' (*SD*, 212). The emotional resolution and the salving of years of distance are distilled out of this shared joy at 'sighting' the salmon. And the final piece of dialogue in the novel confirms the hopeful impulse of the narrative's ending: 'He tied the fly on. He was whispering, "Did ya see it, son?" I looked over and said to him: "Yeah, I saw it"' (*SD*, 212). In the final actions of the novel, which is often marked by personal and familial rancour and physical distance, the poetic and the prosaic cohere in a hopeful, redemptive conclusion. With the experience of exile Conor's return home, specifically to the taut emotional relationship with his father, is eased – travel tempers his bitterness towards 'the old man'.

NOTES

1. Pnina Werbner, 'Introduction: The Materiality of Diaspora – Between Aesthetic and "Real" Politics', *Diaspora*, 9, 1 (2000), p.5.
2. Eamonn Wall, 'Winds Blowing from a Million Directions', in Charles Fanning (ed.), *New Perspectives on the Irish Diaspora* (Carbondale and Edwardsville, IL: Southern Illinois University Press, 2000), p.83.
3. Colum McCann, *Songdogs* (London: Phoenix House, 1995), p.26. All further reference to *Songdogs* will appear in parenthesis as (*SD*).
4. Franco Moretti, *The Way of the World: The Bildungsroman in European Culture* (London: Verso, 2000 [1987]), p.vii.
5. Ibid., p.xii.
6. Ibid., p.6.
7. Ibid., p.15.
8. Ibid., p.230.
9. Gregory Castle, *Reading the Modernist Bildungsroman* (Gainesville, FL: University Press of Florida), pp.4–5.
10. José Santiago Fernández Vázquez, 'Recharting the Geography of Genre: Ben Okri's *The Famished Road* as a Postcolonial Bildungsroman', *The Journal of Commonwealth Literature*, 37, 2 (2002), p.86.
11. See Aidan Arrowsmith, 'Photographic Memories: Nostalgia and Irish Diaspora Writing', *Textual Practice*, 19, 2 (2005), pp.297–322.
12. On photography in *Songdogs*, see Jack S. Flack, 'Telling Shots: Photography in/as/and Literature in Colum McCann's *Songdogs*', *Nua: Studies in Contemporary Irish Writing*, 4, 1 and 4, 2 (2003), pp.77–88.
13. Cited in Timothy Dow Adams, 'Introduction: Life Writing and Light Writing; Autobiography and Photography', *Modern Fiction Studies*, 40, 3 (1994), p.459.
14. Victor Turner, 'Dewey, Dilthey, and Drama: An Essay in the Anthropology of Experience', in Victor W. Turner and Edward M. Bruner (eds), *The Anthropology of Experience* (Chicago: University of Illinois Press, 1986), p.41.
15. James S. Brown, 'Things Not Meant To Heal: Irish "National Allegory" in Doyle, McCabe and McCann', *Nua: Studies in Contemporary Irish Writing*, 1, 1 (1997), p.33.

3

The Retrieval of Dignity:
This Side of Brightness (1998)

NATIONALITY AND ETHNICITY

In the first part of his poetic sequence, 'The Hudson Letter', Derek Mahon summons the diversity of aural and artistic voices that congregate on his New York horizon of the mind. From Dylan Thomas and Charlie Chaplin, we progress to the tones of Respighi and of Lorca – a clamorous dawn chorus in Manhattan for the visiting poet. This section of 'The Hudson Letter', then, is a call to creativity; it is a paean to the international artistry that navigates through New York City, and that takes the metropolis as its stage and as its surrogated home place. Mahon writes:

> The lights go out along the Jersey shore
> and, as Manhattan faces east once more,
> dawn's early light on bridge and water-tower,
> Respighi's temperate nightingale on WQXR
> pipes up though stronger stations throng the ether –
> a radio serendipity to illustrate
> the resilience of our lyric appetite,
> carnivalesque or studiously apart,
> on tap in offices, lofts and desperate 'hoods
> to Lorca's 'urinating multitudes'
> while I make coffee and listen for the news
> at eight; but first the nightingale. Sing, Muse.[1]

Mahon gathers the lyrical impulse and he extols its fortitude as part of the human spirit; technology brings this 'resilience' to the poet's attention. In the midst of the sprawling urbanity of contemporary New York City, Mahon divines the precious durability of fragile art, and out of this sourcing his own lyric emerges. 'The Hudson Letter' is the product of

Mahon's various teaching assignments in New York in the early 1990s and 'is in the first instance a personal letter, written to his close friend Patricia King during his recovery after his severe alcoholic crisis in New York. It is also, however, a report by a city poet on the crisis of the late twentieth-century metropolis.'[2] So, while the poetic emanates from the brisk trade of musicality and aurality on this New York morning, there is a darker, more ominous side to the city temporarily inhabited by Mahon. The poetic sequence is inspired by a deep personal crisis, as Hugh Haughton reveals, which, in turn, takes its poetic form in a meditation on the decline of the urban throng that is New York. During the period in which the poem was written New York was in a crisis of its own, and 'The Hudson Letter' treats of a geography characterized by degeneration. Again, Haughton provides a useful gloss: 'during the early '90s in…subways and squares the social fall-out from post-Reaganite, postmodern America was personified in the homeless, released psychiatric patients, drug addicts, and HIV victims visible in the public spaces across the City. This is the New York of Mahon's poem.'[3] In many ways, this is also the New York of *This Side of Brightness*. While Mahon's poem is a work of profound displacement and crisis, McCann's novel, though written from the vantage point of an Irish writer resident in New York, is less about the author's sense of dislocation than a writer's willingness to immerse themselves in the least visible fastnesses of the city. Written from first-hand experience of the subway tunnels, *This Side of Brightness* certainly deals with urban decay, personal crisis, and the array of social problems listed by Haughton, but it tends towards a commitment to redemption rather than accepting collective and individual atrophy. Both Mahon and McCann foreground the forgotten edges of New York's urban squalor in texts that, through the charge of the aesthetic, bestow a renewed dignity on such locales.

Bringing Mahon's and McCann's literary New Yorks into a tenuous conversation not only raises the squalid environs and moral corruptions of the city over the duration of the last century, but also allows the issue of their nationality to enter the discussion. Both Irish authors deliver differentially displaced perspectives on the city, but what their respective experiences also impress is the variety of New York's historical internationalism, and, implicitly, both texts highlight the levels of impact Irish emigrants have made on the city's culture and society. *This Side of Brightness* may well have been greeted as McCann's least 'Irish' work up to that point, but such a contention is all but defunct. As we shall see, though the narrative action unfolds exclusively within the city, the genealogies of its protagonists are cosmopolitan. The earlier works, *Fishing the Sloe-Black River* and *Songdogs*, both track Irish migrancy in the mid- to late twentieth century, but *This Side of Brightness* gives us the earliest historical account of Irish emigration, and its legacies, in McCann's fiction. Taken as a body, the three early texts confirm the heterogeneity of Irish emigration, and can be read as exemplary of the fact that even within one 'national' diaspora, individual experiences are vastly different. In other words, one of the lessons of McCann's first three books is that we cannot speak lazily of an undifferentiated 'Irish diaspora'. Fintan O'Toole might well argue that 'Ireland is a diaspora...Ireland is often something that happens elsewhere', but such a 'diaspora' and 'elsewhere' are not uniformly identical across histories and geographies of diverse dispersals.[4] Yet neither is *This Side of Brightness* intent on labouring any narrow-gauge variety of Irish identity in contradistinction to those 'alien' or 'other' ethnicities encountered on foot of transatlantic movement. The novel does not conform to any strict dichotomous presentation of incommensurable nationalities or ethnicities and, in this way, anticipates *Let the Great World Spin*. Rather, McCann's narrative displays the common humanity of displaced communities; there are tensions and violences, but *This Side of Brightness* allows differences to blend and to commune. Irish, African-American, Italian communities intermix, contributing and challenging any overarching idea of a pure American national identity. Naturally these are not unproblematic processes but, as Kelly McGovern argues, the novel succeeds in scrutinizing political and cultural hierarchies through its narration of international communality. Invoking the shared solidarities of colonized peoples, McGovern suggests: 'The Irish are only one of many groups that converged, diverged, and transformed identities with respect to each other during that century. These lateral alliances disrupt binary relations between formerly colonized and colonizing national identities that have attempted to contain complex identities as postcolonial hybrids.'[5] The central protagonist, Clarence Nathan Walker, or Treefrog, is the embodiment of this ethnic exchange underscored by McGovern, with his combined Irish and African-American family lineage. But what is crucial is that McCann does not retail international travel as an escape from, or a transcendence of, Irish nationality, but as a process of interrogation of that identity as it comes into contact with a skein of other mobile national identities. Travel does not mean that Irish identity is cashed in in favour of another, less rooted identity, but that its bases are, variously, questioned, adhered to, and/or modified.

THIS SIDE OF BRIGHTNESS

This Side of Brightness is the most expansive treatment of New York City in McCann's fiction up to this point. Both *Fishing the Sloe-Black River* and *Songdogs* have characters who reside in the city, but *This Side of Brightness* takes New York City as its sole setting. McCann portrays a burgeoning, but threatening, urban centre across the twentieth century, as the novel captures the teeming cityscape that is acutely divided along racial and class lines, and that is wracked by violence, drug trade and prostitution. And the novel alights on a variety of characters and locations across the city as it attempts to divine some degree of hopeful resolution to the loneliness and abjection of these lives. The narrative, then, accords with Andreas Huyssen's suggestion that 'no real city can ever be grasped in its present or past totality by any single person. That is why urban imaginaries differ depending on a multitude of perspectives and subject positions.'[6] The novel represents the plural chaos of New York and the city is diverse and segregated, but its plenitude is not devoid of potential future community and hope. Again Huyssen captures the multiplicity evident in the novel: 'All cities are palimpsests of real and diverse experiences and memories...They consist of a cacophony of voices and, more often than not, feature a multiplicity of languages...Urban space is always and inevitably social space involving subjectivities and identities differentiated by class and race, gender and age, education and religion.'[7] For McCann, it is this differential texture of urban space that can alienate, but that ultimately can offer opportunities for solidarity and mutual empathy. Difference, as we see throughout his fiction, is not the basis for cultural hermeticism, but is potentially redemptive and mutually empowering through the sharing of stories. McCann is concerned with examining the metropolitan sub-histories of New York, which can possibly yield narratives of recovery. And one of the ways to conceptualize the novel is in terms of the 'spatiality' suggested by Huyssen. New York City is defined by spatial boundaries of race and class, yet despair and the stirrings of communal or shared redemption are seen to traverse these socially engineered lines of separation. The 'spatiality' of *This Side of Brightness*, then, manifests in the political concerns of the novel. Space and its production are functions of power, and McCann is interested in mining the shadowed spaces of powerlessness that proliferate across New York City. From a theoretical viewpoint, the critical impetus of McCann's novel has affinities with Edward Soja's contention that: 'Spatiality is not only a product but also a producer and reproducer of the relations of production and domination, an instrument of allocative and authoritative power.'[8] Soja's case is laced with Marxist rhetoric, and it would be misguided to pitch McCann's novel in these starkly Marxist terms. But as Soja continues: 'Class struggle, as well as other social struggles, are thus increasingly contained and defined in their spatiality and trapped in its [the State's] grid. Social struggle must then become a consciously and politically spatial struggle to regain control over the social production of space.'[9]

In his collection, *District and Circle*, Seamus Heaney extends his excavation of personal, communal and topographical memories from the peaty repository of bogland to the mortared arteries of the London Underground. In the title poem, 'District and Circle', Heaney narrates the industrial sensuousness of the subterranean transport system. It is a poem in which past, present and future collide in the forms of a fleeting remembrance of the poet's father, a minor moral qualm for the poet in his descent into the humid entrails of the metropolis, and the symbolism of the train's mobility as it hurtles forward with a relentless and shuddering force. The symbolic form of the underground takes on a re-furbished, updated, guise in 'District and Circle', but the content remains as resonant for the poet. Rather than narrating, or re-imagining, archaeological and memorial exhumations, and infusing such 're-births' with moral and historical valences, Heaney now physically descends into the underground himself. The poet enters the liminal zone of evolution, he boards the channels of transportation that ferry people between concrete destinations. Both the initial process of escalatory descent and the herd-like crowding on the underground carriage are spurs to poetic self-consciousness. While the brachiating lines of the metropolitan transport system are facilities of the functioning of capitalist modernity, and, as such, generate anonymity, silence, facelessness, and atomization among the population of users, the poet's encounter with the underground busker and his facial reflection in the door window foster a sense of individual awareness and reflection, perhaps even crisis. It is telling that in this most public of transitional spaces Heaney is brought to a renewed pitch of personal, intimate self-reckoning.[10] And in his novel *This Side of Brightness*, McCann's characters inhabit just such a landscape – a subterranean space of transition, remote from, yet coeval with, the normative patterns of metropolitan life in New York City. McCann's fictional portrait of this submerged urban landscape is based on the author's own personal research into life in the recesses of New York's subway tunnels. Entering the tunnels as much as four or five times a week, tentatively at first, McCann has testified to the variety of life pulsing through the redundant space of the tunnels. From both McCann's testimony and, of course, his fictional rendition, the subway tunnels are spaces in which despair can find refuge and escape, but also redemption and rebirth. In many ways they are exiled from the rhythms of everyday life, with its attendant pressures, routines, and expectations – locations where alternative modes of behaviour are pursued. Likewise, as McCann remarks below, a certain solidarity is palpable between the fragmented residents of the tunnels; their combined situation in the underground is an affront to, an indictment of modern society's hypocrisies:

> I met all sorts of people – junkies, war veterans, people who'd recently been let out of mental asylums, others who had just lost their jobs. I was put in all sorts of different situations. But being Irish helped me – I was never seen as part of the established order, the system. I was outside. And they were outsiders too. So often I felt aligned with the people who were living underground.[11]

A little beyond the halfway point of the novel, one of the central protagonists', Treefrog's, fellow subway dwellers, 'Faraday', is killed in a gruesome and spectacular accident. Living up to his nickname, Faraday 'had gone fishing for electricity way downtown in the Second Avenue tunnel. He went to help someone hook up a transformer but on the way he found a fishing rod in a Bowery dumpster.'[12] But like many tunnel residents, Faraday was afflicted by a drug problem, heroin in his case, and on this occasion it cost him his life. Disoriented and stumbling while he was casting the fishing line across the rail tracks, Faraday's hand touched the third rail and 'the current sucked him in and his body went lengthwise against the metal and the fishing rod completed the circuit and he must have been a corpse of wild blue sparks. Every fluid in his body boiled first, all the blood and water and semen and alcohol dying to nothing. Six hundred volts of direct current blew a hole in the top of his head' (*TSB*, 129–30). Not only is his death graphic and pyrotechnic, but in figuring it in terms of the grace notes of fishing, McCann alludes to both of his previous publications. But the distinction in this case is in the brutality of Faraday's demise. Faraday's death is reported to his fellow tunnel residents by the New York Police Department (NYPD) and it is the routine exchange between the forces of the law and the tunnel 'moles' that throws into relief the divided moral economies of the city. McCann draws out the encounter between the police and the 'moles' in a protracted exchange in the tunnels. The dialogue that ensues captures the presiding tension that the 'moles' elicit from 'topside' life.

After their initial disorientation on entering the tunnels, the police interrogate the 'moles' about Faraday: 'You all know James Francis Bedford?' (*TSB*, 127). Gradually it becomes clear who James Francis Bedford was, and, more importantly, who he became – 'Faraday'. In an equivalent manner to Treefrog, Faraday's identity is obscured by his isolation, his nickname, and his abdication from 'topside' life. There may be echoes of communality in the tunnel, but there is rarely any sustained intimacy. This is also another instance where the back story of another of the tunnel 'moles' is filled in before we get a full revelation of Treefrog's background. Faraday was a police officer in his former life above ground and this, perhaps, makes his descent more acute than many of his co-residents in the subway. Faraday/Bedford was part of the machinery of law and order outside of this netherworld, a fact not lost on his erstwhile colleagues: '"He was good people," says the cop. "Had himself an accident once. Lost his nerve. Shot someone. Never recovered. His family asked me to come down and get his stuff. Good people, Bedford's family. They was all good people. Even Bedford was good people once. Before he came down here"' (*TSB*, 128). What is most striking is the ease with which the police officer damns his former colleague; once Faraday entered the tunnels he is beyond redemption. The tunnels are emphatically figured as 'other' and as immoral in the minds of those that are removed from their reaches. What this abrupt and unforgiving conclusion on the tunnels exposes is an inability to imagine any circumstance in which they may act as a sanctuary for their dwellers.

The tunnels are blindly viewed as forbidding locales that simply accumulate the detritus and damaged of the 'topside' world. In a sense, Treefrog's narrative is, as we shall see, a rebuke to this conviction. Rather than portraying an unyielding geography of damnation and despair, in McCann's tunnels we can glimpse redemption and hope.

Opening in 1916, a year with obvious historical resonances in an Irish context, *This Side of Brightness* is a lyrical narrative of individual trauma and alienation, and it is characterized by a narrative discontinuity in which liminal experiences occasion forms of personal redemption. McCann has commented that the novel is the story of a family, and that he was interested in the idea of dignity, particularly as seen through a family's experience of life.[13] The novel is divided into two seemingly disparate but in fact deeply related narratives: as mentioned, an historical narrative commencing in 1916 and a contemporary narrative. Crucially, the historical narrative is more panoramic in its focus, providing a lateral communal and family history, while the contemporary narrative is contracted to the tortured consciousness of one legatee of the family history. These combined narratives embrace diverse social discourses including race, economics, marginalized populations, immigrants, poverty, miscegenation, drug addiction and mental illness. McCann's mise-en-scène is the multi-ethnic communities of New York City's emerging migrant quarters. And in keeping pace with the demands of its own industrial growth, the city's infrastructural architecture is physically completed by these very migrant underclasses of Irish, Italian and African-American labourers. We witness the unfurling social fabric of mid-century and latter-day New York simmering in the background, only occasionally penetrating the central narrative of urban subalternity – a social class that is epitomized by the sandhogs, black communities, economic under-class, and essentially the contemporary subway moles. It is a portrait of the transgressive heterogeneity of the urban sprawl that is New York City. In contemporary New York the discarded, and defunct, transportation arteries of the city house the cast-offs of modernity's shadowy underside. Peopled by criminals, psychotics, prostitutes, alcoholics and sexual deviants, the network of disused tunnels constitutes an urban gothic terrain. Recessed within its 700-mile geography we find society's combined repressions and guilt, whose actions and appetites are affronts to the horizons of social acceptability. These subaltern lives persist as chafing reminders of society's complicity in their subterranean abjection.

LIMINALITY AND RECOVERY

In *This Side of Brightness*, McCann's characters cling to forms of moral and emotional hope, and, from a thematic perspective, the narratives register the durability and, most significantly, the possibility of hope. Furthermore, in ventilating his testified belief in hope, or personal redemption, McCann's text can be read as evidential of liminal processes of both moral and emotional awakening. Separation, anonymity, silence, ambiguity, and repetition are the watchwords of McCann's liminal spaces, in which his characters alternatively seek moral and emotional redemption. The viscid darkness in the tunnels of *This Side of Brightness* is pregnant with redemptive silences, and the disintegration of interpersonal relationships impels the protagonist of McCann's text towards the liminal, and its attendant confrontation with the ambiguities of memory, identity and place. My concern, then, with the issues of identity and memory extends to Clarence Nathan Walker, or Treefrog, the product of his grandparents' interracial marriage, and his grandfather Nathan.

The anthropologist Victor Turner characterizes the experience of liminality as 'a stage for unique structures of experience in milieus attached from mundane life and characterized by the presence of ambiguous ideas, monstrous images, sacred symbols, ordeals, humilitions, anonymity'.[14] Physical estrangement and emotional dislocation are inherent to the liminal experience, through which the individual is exposed to ambivalent social and physical spheres, and thereby endowed with a *potentially* liberating sense of anonymity. The structural fecundity of the liminal space, or the essential experience of liminality, is in its diversion from the indicative forms of the everyday. As Turner later suggests: 'the liminal phase is the subjunctive mood of culture, the mood of maybe, might be, as if, hypothesis, fantasy, conjecture, desire'.[15] The ritual, liminal experience, then, offers the possibility of change, but does not promise. As I outline below, in McCann's narrative the subjunctive liminality detailed by Turner is concretized in the somatic experience of estrangement, of alienation and of emotional displacement. In the novel we witness the liminal as somatic immersion in the unfamiliar, or, in arenas of re-configuration and subversion. However, the ambiguity or fructile chaos of the liminal context is not in any sense random. While the indicative operations of cause and effect are eschewed in lieu of conditional modes, the subjunctive liminal remains '[a] storehouse of possibilities', what Turner terms 'a striving after new forms and structures, a gestation process, a fetation of modes appropriate to postliminal existence'.[16] The isolation, or perhaps invisibility, engenders a degree of spontaneity as detachment from the constricted mores of the quotidian occasions a dissipation of social responsibility.[17]

McCann's fiction is concerned with remembrance and redemption, and he composes in a narrative style that registers the intimacy of the immediate landscape with the formation of memory. The disintegration of interpersonal relations impels the characters towards the liminal, and its attendant confrontation with the ambiguities of memory, identity and place. The 'limen' then is both the known and the unknown as it problematizes the familiar and domesticates the unfamiliar. My concern with the concepts of identity and liminality extends to the two male protagonists of the novel, Nathan Walker and Treefrog. Firstly, the liminal experience serves as a transitional phase for the younger generations of the Walker family. Equally, the isolation of old age precipitates a yearning for erstwhile sandhog comradeship by Walker. Walker remains detached from the vagaries of an external world through totemistic dedication to desire and fantastic reverie. But in an adjacent manner the tunnels are the 'in-between' spaces cited by Turner, in which the normative protocols of society are summarily suspended in a 'democracy of darkness' (*TSB*, 5). They are both peripheral and central to the everyday routines of New York; they are 'really the subconscious or unconscious mind of New York City. It contains all that the city above ground chooses not to think about. It is a world apart yet it is also the root.'[18] In Nathan Walker's eyes the tunnels resonate with utility and community in the art of digging. The work of the tunnels lies athwart the topside social mores, but, simultaneously, it is ultimately pivotal to the functioning of the evolving metropolis. Further, we uncover the sanctuary afforded by the darkness, specifically in the tunnels beneath the East River, which proves central to McCann's portrait of these urban liminal spaces. The torrid emotional and psychological traumas of two generations of the Walker family are satiated by the repose of these tunnels that are 'high and wide and dark and familiar' (*TSB*, 2). Nathan Walker spends most of his adult life as a sandhog, preparing the underground for New York's burgeoning modernization. And yet upon retirement, the topside world holds little appeal for him. Above ground his mixed-race marriage and progeny, and his own racial ethnicity, are exposed to the ravages of mid-century bigotry. Equally, at a physical level, the decades of subterranean digging have crippled his body and the only physical movements available to him are his occasional jaunts on the underground trams, supplemented by his daydream reminiscing about his years spent rhythmically excavating the New York underground. The tunnels facilitate an 'equality of darkness' (*TSB*, 37), a non-prejudicial space in an acutely divided city and nation. A culture of mutual respect and toleration among the 'sandhogs' is engendered by the threat of death and the prospect of overwhelming natural violence beneath the East River. The perverse democracy of Walker's working environment beneath the river persists in Treefrog's dank liminal space a generation later, as he 'feels the darkness, smells it, belongs to it' (*TSB*, 23). Conventional social contours are dissolved and anonymity provides shelter from judgement, as a muted solidarity is fostered in the tunnels by the equalizing proximity of life-threatening violence.

Walker's vocational digging exhibits the intimacy that existed between the sandhog and his labour, just as it reveals the uncomplicated communality of the harsh occupation. We note Walker's emotional recollections of his laborious working life as they intertwine with an imaginative digging of childhood memories of Georgia which, 'by remembering he invented and by inventing he remembered' (*TSB*, 82). The natural isolation of his childhood with its rustic physicality echoes in the brutish physicality of his years as a sandhog. Walker facilitates the liminal experience endured by his grandson, as the tunnels become a cross-generational palliative space. But while Treefrog's experience results in some form of 'resurrection', Walker's yields only his nostalgic yearning for a return to 'the miasmic dark' (*TSB*, 2). Walker's memories are crystallized in the mid-day reveries of his romantic downward glances.[19] His bond with the tunnels is both physically and emotionally satisfying and the temperate sanctuary of damp and darkness measures out Walker's years in the tunnels until it becomes part of him in every sense; we note: '[the] river's muck is cool against his skin...is good to touch and soon he is filthy from head to toe' (*TSB*, 9). The rhythm of the tunnels seeps into his very pores and he 'notes the passing of years by the way the tunnel-dust settles down in his lungs' (*TSB*, 46–7) and by the ever-worsening rheumatic pain that afflicts his every movement. The tunnels are the sole constant in Walker's working life, he moves from dig to dig as little else impinges on the ritual of his daily descent into the tunnels' 'yellowy darkness' (*TSB*, 9). Indeed, there is a cryptic symmetry to the manner of Walker's death in the subway tunnel as both Walker and Treefrog have been surreptitiously walking through the very tunnel in which the 1916 blow-out occurred, during which Treefrog's great-grandfather was killed. The circuitous closure of the call of the consuming darkness resolves the tedium of Walker's convalescent years. In a strange inversion he walks towards and beseeches the assurance of the dark tunnels as a respite, as a grave. Just as the claustrophobic sanctuary of the tunnels offers Nathan Walker a totemic release from the realities of New York, the act of digging itself becomes a resonant image within the text. The crossover between contemporary and historical narratives is dependent on the notion of 'digging', in a physical sense as well as a metaphorical sense. Through the laborious tunnelling of his grandfather Treefrog now has the liminal space in which to perform his own torturous emotional digging and to conduct what becomes a solitary vigil of balance and repetition. Nathan Walker spent his life in the rapture of physical digging and subsequent years obsessed with 'the fluidity of his shovel, wishing to be back down underneath digging' (*TSB*, 120), and similarly Treefrog's existence thrives in the midst of an alternative, underground womb. Order, balance and darkness are the emotional and physical coordinates of Treefrog's subterranean liminal milieu. The private tyranny of pathological balance is untenable in the topside world of daily human interaction. But in a liminal space that is replete with ambiguity, menace and estrangement, Treefrog's compulsive neurosis of repetition and equilibrium can flourish. McCann's descriptions of the tunnels and their vagabond populace capture the disjointed textures of Treefrog's urban underworld, with the sight of snow swirling through the grille into the underground dark, the sound of an out-of-tune piano in an abandoned subway station, and the smell of a steam-filled room deep below Grand Central Terminal.[20]

Treefrog's tunnels are occupied by 'moles': broken individuals who have forsaken or been discarded by topside life. Treefrog and his fellow moles exist contrary to the day-to-day rituals of topside New York; each possesses a narrative, a story of loss or of trauma that has impelled them to this turgid habitat. The proximity of menace in the shape of physical, sexual or psychological violence demands a keen sense of self-preservation. Similarly, it compromises trust and re-focuses the individual consciousness onto the self and the immediate. The incongruity of the liminal space that resides athwart the topside reality indulges excess but ultimately delivers some form of resolution in the form of death, emotional capitulation or recovery. Yet there is an occasional sense of loose and fragile kinship that is predicated on shared experiences of loneliness, misfortune and deprivation. Self-justification is at the heart of Treefrog's liminal experience as he has transgressed in a most obscene manner in a series of acts that have robbed him of his wife and his daughter. The 'leftovers of human ruin' (*TSB*, 56) inhabit Treefrog's subterranean dwelling, as McCann locates the story of traumatic self-redemption within the detritus of urban humanity. Treefrog's vistas comprise 'broken bottles and rat droppings and a baby carriage and a smashed T.V. and squashed cans and cardboard boxes and shattered jars' (*TSB*, 24); it is a brutal underground life of simmering violence, destitution and substance abuse. We are confronted with a stark subterranean landscape, a shattered wasteland that mirrors the anxieties and self-loathing of Treefrog. The environment of disarray and of displaced materials provides an essential liminal context. His search for redemption is tentatively actualized in his assiduous 'mapping' of the tunnels and it becomes 'his most important ritual' (*TSB*, 24). The 'cartography of darkness' (*TSB*, 25) is not a guiding light for Treefrog, but an aspirational mode of self-redemption. It constitutes an attempt to seek out restitution in a purgatorial landscape. The maps are, perversely, composed in blindness, and consequentially their parameters are exaggerated and ambiguous. Treefrog's subterranean retreat represents a cessation of the historical narrative in the text and his abdication of topside life is a liminal crisis of identity. The certitude of his own identity can no longer be taken for granted as he descends into alcoholism and mental illness. The rich darkness of the tunnels inflicts a blindness in which 'nothing announces its approach except memory' (*TSB*, 24). Treefrog recedes into a state of personal squalor as he permits his body and his attire to decay beyond normal recognition. The darkness and the routine of equilibrium serve as psychological placebos to the torturous emotional confrontations of topside life. And a lifestyle of furtive scavenging, alcohol dependence and physical isolation is accommodated within the 'clarifying dark' (*TSB*, 25) and is symptomatic of his overwhelming guilt. Within the tunnels, '[the] blackest blackness' (*TSB*, 237) permits the stealthy and shattering approach of memory, or as he terms it, 'the ancestry of song' (*TSB*, 242). The two-fold guilt that assails Treefrog is assuaged by this search for ancestry and he legitimates his own redemption by entwining the motive of one failure with the guilt of the other.

Treefrog betrays the anonymity of the tunnels by confessing his guilt to Angela and she becomes a ghost or an angel of absolution through whom he can mediate his burgeoning resurrection to Nathan's ghost and to his absent wife and daughter. Thus Turner argues that 'liminality is frequently likened to death, to being in the womb, to invisibility, to darkness, to bisexuality, to the wilderness, and to an eclipse of the sun or moon'.[21] It is an idea that McCann has actually alluded to elsewhere, suggesting that 'the dead are the only family that the tunnel residents have';[22] indeed, the moles themselves resemble a community of subterranean revenants. Treefrog's self-absolution, facilitated through Angela, is realized in the hemmed-in darkness of his confessional-like nest. Angela's presence, her recognizable consciousness, is all that Treefrog requires in order to convince himself of the possibility of resurrection. Her proximity to, and intimacy with, Treefrog fosters a sense of liminal *communitas*, whereby a tenuous mutual recognition of transition or 'otherness' is forged. As Turner concludes, the *communitas* of liminal entities manifests itself in 'a blend of humility and comradeship'.[23] Equally, the suspension of chronological dependence within 'alternative social arrangements'[24] engenders a feeling of motionlessness. Treefrog's 'ancestry of song' tunnels its way from topside past to underground present during days that are replete with dysfunctional time, and are sundered of temporal functionality. Slowness allows memory to percolate through our consciousness, whereas speed or urgency prevents the stealthy approach of memory: 'place is bound up with pace. The more you seek to get away from a place, the faster you go...the slower you go, the more you become aware of place...the more you become aware of the place of memory.'[25] Some semblance of re-location is only achieved underground in the thrall of incessant repetition and rhythm. The micro-communities of liminal space, where race, class and sexuality are rendered redundant, and ultimately inconsequential, are attuned to this sense of rhythm and repetition. Simultaneously, however, the stark underground sanctuary acts upon the fatigued and tortured individual. The music of the tunnels, just like the persistent din of passing trains, echoes through generations from Walker's spirituals down to Treefrog's renditions on the harmonica in the ancestry of song. Through a startling imbrication of music, rhythmic digging and balance, McCann enhances the idea of a profoundly spiritual as well as physically affective liminal space.

MUSIC AND HOPE

As Treefrog prepares to depart his underground cavern at the end of the novel, as he concludes the narrative with a resolution to leave his fellow tunnel dwellers 'to their own brutalities and all the winters yet to come' (*TSB*, 242), he is assailed by a piercing memory of his 'topside' life. His departure from the tunnels takes him past 'the piles of cans and the shopping trolley and the baby carriage and the dead tree and the scent of shit and piss and every other ounce of imaginable worldly filth' (*TSB*, 242). The discarded materials of everyday life stand hoarded along his exit from the subway system. But as Treefrog processes away from this physical carnage, his past re-appears in the bracing, intangible form of the 'ancestry of song' (*TSB*, 242). The musical inheritance that originates, in this narrative, in his grandfather, Nathan Walker, surfaces as a sign of Treefrog's impending, perhaps imperfect, resurrection from his abject condition. Not only does this musical lineage discharge from the recesses of Treefrog's memory, it issues with equal force from the history of the tunnels. As we shall see, the tunnels were and are transformed into chambers of music by Nathan Walker during his sandhog days excavating their grand contours. In a sense, the durable musical motif in the novel is an essential element of the utopian geist of the narrative. From an intertextual point of view, the space that music arrogates for itself within the figurative economy of *This Side of Brightness* marries it to the musical figurations present in *Fishing the Sloe-Black River*; *Zoli*; and *Dancer*. But what is also notable is the nature of the musical culture invoked by McCann, because this impacts upon our readings of the cultural politics of the novel. Music and lyricism may, at first glance, be of a piece with the intertextual self consciousness apparent in *Fishing the Sloe-Black River* and *Songdogs*, but it is also deployed to specific political ends by the author. The 'ancestry of song' referred to above by Treefrog, then, spools us back to the beginning of the novel.

The generations of the Walker family are, then, connected by an 'ancestry of song', a lyrical and corporeal adhesive that binds the memories of the family unit across the century. And it is worth dwelling on the trope of musicality in terms of how it contributes to the rite of redemption undergone by Treefrog. In more expansive terms, we might query, where and how does McCann assert the utopian potentials of the musical in the lives of his socially excluded characters? In the opening sequence of the novel, McCann convenes some of its most resonant figurations: Treefrog finds a dead crane and sets it free on the frozen waters of the Hudson River; he subsequently returns to his tunnel lair to hear 'a train rumble in the distance' (*TSB*, 2). The carcass of the once graceful bird is a mockery of its poise in flight and its deathly condition is a natural correlative of Treefrog's wretched state. The iced stasis of the river is qualitatively different from the fluvial figurations elsewhere in McCann's work, as here it is further suggestive of Treefrog's subterranean limbo. Yet there is a counterpoint to the intrusive discordance of the timbres of the passing train and the carcass of the deceased bird. The violent pitch of the locomotive is matched and superseded by the grace notes of a Hohner harmonica. As the short first chapter draws to a close, music revivifies Treefrog and his underground habitation; it acts as a corrective to the silence of death and the noise of mass transportation:

> From the depths of the drawer Treefrog took out a small purple jewellery bag, undid the yellow string. For a moment he warmed the harmonica in his gloved fist above the fire. He put it to his mouth, tested its warmth, and pulled in a net of tunnel air. The Hohner slipped along his lips. His tongue flickered in against the reeds and the tendons of his neck shone. He felt like the music was breathing him, asserting itself through him. A vision of his daughter whipped up – she was there, she was listening, she was part of his music, she sat with her knees tucked up to her chest and rocked back and forth in childish ecstasy – and he thought once again of the frozen crane in the river. Sitting there, in his nest, in the miasmic dark, Treefrog played, transforming the air, giving back to the tunnels their original music. (*TSB*, 2)

The music is connective and it is regenerative. Treefrog's musical interlude is, in fact, a precise and necessary personal ritual – among others he adopts in the tunnel. In his description of the ritual, McCann captures beautifully the interplay of the musician's body and the musical instrument. There is also a vividness to the catalyzing effects of music on human emotions and on human memory. In this instance, the cadences of the Hohner harmonica summon memories from Treefrog's past – the presence of his daughter; the harmonica is a family heirloom from his grandfather; and the tunnels that were once animated by the music of Nathan Walker's singing. But these memories are not passive nostalgic effects inspired by the music; rather they are part of Treefrog's painful, sustained reckoning with his past failings. The 'ancestry of song', the musical inheritances are sustenance during, and inspiration to persist with, his purgatorial sentence. Built into the very fabric of all musical expression is the motive force of desire and, as Vincent Geoghegan explains: 'Desire for that which is missing is therefore present at the very birth of music.'[26] Treefrog's musical initiation of the novel should not be read as a powerless lament for that which has gone, but, alternatively, as a keen expression of desire for renewal and for reconciliation. In personal terms, there is a singular utopian impulse evident at the outset of *This Side of Brightness*, one that propels many of the characters towards personal change, personal redemption, and simple levels of personal happiness. Treefrog strikes another keynote at this early stage, interblending desire and music in a novel that is populated by a marginal, racialized working-class family. It is the key conjunction of desire and music that Ernst Bloch has in mind in his social critique of music in *The Principle of Hope*. In a curiously apposite argument, Bloch writes: 'music, by virtue of its so immediately human capacity of expression, has more than any other art, the quality of incorporating the numerous sufferings, the wishes and the spots of light of the oppressed class.'[27] While McCann's narrative cannot be conscripted to the Messianic Marxism of Bloch, the consonance between their relative faiths in the power of music as a redemptive agent allies their vision of the utopian in the most remote corners of the everyday. Highlighting the affectiveness of music, then, is a self-conscious celebration of the power of the aesthetic by McCann, but it is also, in tune with Bloch, a part of his political commitment and social conscience as a literary artist.

As the narrative winds backwards to the historical back story to

Treefrog's life we reach 1916 and the period in which the tunnels were designed, dug-out and completed. And in this context too, the juxtaposition of industrial or natural aural dissonance with the soothing redemptive tones of the musical is apparent. The East River, and its underground territories, looms as overwhelming forces that diminish and destroy sound. Descent underground, under the river via modern technology, is a disorienting process: 'The foreman nods at the two sandhogs and they join the group at the mouth of the shaft. They stand close together and move forward. Walker hears the whine of the compression machine from underground. It's a long hard high sound that will soon become nothing in his ears – the river is a grabber of sound, taking it, swallowing it' (*TSB*, 4). But on reaching their appointed labouring point underground, and as the four lead sandhogs chisel away incrementally at the formidable underground obstacles in the way of modern progress, Nathan Walker's fluid digging motion is accompanied by his mellow singing voice. Walker's musical enunciation acts, firstly, as a respite, a welcome lyrical distraction from the repetitive graft of their labour. But it is also an expression of unverbalized desire. The rhythmic union of body and voice beneath the East River is a gesture of futurity as it transcends the stark, endarkened and cloistered limits of the tunnel space. Walker's singing is a defiant assertion of individual identity and performs as 'a tool for the creation or consolidation of a community'.[28] The spare physicality and the expendable anonymity of the sandhog populous is refined in Walker's cadences, as Hepburn argues:

> Singing effaces neither the body, nor instincts, nor passions, nor reason, nor cognition; it remains the gesture of emotion, unlike speech, which flattens, regularizes, grammatizes, and declaims. Singing obviates identity (any number of singers can perform the same song) and expands it (no two singers sing alike). Singing announces the secret wishes and desires that cannot be spoken in straightforward speech, and these wishes arise from the flesh. Music, especially sung words, embellishes and re-invigorates prosody with emotion. Music is corporeal, not linguistic.[29]

The reduction of the sandhogs' bodies to functions of the progressive geographical vectors of modernization is countered by the 'secret wishes' nested within the vocal lyricism of Nathan Walker. Hepburn's argument retrieves the Blochian fixation of desire and hope with the impacts of the musical and also recovers the essential 'embodiment' of all musical performance. Music does not exist without performance; it may be out-lined in notation, but this never achieves the affective embodied agency of performed lyricism. In a manner that anticipates the performances of both Rudi in *Dancer* and Zoli Novotna in *Zoli*, McCann's utopian mobilization of music in *This Side of Brightness* reminds us of Daniel Barenboim's conclusion: 'Music has a power that goes beyond words. It has the power to move us and it has the sheer physical power of sound, which literally resounds within our bodies for the duration of its existence.'[30] In these brutal subterranean surroundings, music coa-lesces with the multicultural 'democracy of darkness' as a viable utopian energy. Music, from a utopian viewpoint, is a manifestation of what Bloch termed the 'Not-Yet'. It is expectant and hopeful and is a sensual language that is loaded with the promise of something and someplace better. Soja's explication of the spatial politics of modernity is evident, physically and figuratively, in the occupational entombment of Nathan Walker and his international band of fellow sandhogs. However, with the timbres of singing and lyricism resonating through the claustrophobic spaces of the subway tunnels, an anticipatory consciousness is in evidence. In these ways, music 'is not simply an interlude of consolation but one that drives forward to transformation, rebellion and revolution'.[31] In *This Side of Brightness* we are not witness to any outright 'rebellion', but the transformative spirit of music is impressed by McCann.

In the months and years after the fatal tunnel blow-out in 1916, Walker returns to his habitual sandhog lifestyle; he descends into the city's entrails and is always mindful of his deceased friend entombed in the river-bed above his head. Con O'Leary's missing body solemnizes the underground landscape, turning the tunnels into a grave at the same time as they perform as arteries of the city's transport system. Death and punishing labour are constant presences in the tunnels, but Walker finds relief in the co-location of memory and desire in the rhythmic somatic articulation of his digging. Walker's lyrical expressiveness in McCann's narrative, then, recalls Alex Aronson's suggestion that: 'the en-counter between auditory stimuli and the visual associations or mental processes they evoke is...of growing concern to the novelist who no longer acknowledges any uniform division between what is past, passing or to come. For the musical experience frequently occurs at the still point where memory and desire meet.'[32] So as Walker begins another day by saluting his deceased friend, and future father-in-law, his body commences its fluid digging motion in silence: 'but – after a while – he begins to feel the rhythm seep into him and he lets his tunnel song escape his lips, Lord I ain't seen a sunset since I came on down, no, I ain't seen nothing like a sunset since I came on down' (*TSB*, 34). There may be a plaintive quality to Walker's 'tunnel song', but its relieving rhythm is married to the physical toll of his occupation. The song represents a resistant lyrical affront to the physical marginality of his occupation, his race, and his class. The song itself is an inheritance, assumed by Walker along the 'ancestry of song', which will be endowed to future generations of his family.

As the years pass, McCann's narration of Walker's life encompasses many of the key social thematics of mid-century American life: institutional racism, popular culture, and the growth of the urban working underclass. And Walker's, and his family's, lives are microcosmic of these larger social patterns. At the height of Prohibition, Walker is living and working in Manhattan, and his life has taken on a regular, if sometimes brutal, routine. He is confronted with both casual and institutionalized prejudice: 'Occasionally he ends up in a tunnel fight that is not of his making, and he only fights if he absolutely has to. Still, he flings a powerful punch, puts all muscle into it…He puts away money in a Negro bank – it gains less interest, but at least it is with his own and he feels that it is safe' (*TSB*, 46). These combined pressures and grievances will admit of no publicly verbalized outrage or protest by Walker; he must endure these socially sanctioned assaults. But the private vigour provided by his love of music can be read as a residue of personal desire, which runs counter to the violent trammelling of social options available elsewhere. In the same paragraph as the litany of racism cited above, we learn that: 'On his twenty-fifth birthday he splurges on a Victrola in a Harlem store…Let it roll. Let it sound on out. Two years later, he buys an even finer model with a special stylus. He carts it home and winds the handle carefully. Jazz music erupts around him and he does wild solitary dances around his apartment' (*TSB*, 46). Walker's predilection for jazz music can easily be figured in terms of his racial ethnicity and his socio-economic status, but as has been widely documented, jazz assumed political resonances in popular American culture: 'jazz could lay claim to developing a musical language more capable of inscribing the sensuous life of the modern city, the feelings of ordinary people, their hopes, affections, fears and griefs; it could lay claim to being an authentic voice of the subject in the modern metropolis, of being a vehicle for the spirit and a reservoir of subjective energies.'³³ Witkin's précis of the utopian capacities of jazz music resonates with McCann's employment of musicality. It establishes the social and cultural credentials of his protagonist, Nathan Walker, and it successfully contributes to the creation of the metropolitan New York City milieu of the novel's historical narrative. Jazz becomes a cultural coordinate and partakes of the musical utopianism of the novel. The juxtaposition of fevered racial hatred and private musical respite dramatizes the redemptive dynamics of McCann's narrative. The context of Witkin's argument is also revealing in that it is drawn from a book on Adorno, and Adorno would admit to none of the utopian possibilities of jazz music. According to his refined musical palate, jazz was nothing besides a commodified musical variety. In Witkin's terms, jazz 'was the very antithesis of the modernist project in music to which he was committed...jazz was essentially a formulaic music, a ritualized and impoverished performance.'³⁴ Yet *pace* Adorno, McCann's deployment of 'low' musical culture in the form of jazz might not be high modernist, but it contains the utopian knots espoused by Bloch in his critique of music. Superficially, popular musical elements in the narrative may provide necessary cultural background for McCann's historical narrative, but they also are facets of his utopian political exercise.

The presence of jazz as a palliative refuge for Nathan Walker mirrors the sanctuary of the uterine spaces of the tunnels. And this sense of respite and hope nourishes the younger Walker and fills out his later years, when his mobility has been severely limited and his family circumstances have been tragically altered. As the 1950s begin in Chapter 8, the middle-aged Walker has become a prisoner in his own body; the decades of extreme physical effort in the tunnels have broken him. He sits inside his apartment, confined to a daily routine of domestic inertia, intruded upon by the discordant soundscape of the city on his doorstep. As he rests on his sofa, he is perched above the street that has become 'maddened in recent years by motor cars' (*TSB*, 108). Nathan is physically paralyzed and is animated only by the return of memories provoked by music. In a frank but suggestive description, McCann establishes Nathan's dependence on jazz music and, equally, conveys the severity of his withered physicality:

> The stylus of the record player tumbles across an old jazz record. Louis Armstrong. The pulse of the man. The gorgeous rhythm. The syncopated slide. Walker moves his head to the beat and the silver cross sways gently against his neck. When the record finishes he stands up from the sofa to break the cramp in his knees and stretches wide, bending the pain from his fingers. Carefully he places the needle in a groove just beyond a scratch in the vinyl. Last week the needle began to skip, but the jabs were so terrible in his knees that he just let it sound over and over and over again at the point of a shrill trumpet note – it got to the stage where he didn't hear it anymore, he was back underneath a river, he was digging, his friends were around him, it was the compressor sounding out. (*TSB*, 108–9)

For Nathan, music and the tunnels are inextricably linked; music belongs in the tunnels, it aided the excavation of the tunnels, and it is a contemporary prompt to those earlier days in his life. Louis Armstrong's 'pulse', 'the gorgeous rhythm', might equally be referring to the steady lyricism of Nathan's youthful digging routine, and recalls the rhythmic physicality of Heaney's 'Digging'. Music becomes a way of communing with the past for Walker; it enables him to resist the degenerating confines of the present in his bodily decline. As McCann puts it at another point: 'Walker lets the music roam in him' (*TSB*, 109). Music is an energizing force in the narrative; it propels, it relieves and it liberates in many different ways and contexts across the Walker family lineage.

This Side of Brightness narrates the lives that populate an urban netherworld in New York City, and this invisible landscape is wracked by the fears and indignities of its junked population. Homeless and impoverished, this loose community is individually and collectively flensed of human dignity and they occupy the ultimate site of social marginalization. In his *Reith Lectures*, the Nobel Laureate Wole Soyinka foregrounds the precariousness of just such human dignity in the face of overwhelming political and economic power in the contemporary world. At a general level, there seems to be a moral consensus between Soyinka's philosophical argument and McCann's literary ethics. Central to Soyinka's contentions are the mutuality of dignity, freedom, respect, and community, and he foregrounds these as the basic units of functional human collectivities. In his view, the late twentieth century is a period during which these have been denied or threatened with ever-greater acceleration and alacrity. He diagnoses a 'global climate of fear', which 'owes much to the devaluation or denial of dignity in the intersection of Communities, most notably between the stronger and the weaker ones'.[35] Marginalization, victimization and disenfranchizement are processes that are instrumental within this 'climate of fear' and they are central themes of McCann's fictions. Specifically, the urban nether-world of *This Side of Brightness* is haunted by permanent menace and fearfulness, and the conditions of the urban subalterns charted by Mc-Cann seem at odds with the fundamental requirements of respecting human dignity essayed by Soyinka. In his view: 'it is within human re-lationships that the essence of a human attribute, such as dignity, is most meaningfully sought, not within the self as some mystic endowment, but as a product of social interaction.'[36] McCann attempts to restore a level of dignity and of humanity to the marginalized populations of twenti-eth-century New York City by embracing and by representing their sto-ries in his narrative. Their impoverished anonymity is remedied to some extent by McCann's narration of the micro-history of three generations of the Walker family. He points towards the vitality and the tragedy of New York City's 'unconscious' populations, and, once more, brings a democratic spirit to his storytelling. McCann preserves a narrative space for those that inhabit the nowhere and liminal territories of a cosmopolitan, global city. As an authorial action and as a specific plot, *This Side of Brightness* is a gesture of redemption and chimes with Soyinka's ethical imperatives towards human dignity.

NOTES

1. Derek Mahon, 'The Hudson Letter', *Collected Poems* (Loughcrew, Oldcastle: Gallery Press, 1999), pp.186–7.
2. Hugh Haughton, *The Poetry of Derek Mahon* (Oxford: Oxford University Press, 2007), p.226.
3. Ibid., p.228.
4. Fintan O'Toole, *The Lie of the Land: Irish Identities* (Dublin: New Island Books, 1998), p.12.
5. Kelly McGovern, 'Burying Con O'Leary: New York Cartographies of Identity in Colum McCann's *This Side of Brightness*', in Gerhard Stilz (ed.), *Territorial Terrors: Contested Spaces in Colonial and Postcolonial Writing* (Wurzburg: Verlag Konigshausen & Neumann, 2007), p.176.
6. Andreas Huyssen, 'Introduction: World Cultures, World Cities', in Andreas Huyssen (ed.), *Other Cities, Other Worlds: Urban Imaginaries in a Globalizing Age* (Durham, NC and London: Duke University Press, 2008), p.3.
7. Ibid.

8. Edward Soja, 'The Spatiality of Social Life: Towards a Transformative Retheorisation', in Derek Gregory and John Urry (eds), *Social Relations and Spatial Structures* (Basingstoke: Macmillan, 1985), p.110.
9. Ibid.
10. It is not insignificant that Heaney is positioned in the underground in London, which is part of a longer history of Britain's transportation network that was built with the employment of the labour of emigrant Irish populations.
11. Colum McCann, '*This Side of Brightness* Interview', *Colum McCann Official Author Website*, www.colummccann.com.
12. Colum McCann, *This Side of Brightness* (London: Phoenix House, 1998), p.129. All further references to *This Side of Brightness* will appear in parenthesis as (*TSB*).
13. Eileen Battersby, 'Coming Up for Air: An Interview with Colum McCann', *Irish Times*, (15 January 1998).
14. Victor W. Turner, 'Dewey, Dilthey, and Drama: An Essay in the Anthropology of Experience', in Victor W. Turner and Edward M. Bruner (eds), *The Anthropology of Experience* (Chicago: University of Illinois Press, 1986), p.41.
15. Ibid., p.42.
16. Ibid.
17. Victor W. Turner, 'Liminality and Community', in Jeffrey C. Alexander and Steven Seidman (eds), *Culture and Society: Contemporary Debates* (Cambridge: Cambridge University Press, 1990), p.153.
18. McCann, '*This Side of Brightness* Interview'.
19. John F. Healy, 'Dancing Cranes and Frozen Birds: The Fleeting Resurrections of Colum McCann', *New Hibernia Review*, 4, 3 (2000), p.113.
20. David Willis-McCullough, 'Tunnel Vision', *New York Times on the Web* (5 April 1998). www.nytimes.com/pages/readersopinions/index.html. Accessed 22 May 2005.
21. Turner, 'Liminality and Community', p.147.
22. Colum McCann, 'The Tunnels Under New York City', *Fotoshoot Magazine*, A.1 (5 February 1995). www.fotoshow.com/magazine/tunnels_a.html. Accessed 11 Febtuary 2006.
23. Edith L.B. Turner, *On the Edge of the Bush: Anthropology as Experience* (Tucson, AZ: University of Arizona Press, 1985), p.173.
24. Victor W. Turner, *Drama, Fields, and Metaphors: Symbolic Action in Human Society* (Ithaca, NY: Cornell University Press, 1974), pp.13–14.
25. Michael Cronin, 'Inside Out: Time and Place in Global Ireland', in Éamon Maher (ed.), *Cultural Perspectives on Globalisation and Ireland* (Bern: Peter Lang, 2009), p.12.
26. Vincent Geoghegan, *Ernst Bloch* (London: Routledge, 1996), p.53.
27. Ernst Bloch, *The Principle of Hope* (Cambridge and London: MIT Press, 1986), p.1063.
28. Allan Hepburn, 'Noise, Music, Voice, *Dubliners*', in Sebastian Knowles (ed.), *Bronze by Gold: The Music of Joyce* (New York and London: Garland Publishing, 1999), p.196.
29. Ibid., pp.205–6.
30. Daniel Barenboim, *Everything is Connected: The Power of Music* (London: Weidenfeld & Nicolson, 2008), p.115.
31. Ruth Levitas and Tom Moylan, 'Introduction: The Once and Future Orpheus', *Utopian Studies – Special Issue: Music and Utopia*, 21, 2 (2010), p.213.
32. Alex Aronson, *Music and the Novel: A Study in Twentieth-Century Fiction* (Totowa, NJ: Rowman & Littlefield, 1980), p.x.
33. Robert W. Witkin, *Adorno on Music* (London: Routledge, 1998), p.161.
34. Ibid., p.171.
35. Wole Soyinka, *Climate of Fear* (London: Profile Books, 2004), p.95.
36. Ibid., p.92.

4

Hope and Youth: *Everything in This Country Must* (2000)

LITERATURE, HOPE AND THE 'TROUBLES'

The Northern Irish 'Troubles' have been well narrated within the novel form. Michael Storey estimates that as many as five hundred novels deal with the cultural geography and the political history of the conflict,[1] while Aaron Kelly suggests that in the region of 'four hundred thrillers have been produced over the last 35 years in response to the current phase of political upheaval in Northern Ireland'.[2] In equal measure, the conflict has been widely poetically mediated, as well as being dramatized theatrically – and each of these differential genres have received considerable literary critical attention, both comparatively and in their own right. However, with a few exceptions, the representation of the 'Troubles' in the short story form has received considerably less critical attention.[3] Most recently, Ronan McDonald has published an accomplished essay, 'Strategies of Silence: Colonial Strains in Short Stories of the Troubles',[4] while Storey's *Representing the Troubles in Irish Short Fiction* is the sole book-length survey of this literary genre and the striven history of the Northern 'Troubles'.[5] Notwithstanding the relative merits, and limitations, of these two interventions, McCann's collection *Everything in This Country Must* has not been represented in critical accounts of the fictional heritage of Northern Ireland. My primary foci in this discussion will be the logic of operating within the abbreviated parameters of short fiction in narrating the historical origins and enduring divisions of Northern Irish society. In addition, because of the intensity of carceral violence attendant to the 'Troubles', the discussion will highlight 'the body' as a recurrent thematic presence in the collection, and discuss how it is differentially exhibited as a site of political and cultural contestation, and as a resource for possible political solidarity in the Northern Irish context.

While much of the literary heritage of the 'Troubles' catalogues and ex-plicates the varieties and excesses of savage hatred and violence, writers like Eugene McCabe, Eoin McNamee, Benedict Kiely, and Ciaran Carson, among legion others, have tracked the performance of sectarian conflict across the Northern province over the duration of the 'Troubles'. However, in the current context, and returning to the 'aesthetics of redemption', we will turn briefly to the poetry of the 'Trou-bles' – specifically a cursory glance at a poem by Seamus Heaney. By looking at Heaney's poem 'Keeping Going', and by providing some critical positioning of the poem, one can glean some sense of context for the subsequent arguments. In other words, Heaney's poem offers a poetic keynote to the broader treatment of the 'Troubles' in McCann's short fictions. One of the abiding features of 'Keeping Going' is the endurance of hope as embodied by the poet's brother and, by implication, the poet's own artistic/poetic tribute to that unsullied ordinariness. Literary art is essentially hopeful, even utopian, in its desire and its capacity to imagine alternative social worlds and ethical systems, as well as its facility for radical political and cultural critique. So while Hugh Heaney is offered as an embodiment of redemptive hope, literary art is affirmed as a commensurate utopian form.[6]

In his 1989 Oxford Lecture, *The Redress of Poetry*, Seamus Heaney addresses the ethical capacities of the poetic imagination. Drawing on the work of Simone Weil, Heaney writes:

> 'Obedience to the force of gravity. The greatest sin.' So Simone Weil also writes in *Gravity and Grace*. Indeed her whole book is informed by the idea of counterweighting, of balancing out the forces, of redress – tilting the scales of reality towards some tran-scendent equilibrium. And in the activity of poetry too, there is a tendency to place a counter-reality in the scales – a reality which may be only imagined but which nevertheless has weight because it is imagined within the gravitational pull of the actual and there-fore hold its own and balance out against the historical situation.[7]

It is perhaps inevitable that Heaney advances such a measured précis of the potentials of poetic art given the extreme disequilibrium that obtained in the North of Ireland during the greater part of his life and artistic career. And indeed, his 1996 collection *The Spirit Level* is the most obvious instance in which the very notions of balance and equilibrium are creatively explored at length. Again there is a thematic symmetry here with McCann, in whose works, particularly *This Side of Brightness* and *Let the Great World Spin*, balance and equilibrium are primary motifs. Art, for Heaney, retains material political import in its ability to engender languages of hope in those that expose themselves to its simple truths. Hope, in other words, is a profoundly enabling political cohesive, 'a protest against necessity'; and art, in its turn, embodies a Blochian 'principle of hope'.[8] In *The Spirit Level*, Heaney provides us with one of his most personal, and affective, symbols of such durable hope in 'Keeping Going'.[9] The poem is dedicated to the poet's brother, Hugh, who unlike Heaney, decided to remain resident in Northern Ireland during the course of the worst excesses of the 'Troubles'. 'Keeping Going' is a six-part piece that catalogues Hugh's personal virtues of stoic endurance, good humour and commitment to hard work, while at the same time detailing the encroachment of various forms of moral evil, in the form of Pre-Christian superstition, Macbeth and the witches, and a cold sectarian murder in the local village. The binding agent in all of these is, of course, Hugh's quiet resilience in the face of such moral outrages. 'Keeping Going', Helen Vendler suggests, 'is in part an investigation of the qualities that go to make up that sort of emotional stamina [Hugh's stamina], in part an overview of the atrocious conditions which make the stoic response an heroic one'.[10] She further notes that: 'a great deal of weight in favour of Hugh's choice of life is exerted by this habitual present of decency, exuberance and hard work: one feels Heaney's deep admiration for his brother's restoration of equanimity to everyday existence.'[11]

The formal structure of the poem itself dramatizes the act of equilibrium cited by Heaney above; the aggregated menace of intangible and tangible agents of threat is balanced by the uneroded everydayness of Hugh's routines. Heaney presents naturalistic descriptions of wanton sectarian murder and unalloyed agricultural habits, as they unfold within the same urban space, 'the Diamond'. Countervailing the oppressive burden, and persistent threat, of internecine murder is Hugh's stoic banality, unremarkable yet inspirational for that very reason. Hugh's environs are not unscarred by the legacies of the 'Troubles' and Heaney provides a protracted, almost slow motion cinematic rendition of a particular assassination:

Grey matter like gruel flecked with blood
In spatters on the whitewash. A clean spot
Where his head had been, other stains subsumed
In the parched wall he leant his back against
That morning like any other morning,
Part-time reservist, toting his lunch-box.
A car came slow down Castle Street, made the halt,
Crossed the Diamond, slowed again and stopped
Level with him, although it was not his lift.
And then he saw an ordinary face
For what it was and a gun in his own face.
His right leg was hooked back, his sole and heel
Against the wall, his right knee propped up steady,
So he never moved, just pushed with all his might
Against himself, then fell past the tarred strip,
Feeding the gutter with his copious blood.[12]

Amid the early morning rituals of this rural streetscape, Heaney charts a more sinister ceremony of evil. The density of Heaney's description engenders a sense of simultaneity in the poem – although the poem proceeds over time, the narrative is building in texture rather than unfolding chronologically. That is not to say that the temporal or the historical are elided, they are signalled in the reference to this morning's similarity to any other morning. But the killing is figured in terms of a spatial act; the brutal violation of the carceral within the intimate social space of the town square. Significantly, the act of murder is narrated in terms of the dismemberment of the victim's body; his brain, face, knee, sole, heel and blood are the constituent elements that are invoked in this local theatre of sectarian death. Indeed this is a theme that we will return to below with respect to McCann – the unrelenting assault on the somatic and the figuration of the body as a political site of oppression and resistance are recurring tropes within literary, historical and anthropological engagements with the Northern 'Troubles'.

However, the symbol of hope in the poem is the poet's sibling, to whom he offers the following address:

My dear brother, you have good stamina.
You stay on where it happens. Your big tractor

Pulls up at the Diamond, you wave at people,
You shout and laugh above the revs, you keep
Old roads open by driving on the new ones.[13]

Hugh's routines reclaim the violated space of murder, the defiled
'Diamond', from the unnatural and the unspeakable. Delivered by
Heaney in the reassuring, and affirmative, register of the present tense,
the scene conveyed above is a testament to the possibility of hope and
resolution. Heaney's brother, then, is physically implanted in this
locale and within this community; and again the image of Hugh, akin
to the scene of the earlier murder in the town square, is articulated in
performative terms. But the protestant gestures are not aggressive, they
are not staged-managed; Hugh's resilience is effected through affective
means, through the recalcitrance of moral courage. He is a figure of
equilibrium within a society of unreason; his is a silent resistance,
which is no less viable than the languages of violence and political
discourse. As we shall discuss, there are similar symbols of change, of
futurity nested within McCann's short fictions – individuals whose
bodies become sites of contestation and of resistant hope.

'EVERYTHING IN THIS COUNTRY MUST'

The American academic and writer Joyce Carol Oates has suggested that
the short story is an endangered species of literary expression; the fact
that it is essentially more 'literary', or genuinely 'artful', than the novel
militates against the generation of broad constituencies of readers.[14]
Not only, then, as Frank O'Connor maintained, is the short story
the province of 'outlawed figures wandering about the fringes of
society',[15] but the form itself has acquired the status of a marginal
literary mode. Equally, narrative exposition within the short story is
typically elusive and suggestive, rather than deliberate and detailed, a
device that provokes the reader into the fertile possibilities of imagination. In this way the part, or the fragment, is allowed to speak
for some absent, but implied, whole; in Sean O'Faoláin's terms, the
dilatory capacities of implication replace the spareness of telling.[16] The
attenuated formal structure of the short story permits snapshot expo-
sures to the lives, motives and emotions of the characters involved.
Denied the narrative scale of the novel form, the short-story writer
portrays fragments of human experience in densely compressed

moments of representation. The aggregation of these characteristics, it might be argued, explains the radical political possibilities of the short story as a literary genre; its marginal status and ambivalence of articulation confer a level of unpredictability that has been well domesticated within the realist aesthetic. In this sense, 'the essential deviousness of the short story form, in which so much needs to be suggested by so little, houses a radical potential: through its reticence, its instinctive chariness of normative representation, the short story can slip through the totalizing narratives of the dominant culture.'[17] The apparent peripherality of the short story form coupled with its stylistic and formal embrace of unconventional representational codes facilitates the narration of trauma, excess, violence and dislocation – all of which are abiding presences in McCann's short fiction. In tackling the embedded contradictory convictions of the Northern 'Troubles', McCann avails of the suggestive and localized form of the short story, allowing its compressed borders of revelation to illuminate basic human truths in fragmentary moments of crisis. In the end, the combined formal and the thematic contents of McCann's collection compels the reader to imagine beyond the parameters of the immediate, beyond the horizons of burdensome ideologies and to interrogate how the present, and *possibly* the future, have been disfigured by repressive, oppositional politico-cultural histories in the past. In McCann's case it is possible, and this was the author's explicit intention, to discern the stirrings of resolution or accommodation across antagonistic communities. In these stories McCann's utopian ambitions are literally 'embodied'; an unspecified, yet implicit, utopian investment is made by McCann in the fertile, emergent bodies and imaginations of these youths, and McCann points towards an as yet to be imagined future social conjuncture.

With the publication of *Everything in This Country Must* in 2000, McCann returned to the literary province of short fiction, a form that had initially launched him as a writer of considerable promise in 1994. The later collection, however, is not confined to the short-story mode; *Everything in This Country Must* contains two short stories, 'Everything in This Country Must' and 'Wood', and a novella, 'Hunger Strike'. Indeed both collections embody what McCann has called the 'implosive moment' of the short story; points of ferocious energy.[18] Yet, it is not just at the level of form that McCann strikes a note of continuity between the two editions. The earlier collection ends with a story entitled 'Cathal's Lake', a story that concerns itself with the violence of the Northern 'Troubles'. 'Cathal's Lake', like many interventions on the cultural politics of violence, probes the mechanics of individual and communal rituals. Drawn from an old Jewish myth, it tells of the existence of thirty-six hidden saints who bury the world's sorrows so that it can continue to function, as well as bringing to mind the Irish myth of the Children of Lir. The story is narrated from the point of view of a middle-aged man, the eponymous Cathal, whose ritualized rural existence is tethered to the cyclical violence of urban civil unrest in the North. McCann's importation of such mythic structures, however, is not confined to this story – his use of magic realism is a recurrent feature in his first collection of stories. But his employment of the magically real transfuses realist representation with the narrative contingency of myth, magic and folklore. Significantly, McCann's co-option of magic realism into the minor art form of the short story, specifically in 'Cathal's Lake', is, then, both politically and aesthetically enabling. It is a coupling, at the levels of form and content, which eschews the aridity of telling in favour of the fertility of imaginative suggestion.

The narrative begins with the ambiguous reflection by Cathal that: 'It's a sad Sunday when a man has to find another swan in the soil' (*FSBR*, 173) – a statement that only assumes its full meaning at the end of the story. Its magically real connotations are replaced for the majority of the narrative by a realist approach from McCann, whose style is most often noted for its linguistic sensuality and its rich symbolism. However, in this story, McCann stylistically melds the magical, the real and the mythic within the limits of the short-story form. As we have seen, and as is well attested to, the accommodation of marginal individuals and constituencies within the narrative codes of the short story is abetted here in the coupling of narrative realism with the non-realist register of the magically real. This stylistic turn to magic realism imports another literary register that is traditionally associated with narratives of oppression, exile, displacement or cultural resistance. And that points to 'other' ways of living; Cathal's physical remoteness to the violence is narrated as a parallel redemptive space, an imagined space where the defiled, dismembered carceral of the victim of violence is transfigured into a body of grace and beauty. The visceral brutality of the body under violence mutates into a figure of delicacy as the victim moves out of the brute realities of sectarian ideology into the purgatorial or mythological space of Cathal's lake. In a sense, we might suggest that one suite of myths is usurped by another – but it is in the contrast between the two that McCann's utopian hopes exist.

In a fashion recollective of the works of Michael McLaverty, McCann's story navigates both the urban and the rural in the northern province. The urban is portrayed as an incendiary venue of intercommunal aggression, while the rural, almost Arcadian, milieu in which the enigmatic figure of Cathal lives is a sanctuary of calm and renewal. In contrast to these regenerative surroundings, on hearing of the death of a teenage boy in sectarian disturbances in Derry, Cathal imagines the mise-en-scène of the youth's demise:

> Maybe a head of hair on him like a wheat field. Or eyes as blue as thrush eggs. Young, awkward and gangly, with perhaps a Liverpool scarf tied around his mouth and his tongue flickering into the wool with a vast obscenity carved from the bottom of his stomach. A bottle of petrol in his hands and a rag from his mother's kitchen lit in the top. His arms in the beginnings of a windmill hurl. (*FSBR*, 173)

The boy's strained, physical posture, poised in the act of violence, is, however, abruptly altered in the next line: 'Then a plastic bullet slamming in his chest, all six inches of it hurtling against his lung at 100 miles per hour. The bottle somersaulting from the boy's fingers. Smashing on the street beneath his back. Thrush eggs broken and rows of wheat going up in flames' (*FSBR*, 173). The verbal intensity of McCann's language here, together with the report of the statistical specifics of the plastic bullet, enforces the brute physicality of this uneven suburban military exchange. The image drawn by McCann is clearly that projected time and again on news footage from any one of hundreds of civil riots across the North of Ireland since the late 1960s. But also, the description recapitulates Heaney's earlier cited image of the random murder victim in 'Keeping Going', wherein the body-as-image is dismembered and fractioned.

And the later stories resume this thematic preoccupation; all three narratives are meditations on the physical, emotional and geographical stresses of the internecine conflict in the North of Ireland. In a manner similar to the structure of Eugene McCabe's *Christ in the Fields*, McCann's own 'Troubles' trilogy explores, and articulates, entrenched intercommunal beliefs from both sides of the sectarian divide.[19] Specifically, 'Everything in This Country Must' is told from the point of view of a Catholic teenage girl; 'Wood' is narrated by an adolescent Protestant boy, while in 'Hunger Strike', another adolescent boy relates the most ambitious, and also problematic, of the stories, this time a Catholic youth. In these stories McCann's youthful protagonists straddle the border between a mature comprehension of the deep-seated forces that nourish the respective sectarian convictions of their families and localities, and a childlike lack of apprehension of the severity of these naturalized passions.[20] And again, in this sense McCann's narratives recollect the childhood and adolescent emotions and territories of McLaverty's short story, 'Pigeons', and the novel into which the earlier story developed, *Call My Brother Back*.[21] Yet more crucial to McCann is the possibility that these formative consciousnesses might imagine alternatives to their apparently naturalized historical inheritances. These are people in process, who, respectively, eschew, misunderstand, or naively experiment with the well-furrowed rituals and expectations of their political communities, but who retain the possibility of escaping such future roles.

The titular story, 'Everything in This Country Must', opens the collection and establishes a frantic tone in its opening paragraph.[22] McCann initiates the story with a panicked scene in which the young girl and her father are faltering in their combined efforts to save their old draft horse from drowning in the flood-expanded waters of a nearby river:

> A summer flood came and our draft horse got caught in the river. The river smashed against stones and the sound of it to me was like the turning of locks. It was silage time and the water smelled of grass. The draft horse, Father's favourite, had stepped in the river for a sniff maybe and she was caught, couldn't move, her foreleg trapped between rocks. Father found her and called *Katie!* above the wailing of the rain.[23]

Besides the obvious idiom of entrapment deployed in this extract by McCann, he also reprises the verbal intensity of 'Cathal's Lake' cited above; there is a sense of urgency and of violent movement to the beginning of the narrative. The horse itself is of limited practical use on the family farm, but the frenetic rescue is actually fomented by the animal's symbolic value to the girl's father.

As we learn subsequently, and as is a thematic constant in 'Troubles' fiction, the low intensity warfare of the conflict has invaded the domestic space. In this context the girl's mother and brother were killed in a collision with a British Army vehicle some years previously, an incident that was adjudicated to have been accidental. And this is a motif that McCann employs in each of the stories in the collection: in 'Wood', the family remains integrated, but the boy's father has suffered a stroke and is effectively paralysed from the neck down, and in the novella, the boy's biological father is also deceased and has been surrogated by the boy's uncle, an imprisoned hunger striker whom the boy has never met.[24] In telescoping the fractured contours of these familial situations, McCann demonstrates how 'political and power structures infiltrate familial and sexual relations'.[25] In a colonial context, a context in which the fundamental historical dispute is rooted in the division and occupation of territory, the politics of repro-duction and the constitution of communities of ethnic, racial or confessional solidarity are foundational matters. Equally, from a formal perspective, the 'deep' representational horizons of the short story mode find suitable material within the domestic privacies of the family unit, rather than in the more social landscapes of the novel form. And as McDonald mentions, the insinuation of the political onto the topographies of the domestic can be either explicit ideological presences or more non-political and practical in nature.

The fulcrum of the dramatic tension in McCann's narrative is the unexpected arrival of a British Army patrol onto the aforementioned rescue site. As the headlights of their vehicle approach it is assumed by both father and daughter to be those of a neighbour's vehicle. But when they catch sight of the uniformed figures exiting the jeep in order to aid their efforts, the father recoils from his attempt to save the animal. Essentially, the draft horse's affective worth to him is negated by its rescue by the British soldiers, accomplices, however obliquely, to his more acute familial loss several years before. In this sense, then, the father is representative of congealed forms of cultural memory – embedded in divisive simplicities, which foreclose any semblance of political rapprochement, even at the level of the practical and interpersonal. While his perceptions of the soldiers are coloured exclusively by the pained hatred of his own private loss, his fifteen-year-old daughter, the first-person narrator of the story, is of a more inclusive disposition. As she observes the various military bodies disperse in their rescue strategy, she christens each of them according to their physical features: one becomes 'Hayknife' because he 'had a scar on his cheek like the bottom end of Father's barn hayknife'; another 'had a moustache that looked like long grasses' and, therefore is dubbed 'LongGrasses', and yet another, whose 'hair was the colour of winter ice', is 'Icehair' (*ETCM*, 6–7).

Rather than retreat to the distance of anonymity, a silent idiom that engenders only suspicion, the girl personalizes each of the soldiers in a catholic language of her own. And again, this explains McCann's formal logic – he relates this incident within the abbreviated form of the short story, but tellingly does so through the narrative device of the first-person testimony of an adolescent. The language of the young girl, then, suggests the possibility of hope through its very playfulness, yet it is not entirely the language of childhood. Nested within her colloquial attribution of names are the murmurings of an autonomous adolescent female sexuality, an energy that has, traditionally, been diagnosed as politically, culturally and morally subversive. In her father's jaundiced view, Kate's sexuality is to be protected and fenced off from the contaminating advances of these British soldiers. In the apparently conciliatory gesture of offering her the warmth of a British army jacket, Kate's father divines an ulterior, transgressive intent: 'LongGrasses was standing beside me and he put Stevie's jacket on my shoulders to warm me, but then Father came over and he pushed LongGrasses away. Father pushed hard' (*ETCM*, 8). Rather than permit his daughter to be shrouded in the protective garments of this illegitimate occupying force, the father is driven to exact violence. Clearly the episode has multiple ideological resonances; the girl's emergent female body is transformed into a political document onto which the competing ideological freights of the 'Troubles' are projected. Furthermore, the scene is an enactment of a prevailing patriarchal authority, under which the girl's body is subservient to the contestatory designs of two male figures.

The most significant aspect of the passage cited above is, however, the girl's referral to one of the soldiers as 'Stevie'; during the rescue operation she has learned his real Christian name and is suitably impressed with his strident efforts to save the draft horse. As a consequence, she invites the group of soldiers to return to her house for tea and in order to dry off, an invitation that understandably infuriates her already indignant father. The other soldiers either remain anonymous or retain their nicknames, but Stevie emerges from the ideological confines of his uniform, his rank and his accent and a brief, but effective, drama of coy flirtation ensues between Katie and him. The theatre for this furtive action is within the domestic geography of a rural Catholic family, a kitchen in which half a dozen British soldiers are sharing tea with an embittered widower and his daughter. What is striking is that the usual scenario in which such a group would be together in such circumstances is under a violently intrusive operation of counter-insurgency, a security search. Predictably, perhaps, the father's belligerent attitude and equivalent remarks provoke one of the soldiers and the scene does, in fact, conclude with a reversion to type. The episodic flirtation between Katie and Stevie is bracketed between two acts of ideological expression. As we have seen, it ends with a sectarian argument, but our first description of the interior of the house, as the men wait for their tea, is of Katie meticulously preparing her father's brew:

> Father likes his tea without bags like Mammy used to make and so there is a special way for me to make it – put cold cold water in the kettle and only cold then boil it then put a small boiling water in the teapot and swish it around until the bottom of the teapot is warm. Then put in tea leaves not bags and then the boiling water and stir it all very slowly and put on the teacosy and let it stew for five minutes making sure the flame is not too high so the teacosy doesn't catch flame and burn. Then pour milk into the cups and then the tea followed at last by sugar all spooned around into a careful mix. (*ETCM*, 10)

The simple act of making tea is elongated into an absurd ritual of domestic control; in effect the girl's past and future unite in this banal household chore. She has assumed the roles of mother, wife and daughter within the domestic economy, but none of these roles, in their current guises, offers her any opportunity of escape, or of change. In this respect, the story, in its delineation of an oppressed female sexuality has a clear historical precursor in Joyce's 'Eveline'. The protracted surgery of brewing tea could easily be re-imagined as a task set for Eveline, in her parallel world of clipped domestic horizons. But whereas Eveline's desires to flee the cramped social and moral conditions of Dublin are still-born, McCann's narrative allows the unsettling capacities of human desire to infiltrate the hardened arteries of political entrenchment. Immediately subsequent to the lengthy rendition of the tea making, Katie describes the energizing thrill of her flirtatious interaction with Stevie – one act of dull repetition is juxtaposed with an act of possibilities: 'My tea fuss made the soldiers smile, even Stevie who had a head full of blood pouring down from where the draft horse kicked him above his eye' (*ETCM*, 10). But his smile is, of course, an affront to her father: 'Father's face went white when Stevie smiled but Stevie was very polite. He took a towel from me because he said he didn't want to get blood on the chair. He smiled at me two times when I put my head around the kitchen door' (*ETCM*, 10). This illicit, and previously uncharted, exchange of sexual tension permits Katie a level of physical and emotional autonomy that has previously been foreclosed under her father's domestic regime. She felt her 'belly sink way down until it was there like love in the barn, and he smiled at me number three' (*ETCM*, 11). This brief emotional transaction between Katie and Stevie provides McCann with a moment of political hope. The privacy of Katie's desires, then, is demonstrative of a secret language of solidarity, and this is a consistent feature of the entire collection; each of the young protagonists retains secrets and privacies from the probing eyes of their parents. McCann is actually employing flirtation as a political device in the narrative, a contrastive mode of behaviour to the rooted, and ruthless, passions of mutual antipathy.

The psychoanalyst Adam Phillips alludes to just such trajectories in his study of flirtation and contingency. Flirtation inaugurates a process of re-scripting, in which previously naturalized commitments to relationships, to ideologies or to vocabularies can be opened to alteration:

> In flirtation you never know whether the beginning of the story – the story of the relationship – will be the end; flirtation, that is to say, exploits the idea of surprise…from a pragmatic point of view one could say that a space is being created in which aims and ends can be worked out; the assumed wish for the more or

less obvious sexual combinations, or commitments, may be a way
of pre-empting the elaboration of, making time for, less familiar
possibilities. Flirtation, if it can be sustained, is a way of cultivating wishes, of playing for time. Deferral can make room.[26]

If, as Heaney maintains above, creative art kindles hope as a political
energy towards the future, in this context the flirtatious act sustains
liberatory impulses in the form of desire – both primary ingredients of
any utopian imaginary. Rather than cementing the staid certainties of
their respective cultural codes, these two young people transfuse such
stasis with an ambiguous language of risk. By inserting this erotically
charged passage, McCann multiplies the narrative possibilities that can
ensue from these lives; nothing may come of the episode, an episode
that has other self-evident predecessors in 'across the barricades'
fictional love affairs, but it does invite the chance that something may
transpire.[27] Equally, in eschewing the cautious conservatism of stereotype, Katie and Stevie import an element of contingency into the
narrative; likewise, in sharing this series of moments they display
generosity towards each other in offering a spur to the other's desire.
Under the strained atmosphere of the family's kitchen, which is
suffused by traditional sectarian borders, the vigorous unpredictability
of flirtation provides emotional sustenance for Katie: 'Father is good,
he was just wanting to dry my hair because I was shivering even in
Stevie's jacket. From under the curtain I could see the soldiers and I
could see most of all Stevie. He sipped from his tea and smiled at
me and Father coughed real loud' (*ETCM*, 12). Phillips is keen to
highlight, contrary to Freud, that flirtation is a legitimate idiom of
possibility; it is not merely a frivolous gesture of indecision. 'Flirtation,' he suggests, 'is more than a trivial nostalgia for a world before
the war. Like all transitional performances it is an attempt to re-open,
to rework, the plot; to find somewhere else, in the philosopher
William James's words, "to go from".'[28] In essence, the act of flirtation
leavens the tyranny of certainty, it is consistent with a subjunctive
mood – a mood of maybe, and therein rests its political voltage
for McCann.

'WOOD'

Moving to the domestic terrain of a rural Presbyterian family, McCann's second short story, 'Wood', explores the pervasive secrecy of life in Northern Ireland. As before, the first-person narrator is a youth, an adolescent boy, who narrates the clandestine, nocturnal activities he engages in with his mother at the family wood-mill. The farm on which the drama unfolds also functioned as a wood-mill, until the father suffered a stroke that left him severely disabled, effectively paralyzed – a condition that reverberates with symbolism throughout the story, and again gestures towards the endemic inertia of Joyce's earlier collection. Furthermore, McCann again focuses on the notion of intergenerational tension – in 'Everything in this Country Must' it was a simple binary friction between father and daughter, in 'Wood' the intergenerational dynamics are more complex and fundamentally traumatic for the young boy. 'Wood' imports the rituals and symbolism of loyalism into the familial sphere, rather than explicate the divisive contours of the spatial command of loyalist marches and spectacular seizures of contested public space. McCann's story deals with the private, practical mechanics of preparation involved in organizing these events. He examines how political and moral principles are compromised when stark economic choices are confronted, and even within the remote family unit, new secrecies and deceptions are fostered under the weight of straitened political and economic circumstances. Simply, the boy is compelled to deceive his paralyzed father by his mother, who sees the deception as necessary for the economic well-being of the family.

The dramatic strain is centred on the fact that the local Orange lodge have requested forty wooden banner poles to be manufactured at the mill, a request the mother has agreed to meet. However, as the following exchange reveals, there are political implications within the household: 'Your husband'll be alright with that, then? he asked. He will, aye. He was never mad keen before, was he?' (*ETCM*, 21). While the father may remain permanently physically immobile, his political sensibilities, indeed his political imagination, extend beyond the sectarian paralysis that he sees around him. The family's participation in the triumphalism of loyalism may only extend to the provision of banner poles, but the father is alert to the divisive symbolism of the most mundane of actions. From his perspective, the performance of loyalist identity and the spatial commemoration of past sectarian victories merely service further intercommunal antagonisms. The boy recalls that his father was a proud Presbyterian, but eschewed the 'meanness' of such public commemorations and forbade his children to attend the Orange parades. And here, again, we see a disjunction between the generations; the father's disavowal of triumphalism and the attraction of such theatricality to the boy:

> He doesn't allow us to go to the marches but I've seen photographs in the newspapers. My favourite was the two men in bowler hats and black suits and big thick ribbons across their chests. They were carrying a banner of the King on a white horse. The horse was stepping across a river with one hoof in the air and one hoof on the bank. The King wore fancy clothes and he had a kind face. (*ETCM*, 28)

The boy's waking dreams are electrified by the imagined prospects of the communal carnivalesque of the Orange parades; in the youth's yearning reveries the drama of the spectacle is evacuated of its divisive political connotations and he assumes a role within the parade as the creator of the displayed banner poles: 'Lots of people cheering and blowing whistles and drums playing. Ice cream vans giving out free choc ices. All the crowd would stand up on the tips of their toes and say my oh my, look at that, aren't they wonderful poles, aren't they lovely' (*ETCM*, 33).

In producing the banner poles for the upcoming Orange Order parade the boy and his mother forge a covert bond that sees their activities shielded from his father and also from his siblings. Born of material necessity, even economic desperation, the situation casts the boy into an alien moral dilemma in which he is bound to deceive one parent in his professed loyalty to the other. Thus the complex contradictions of economic urgency, political fealty and sectarian bigotry in the North of Ireland are mediated through the maturing adolescent experience of this youth. And the intimate subterfuge within the family reaches a dramatic climax in the final pages of the story. On the morning of collection by the Orange Order the boy is permitted to shave his prone father. Yet this ritual that seems to resurrect a feeling of guiltless intimacy between the two merely continues the deception. The boy has been instructed to turn on the radio and increase the usual volume so that his father will not hear the stealthy approach of the collection van or the transfer of the poles from the mill. The central tension, then, of McCann's narrative revolves around the stark physical paralysis of the boy's father – confined to bed and a routine of utter dependence on his wife and children, and the political paralysis of his community's repertoire of annual rituals. In effect, the passive, paralytic body of the father houses the imaginative possibility of political progress and hope, while the resolutely mobile bodies of Orange Order commemorative marches, and, of course, those of his wife and eldest son are, to varying degrees, complicit in the sustenance of political stasis. The mobile bodies of the commemorative march are further inscribed by intercommunal history and are politico-cultural texts of popular remembrance. We note the performance of community identity through the reclamation of space – the politically inscribed corporeal enacting the accumulated historical identity of the imagined loyalist community. The banner poles, while obvious symbols of a more lateral cultural group at one level, demand, at another level, the physical participation of the individual in the confessional community. This surfaces in the manufacture and the laborious production of the object, subsequently in its symbolic transformation through detailed decoration, and finally in the somatic articulation of the banner pole bearer during the Orange Order parade.

'HUNGER STRIKE'

In *Hunger: An Unnatural History*, Sharman Apt Russell argues that the physiological experience of hunger is, in fact, a form of articulation – hunger is a mode of somatic speech.[29] Hunger demands to be satiated. Likewise, the choice of hunger in the pursuit of hunger striking takes this communicative essence to an altogether different register. Under circumstances of perceived political and/or cultural disenfranchizement hunger striking is a route through which the always already political, and politicized, body is re-calibrated for terminal acts of resistance. In the Northern Irish context, the mobilization of the body in such extreme forms of political protest belongs to a longer continuum of somatic negotiation. The genealogies of fictions, myths and histories of the northern conflict are all indelibly marked by spatial relations; dispute over territories at the local, provincial and national levels. With the spatialization of power, in repressive and counter-repressive guises, the body became a focal site of contestation. And as Allen Feldman suggests:

> In Northern Ireland the body is not only the primary political instrument through which social transformation is effected but is also the primary site for visualizing the collective passage into historical alterity. The body's material deformation has become commensurate with the deformation, instrumentation and 'acceleration' of historical time.[30]

Both Tom Herron and Scott Brewster have recently explored the body as trope in contemporary Irish poetry – the body as a victim of state and of paramilitary violences.[31] In this section I will turn to McCann's novella, 'Hunger Strike', in order to discuss the degenerative recalcitrance of the incarcerated and hunger-stricken body during the northern 'Troubles'.[32]

In his study of political violence and Northern Ireland, cited above, Feldman charts the ideological consumption and production 'of the body as a political institution'.[33] Part of Feldman's project is to explore the H-Block hunger strikes of 1981 as rituals of re-appropriation by the republican prisoners. What is important about his analysis is that Feldman positions the hunger strikes within the broader framework 'of the cultural construction of violence' in the North, and does not simply draw easy analogies with other, ostensibly non-violent or pacifist protestation. The hunger strikes, then, were elements of a longer process of somatic resistance within the state-governed institutional space of the prison. Prior to the strikes, republican detainees had engaged in lengthy 'blanket' and 'dirty' protests, both of which symbolically and literally saw the prisoners commandeer bodily autonomy – retrieving such authority from the state. The hunger strikes represented the next, and terminal, step in this logic of somatic seizure; incarceration subjected the prisoner to the routines, violences and surveillance of the state's authority, but these three voluntary rituals of bodily self-sacrifice were resistant in their excess. Rather than protest in the hope of a cessation of violence, the prisoners assumed control of the violence inflicted on their own bodies; indeed the violence of the protests exceeded that which the state itself had imposed. Under the conditions of the hunger strike, in particular, the body of the starving prisoner is both biologically terminal in its organic decline and simultaneously ever edging towards a symbolic perpetuity. Again in Feldman's terms: 'The historicized and historicizing body is a pluralized site of torsion and contestation. But it is not a passive site.'[34] In McCann's narrative, the progress of one man's hunger strike is filtered through the consciousness of his teenage nephew, and McCann records the gradual biological decay of the hunger striker together with the resonant symbolic import of his actions for his dislocated adolescent nephew.

The story is remarkable for its consistent channelling of the boy's emotional and cognitive development through the rigours of the somatic. Variously we see the boy engaged in rhythmic boatmanship with his elderly Lithuanian acquaintance, tentative sexual experimentation, and a *faux* enactment of a 'Troubles' riot by the boy. McCann interweaves the troubling bodily landmarks of pubescent development, with their attendant emotional strains, and the combined performances of protest of the youth and his imprisoned uncle. The boy's masturbation on the beach is matched by his illicit theft of his mother's cigarettes, and her money. His attentive curiosity concerning his uncle's bodily degeneration, likewise, is echoed in the detailed descriptions given of the age-ravaged bodies of the elderly Lithuanian couple. McCann realizes that in portraying the growth of the emotional and cognitive intelligence of these young protagonists, one cannot but include the lateral corporeal evolution in equal measure. The boy in this story is not only confounded by the distant, yet intimate, political narratives of the 'Troubles', which are relayed sparingly and second-hand; he is also perturbed by the profound emotional and physical alterations that are intrinsic to his bodily maturation. Yet it is this prospect of maturation in which McCann banks his authorial hope for the future; these are the repositories of McCann's utopian energies. As one body commits to death, and is charted and symbolized through this process, another is a seed-bed of future peace. The narrative action of 'Hunger Strike' unfolds in and around the town of Clifden in County Galway, but the emotional focus of the novella is centred on the North of Ireland, specifically the penal space of the H-Blocks. Having recently left his home in the North with his mother, the anonymous protagonist struggles to adjust to life in the west of Ireland. His accent, his age and his diffident temperament are varying indices of estrangement for the boy. And this period of geographical and emotional teenage transition is amplified by the news that his paternal uncle has committed himself to the hunger strike protests. Although the boy has never met his uncle – he has only ever seen a picture of him – the symbolic voltage of the uncle's sacrifice, as Feldman outlines, transcends the limits of biological time and historical time, and enters epochal time. The mythic aura of this resistant act becomes an obsessive concern of the boy and at one point he initiates his own, unsuccessful, attempt at a hunger strike. In a certain light, the boy's commitment to his uncle is mirrored in the uncle's devotion to his own stable of abstract political ideals. Again, it is significant that McCann chooses to mediate the hunger strikes through the narrative device of a thirteen-year-old consciousness, and through the compressed exposition of the novella. The relative concision of the narrative does not elaborate on the loss of innocence that is at the core of the story [as a novel would], nor does it extensively abbreviate the circumstances of this loss [as a short story would], but offers a constellation of events in which the boy gradually demonstrates the frustrations and confusions that are attendant with all forms of emotional awakening.

The journey to the west of Ireland, which furnishes nostalgic consolations for the boy's mother, is less rewarding for the youth. His detachment from his social and physical surroundings manifests in various, and frequent, acts of delinquency: theft, vandalism and deception. These trivial acts of adolescent immaturity and pubescent defiance are marginal in comparison to the symbolically charged actions that transcend these shallow teenage gestures. Specifically, his imitative enactment of a hunger strike, the short-lived routine of rowing with his elderly Lithuanian neighbour [which is actively fostered by his mother], and at the story's conclusion, his attempt to destroy the old man's kayak. The story signals the very real, but often suppressed, fact that the conflagration in the North of Ireland was not simply confined to the geopolitical limits of the six counties. As Joe Cleary has argued, both British and Irish governments preferred to represent the conflict as a localized dispute, thereby absolving themselves and their own political jurisdictions of any direct responsibility; in effect, quarantining the sectarian warfare within the dysfunctional Northern polity.[35]

As a prelude to his own brief hunger strike, the boy exhibits a fascination with his uncle's body; however, the only material reference point that he possesses is a recollection of previously seen photographs. He calls to mind an image of his uncle's distinctive facial profile, which was 'hard and angular with shocking blue eyes; the hair curled; the eyebrows tufted; a scar running a line of outrage across the bottom of his nose' (*ETCM*, 55) – it is a face that has been indented with unexplained violence. But as the boy realizes, this image almost certainly bears little or no resemblance to his uncle's current bodily state. The dissolving body is now scripted with the resistance of the man's political convictions, his communal obligations. And although the boy can draw on no specific image that will singularize his uncle's individual suffering, he imagines through the lens of a newspaper article, which graphically details the conditions of those who have progressed from blanket protest to dirty protest and are now on hunger strike. In this sequence we see a confluence of the boy's imaginative creation of his uncle's present bodily condition and McCann's insertion of brutal realistic description of a stark historical reality:

> There had been a photo smuggled out of the H-blocks during the dirty protest – a prisoner in a cell, by a window, wrapped in a dark blanket, with shit in swirled patterns on the wall behind his head. The boy wondered how anyone could have lived like that, shit on the walls and a floor full of piss. The men had their cells sprayed down by prison guards once a week and sometimes their bedding was so soaked that they got pneumonia. When the protest failed they cleaned their cells and opted for hunger instead. (*ETCM*, 55–6)

McCann further documents the insistent decline of the hunger striker's body when he notes, in empirical fashion, the gradual loss of weight by the starving prisoner:

> Ranged in a notebook in opposite columns:
> Day One – 147 lb – 66.8 kg
> Day Two – 146 lb – 66.36 kg
> Day Three – 144.9 lb – 65.86 kg
> Day Four – 143.9 lb – 65.4 kg (*ETCM*, 72)

While at one level the prisoner's body, as Feldman maintains, outstrips the material and enters the mythical, McCann's stark, metrical record of the declining mass of the imprisoned body reminds the reader of its actual disintegration. The medical report of the dissolving physiology of the prisoner is continued throughout the narrative, bringing a disarming extra-diegetic feature to McCann's text. As the stricken prisoner's hunger strike continues beyond twenty days and closes in on its thirtieth, extra commentary is added to the textualized account of this resistant somatic act:

> Twenty-seven – 127.3 – 57.81 kg – 110/60
> Twenty-eight – 126.8 – 57.6 kg – 115/68
> Twenty-nine – 126.3 – 57.4 kg – 110/59 – Tonight the fuckers put enough food out to feed an army.
> Thirty – 125.9 – 57.22 – 105/65 (*ETCM*, 97)

The blood pressure of the hunger striker has now been added to the report – a narrative that gradually begins to read like an ongoing biography, or morbid medical diary. The protesting prisoner is some-what replaced by the statistics of his declining physical state; the unrelenting slide towards death is the shadow that is cast across this newly authored biological narrative. Time, weight and blood pressure become imbricated in the mechanics of political struggle – a struggle that is revealed as callous and vulgar by the insertion of a short discursive comment about the prison authorities. Indeed this insertion merely serves to underscore the absence of discourse in this protest; verbal discourse has been abandoned in favour of the fatal narrative of the hungering body's inevitable collapse.

These reports can be figured as the struggle between myth and history that is played out during this hunger strike. And the boy is entangled in this ideological dialectic; the myths that corral around such sacrifices have already been seen to activate the boy's imagination, as when he enacts an imaginary riot of protest, and in his brief but physically real hunger strike. The issue, then, is how to wean the youth from such political trajectories, given the evident inevitability of suffering, if not death. Exile, of course, is one route through which the boy might be sheltered from such a future, and it too belongs to considerations of the somatic; the body is literally removed from the context of threat. But surely that is a partial solution and McCann sees it as so; it is contributive but nothing more. At the end of the story, the long developmental cycle of the boy, which is repeatedly figured in overtly corporeal terms, remains south of the border, but is abetted by the tutelary presence of the elderly Lithuanian couple. At this point he is in the process of vandalizing their kayak, as they watch benignly; but it is their presence, their understanding of the historicity of extreme ideological violence that will offer the boy guidance as he develops physically, intellectually, and emotionally. The final lines of the novella indicate the generosity of spirit and the depth of emotional intelligence that this emigrant couple bear. Their experience, which is always subterranean within the novella, hints at a familiarity with the dynamics of the northern 'Troubles', and the manners in which the boy is assimilating these 'personal' events. It is the conjunction of this catholicity of humane experience and the possibilities rooted in the developing adolescent that represents McCann's 'hope principle'. As he rampages on the beach, destroying their kayak, 'the boy lifted his head from the boat, looked back over his shoulder, saw the light from the house of the Lithuanians, the front door open, the couple stand-ing together, hands clasped, watching, the old man's eyes squinting, the old woman's large and tender' (*ETCM*, 143). It is an indelible and highly charged symbolic set-piece that draws McCann's collection to a close, and, as an imagistic fragment, concisely expresses the under-lying utopian impulse of the whole.

In his critical reflections on the nature of the short story, the Amer-ican author, Raymond Carver, a contemporary master of the genre in his own right, consistently accented the necessity of menace to the dra-matic success of short fiction. Most memorably in his revealing essay, 'On Writing', Carver argues:

> I like it when there is some feeling of threat or sense of menace in short stories. I think a little menace is fine to have in a story. For one thing, it's good for the circulation. There has to be tension, a sense that something is imminent, that certain things are in relentless motion, or else, most often, there simply won't be a story. What creates tension in a piece of fiction is partly the way the concrete words are linked together to make up the visible action of the story. But it's also the things that are left out, that are implied, the landscape just under the smooth (but some-times broken and unsettled) surface of things.[36]

In this sense, it seems entirely apposite for McCann to operate within the abbreviated literary parameters of the genre. We are offered cursory glimpses of ordinary lives lived within or adjacent to the grounds of the northern conflict. Each of the youthful characters in *Everything in This Country Must* operates in an environment that is uncharted and enigmatic. Each is confronted with an emotional and physical situation that harbours potential threat. Similarly, the incendiary unpredictability of the northern crisis, primarily evidenced in the seeming random nature of violence, is played out *in parvo* within the adolescent dramas of McCann's protagonists. Through the recurring motif of the body, initially the fractioned body of the victim, and subsequently the emergent sexual, the prone paralytic, and the resistant starving bodies, McCann's narratives foreground the methods through which the political extremities of the 'Troubles' were scripted onto the carceral. Nevertheless, it is possible, as we have outlined, to divine moments of hope or imagination in the stories beyond the foreshortened mindscapes of sectarianism. McCann seems to insist on the urgency of change and responds to political extremity through the brevity of the short-story form. McCann's fictions are symptomatic of an author who has glimpsed post-'Troubles' Northern Ireland, as they intimate at a will to imagine peace. While we can only definitively 'locate' the novella 'Hunger Strike' in a specific time period, 1981, we can assume that the other stories are set in adjacent years of the 'Troubles'. The age profiles of each of the protagonists in McCann's stories suggests that any form of effective reconciliation is in the medium to long-term future – at least a decade and a half. In this respect, we can view McCann's collection as a literary response to the various tentative steps towards cross-factional accord that took public, material form in the mid- to late 1990s. The emergent bodies and minds defy, or are encouraged to defy, the artificial political and cultural tenets of sectarianism.

NOTES

1. Michael Storey, *Representing the Troubles in Irish Short Fiction* (Washington: Catholic University of America Press, 2004), p.10.
2. Aaron Kelly, *The Thriller and Northern Ireland since 1969: Utterly Resigned Terror* (Aldershot: Ashgate, 2005), p.1.

3. In his essay, 'The Irish Short Story (1980–2000): Ireland Anthologized', Ben Forkner writes: 'As far as energy and conviction are concerned, the Irish short story has little to fear or envy when compared with the celebrated examples of the past', *Études Anglaises*, 54, 2 (2001), p.152.

4. Ronan McDonald, 'Strategies of Silence: Colonial Strains in Short Stories of the Troubles', *The Yearbook of English Studies*, 35, 1 (January 2005), pp.249–63.

5. For a recent summary survey of the Northern Irish novel, see Elmer Kennedy-Andrews, 'The Novel and the Northern Troubles', in John Wilson Foster (ed.) *The Cambridge Companion to The Irish Novel* (Cambridge: Cambridge University Press, 2006), pp.238–58.

6. On the utopian force of literature see Ernst Bloch, *The Utopian Function of Art and Literature: Selected Essays*, trans. Jack Zipes and Frank Mecklenburg (Minneapolis, MN: University of Minnesota Press, 1989). More recently see Bill Ashcroft on postcolonial literature and utopia: 'Critical Utopias', *Textual Practice*, 21, 3 (2007), pp.411–31.

7. Seamus Heaney, 'from *The Redress of Poetry*', *Finders Keepers: Selected Prose 1971–2001* (London: Faber & Faber, 2002), p.259.

8. Ernst Bloch, *The Principle of Hope* (Cambridge and London: MIT Press, 1986).

9. Seamus Heaney, 'Keeping Going', *The Spirit Level* (London: Faber & Faber, 1996), pp.10–12.

10. Helen Vendler, *Seamus Heaney* (London: HarperCollins, 1998), p.164.

11. Ibid., p.166.

12. Heaney, 'Keeping Going', pp.11–12.

13. Ibid., p.12.

14. Joyce Carol Oates, 'An Endangered Species', *New York Review of Books* (29 June 2000), pp.38–41.

15. Frank O'Connor, *The Lonely Voice: A Study of the Short Story* (Cleveland, OH: World Publishing, 1963), p.5.

16. Seán O'Faoláin, *The Short Story* (Cork: Mercier Press, 1948), p.177.

17. McDonald, 'Strategies of Silence', p.250.

18. Colum McCann, '*Everything in This Country Must* – Interview'. http://www.colummccann. com/interviews/everything.htm.

19. Eugene McCabe, *Christ in the Fields* (London: Minerva, 1993).

20. Again Ben Forkner suggests that 'McCann dwells on those inevitable moments when innocence is shattered and the inner self splintered into divided allegiances. These are universal experiences, of course, but far less easy to assume when they arrive too early, and with the brutality of historical fate', p.159.

21. On these two works by McLaverty see Sophia Hillan, 'Wintered into Wisdom: Michael McLaverty and Seamus Heaney, and the Northern Word-Hoard', *New Hibernia Review*, 9, 3 (2005), pp.86–106.

22. This story was adapted into an Oscar-nominated short film in 2005 by McCann and directed by Gary McKendry. It can be viewed in full at: http://www.colummccann.com/media/film.htm.

23. Colum McCann, 'Everything in This Country Must', *Everything in This Country Must*, (London: Phoenix House, 2000), p.3. All further references will appear in parenthesis as (*ETCM*).

24. The dysfunctional family unit is a feature that, again, is apparent in Joyce's *Dubliners*.

25. McDonald, 'Strategies of Silence', p.254.

26. Adam Phillips, *On Flirtation* (London: Faber & Faber, 1994), p.xix.

27. See Joan Lingard, *Across the Barricades* (London: Hamish Hamilton, 1972).

28. Phillips, *On Flirtation*, p.xxv.

29. Sharman Apt Russell, *Hunger: An Unnatural History* (New York: Basic Books, 2005).

30. Allen Feldman, *Formations of Violence: The Narrative of the Body and Political Terror in Northern Ireland* (Chicago and London: University of Chicago Press, 1991), p.9.

31. Tom Herron, 'The Body's in the Post: Contemporary Irish Poetry and the Dispersed Body', in

Colin Graham and Richard Kirkland (eds), *Ireland and Cultural Theory: The Mechanics of Authenticity* (Basingstoke: Macmillan, 1999), pp.193–209 and Scott Brewster, 'Rites of Defilement: Abjection and the Body Politic in Northern Irish Poetry', *Irish University Review*, 35, 2 (2005), pp.304–19.

32. For a detailed historical account of the 1981 Hunger Strikes, see David Beresford, *Ten Men Dead: The Story of the 1981 Irish Hunger Strike* (London: Grafton Books, 1987).

33. Feldman, *Formations of Violence*, p.8.

34. Ibid., p.177.

35. Joe Cleary, *Literature, Partition and the Nation State: Culture and Conflict in Ireland, Israel and Palestine* (Cambridge: Cambridge University Press, 2002), pp.97–141.

36. Raymond Carver, 'On Writing', *Fires: Essays, Poems, Stories* (New York: Vintage Books, 1984), p.17.

5

Representation and Performance: *Dancer* (2003)

THE NOVEL, HISTORY AND BIOGRAPHY

Introducing the work of John Banville, Derek Hand invokes the protracted genealogy of the novel in locating the formal and thematic loci of Banville's fictions. Hand alludes to Harold Bloom's recent thoughts on the significance of Miguel de Cervantes' *Don Quixote* as an aesthetic symptom of European cultural modernity.[1] Specifically, Hand is keen to highlight the internal paradox that is at the core of the novelistic tradition: 'On the one hand, it aspires towards certainty, unity, knowledge, and completeness, while on the other, obvious epistemological anxieties and ontological uncertainties are deeply bound up with it.'[2] Latterly, much postmodernist, or self-reflexive, literary fiction has tended towards the latter pole, reflecting philosophical and theoretical scepticism about the natures of modern society and the so-called modern 'subject'. The desire to cohere within the limits of a generic form are perpetually confounded by internal anxiety that meaning is always elsewhere, that there is always something absent. Thus, when one approaches the novel, one encounters a deeply anxious and/or defiantly playful form – one that is increasingly conscious of its provisionality. Hand continues: 'The novel hopes to succeed in its efforts to tell readers everything. However, in the end, it can offer nothing but shards and moments of possible insight.'[3] Yet such comments should not blind us to the utopian and hopeful dynamics of the novel form: the lack of conclusiveness, which is its necessary condition, does not render the novel devoid of political and cultural agency. 'Moments of possible insight' may be provisional but the impulse towards such fleeting epiphanies transfuses the novel with its future-oriented potentialities. From a formal perspective, as Hand maintains, the novel is entirely cognizant of the limits of its unity and the partiality of its representations. But again, this is precisely what makes the novel, potentially, a quintessential democratic aesthetic space. Such issues, then, as formal self-consciousness, narrative anxiety, the politics of representation, and the relationship between the novelist and history are among those that preoccupy McCann's 2003 novel *Dancer*. If the novel as a form 'can offer nothing but shards', then McCann's novel is eminently characteristic. Its narrative teems with a dissonant chorus of voices, which are enunciated through a variety of narrative registers. These 'shards' are, firstly, part of the internal tremulousness of the genre, its recognition of its own failure as a form of conclusive communication. But at the same time, they represent its viability as an inclusive democratic space; *Dancer* provides a representational embrace to a multiplicity of unregistered personal histories. These unrecorded missives from the margins of recent history, then, are not indulged merely as part of an abstracted novelistic system of playful narration, but are representative of McCann's commitment to our titular 'aesthetic of redemption'. *Dancer* is aware of the urgency and legitimacy of novelistic intervention in the sphere of historical writing and representation. The consequences of historical writing can be too politically and ethically incendiary for these two adjacent fields of storytelling to be left in mutual exclusion. As McCann suggests:

> I'd rather not leave my sense of history, and certainly politics, to the talking-heads on the six o'clock news…There is a point, and a valid point, where writers can step in and create another logic or another angle or another question. Why not? There has to be a point where we, as writers, enter what people call 'history'. Not necessarily to legislate it, but certainly to witness it at its stranger, darker, quieter angles.[4]

As the above exposes, McCann's work exhibits an overt concern with the novel's and the novelist's relationship with 'the living stream' of history. Embedded within this historical sense are political and ethical questions about how such history or, more likely, histories, become monumentalized or jettisoned from historical accounts. *Dancer* is, arguably, McCann's most sustained interrogation of the interior workings of memory, historical record and literary representation. At a number of levels, *Dancer* is a frontal confrontation with mainstream complacency about established historical truths. And the novel edges towards a deconstructive mode in many of its formal and thematic features. Indeed, a suitable departure point is to consider the paratextual devices operative in the novel, as they disclose the author's awareness of and sensitivity to the power of representation and narrative record. At the beginning of the text, McCann inserts two paratextual devices: an authorial statement and an epigraph; and there are 'Acknowledgements' at the end of the text. *Per se*, there is little unusual about the inclusion of these three technical features, but if we tackle them as a triangulation of authorial self-consciousness, then we are back to McCann's stated concern for the novelist's role in relation to the flow of history. The unpaginated authorial statement reads: 'This is a work of fiction. With the exception of some public figures whose names have been used, the names, characters and incidents portrayed are the work of the author's imagination' (*Dancer*).[5] This statement effectively approaches the idioms of the legalistic in its clipped assertion of the work's fictional origins. It is a resolutely unambiguous testimony that contradicts any 'truth' value that might be pursued in the ensuing narrative. Subsequent to this paratextual insertion, McCann includes a suggestive epigraph from William Maxwell's novel, *So Long, See You Tomorrow*. The function of epigraphic material is, in general, transparent, as they locate the text quite explicitly in thematic terms. These quotations also invite or summon the reader to make this thematic connection via intuition or interpretation. Apart from obeying these structural requirements of the epigraph, the content of Maxwell's excerpt is consonant with the legalistic assertion of the authorial statement:

> What we, or at any rate, I, refer to confidently as a memory – meaning a moment, a scene, a fact that has been subjected to a fixative and thereby rescued from oblivion – is really a form of storytelling that goes on continually in the mind and often changes with the telling. Too many conflicting emotional interests are involved for life ever to be wholly acceptable, and possibly it is the work of the storyteller to rearrange things so that they conform to this end. In any case, in talking about the past we lie with every breath we take. (*Dancer*)

Emplotment and falsity are, then, integral components of remembrance – at an individual level and in more collective contexts. What cannot be gainsaid, however, is the tenacity of humanity to seek perpetually to organize its diverse histories and recollections, hence the importance of storytellers. But with importance comes responsibility, and while the storyteller – in the guise of the novelist or the historian – can manufacture generous narratives of consolation and celebration, the equivalent storytelling skills are prey to politicization in the service of marginalization or demonization. Yet the underlying truth is that each and all of these 'stories' are arbitrary and false in their forms and contents; it is simply an inconvenient truth we are content to disavow. From the legalistic to the novelistic, we move to the final side of McCann's paratextual triangle, the personal in his 'Acknowledgements'. What is remarkable about this paratext is the degree to which McCann anatomizes the intellectual labour that was invested in the production of the novel, as well as his authorial sensitivity to the power of literary and historical representation. He writes:

> In this novel many changes in names and geographies have been made to protect the privacy of people living and also to give a shape to various fictional destinies. I have, on occasion, condensed two or more historical figures into one or distributed the traits of one person over two or more characters. Some of the attributions to public figures are exact; others are fictional…I was privileged to read a great deal, fiction, non-fiction, journalism, poetry and internet material, in the course of researching this book. (*Dancer*, 291)

Because *Dancer* teases the reader with the prospects of biographical details, McCann is pressed to underline the extents to which he has undertaken authorial licence. As we have said, the passage is an open declaration of McCann's authorial process of research and production, and in this sense, alerts the reader to the laborious nature of creative industry. More pertinently to our discussion, it opens the door to fallibility and incompletion, as the novelist as historical investigator and as narrative creator can only ever aspire to parts of the histories and personalities that they are engaged with as textual content. Furthermore, McCann's undressing of authorial practice foregrounds the 'textuality' of the narrative – it emerges from a diversity of other textual sources and resources into the presented textual format. This last point, again, flags the anxiety and self-consciousness of the novel. But *Dancer* willingly exposes such sentiments in the service of a broader discussion of the roles and functions of all forms of narration and storytelling. In a way the final passage above is an indication of the power of the author, but at the same time an acknowledgement of the limits of that authorial agency – power, in the sense that people invest emotionally in how they, their loved ones and events are textually represented and remembered; powerlessness in the sense that any text is a failure, as well as never being a self-contained autonomous textual assertion. Each of the paratextual devices belongs to a different register and, ostensibly, performs an exclusive task within the overall architecture of the book. Yet these mutually exclusive functions remind us of the 'textuality' of this literary artefact, and therefore the triangulation of passages collectively highlights the anxiety of textuality. Likewise, they are united by their common concern for the politics of remembrance and for the proximity of the vocations and responsibilities of the literary and historical story-teller.

The intersected operations of the literary and the historiographical are most effectively articulated by Linda Hutcheon in her, by now, classic intervention, *The Politics of Postmodernism*. Employing what has become recognizably postmodernist critical rhetoric, Hutcheon reflects that: 'we may no longer have recourse to the grand narratives that once made sense of life for us, but we still have recourse to narrative representation of some kind in most of our verbal discourses, and one of the reasons may be political.'[6] Though much critical and theoretical water may have passed under the bridge between Hutcheon's publication and the appearance of McCann's novel, there are definite traces of common interest. Despite the self-evident unreliability of narrative representation, the claims of narrative representation prove irresistible for a variety of reasons across social and cultural collectives. Hutcheon's point, then, is, perhaps, a truism within contemporary critical theory and literary studies; less so, one might suggest, within mainstream historical studies. And her argument resonates with McCann's stated attentiveness to the democratic opportunities of storytelling. The disestablishment of 'grand narratives' does not necessarily decommission narrative as such, but does democratize, potentially, access to narrative space. Of equal relevance is Hutcheon's later, and more enduring, contention on the phenomenon of 'historiographic metafiction'.[7] While it is difficult to argue, without remainder, that *Dancer* fits entirely within this literary genus, the novel does exist in formal and thematic adjacency to Hutcheon's typology: 'Historiographic metafiction is written today in the context of a serious contemporary interrogating of the nature of representation in historiography. There has been much interest recently in narrative – its forms, its functions, its powers and its limitations – in many fields, but especially in history.'[8] Thus we can situate McCann's novelistic intervention within a longer, and ongoing, series of debates on the very fabric and, in the views of some historians, the very legitimacy of historical writing. Hutcheon's point contests the demarcations of fiction and non-fiction; of the literary and the historical; and of the imagination and factuality. Loss and creativity are key elements of historical writing, and these elements always shadow attributions of certainty and structure in form when it comes to the construction of historical narratives. There is an essential blindness to all encounters with the past, perhaps one that, *inter alia*, energizes and demoralizes those who write about the past. As Hutcheon concedes: 'the absent past can only be inferred from circumstantial evidence.'[9] Without recourse to putative hard evidence, testimony is partial, oblique and susceptible to the workings of imaginative emplotment. And this is precisely the juncture at which McCann enters the past, with his array of authorial and textual techniques aligned in creative representation of recorded and unrecorded histories. If, as Hutcheon maintains, 'Historiographic metafiction...traces the processing of events into facts, exploiting and then undermining the conventions of both novelistic realism and historiographic reference', then McCann's *Dancer* partakes of this act of narrative exposure through its polyphonic and multi-formal structure.[10] *Dancer* is presented as a cacophonous text, or in historiographical parlance, a congeries of documentary evidence, oral testimonies and first-hand accounts. McCann makes a series of formal selections that have consequences for the novel's problematic relation to historical writing, biographical life writing, and, of course, historiographic metafiction.

McCann's paratexts are indicative of the schizophrenic character of the 'historical': a version can be represented in a textually codified approximation, but the past can never be known, it always remains outside, beyond our epistemological grasp. We can fashion narratives about the past, but it is forever absent from these acts of textual containment. Nevertheless, as we alluded to above, acts of textual seizure do possess agency in their own right. But for the moment, it is worthwhile to focus upon the open-endedness that new approaches to historiography bring to our understandings of and ways of re-imagining historical narration. While McCann's text throws into relief the gravity of historical representation, it also exploits the liberty afforded by contemporary critical assaults on the sanctity and empirical fortitude of historiographical theory and practice. The radical recalibration of the constitution of the historical is foundational, for instance, to historian Richard Jenkins' lateral political ambition. Again, vitalized by the concepts and the idioms of contemporary 'postal' theories, his view is that it is 'liberating for the creative imagination that there is no such thing as a correct historical method'; this is because 'it is this failure which allows radical otherness to come, new imaginations to emerge. We ought not to waste this chance of otherness, of newness, in deference to the dead weight of professional, academic orthodoxy.'[11] Out of the ultimate failure, the inevitable incapacity of historical representation, Jenkins imagines a new creative politics of representation; in McCann's terms: a democratic narrative terrain. Despite the feverish deployment of theoretical rhetoric, Jenkins' openness to historical inclusivity and his spotlighting of the 'creative' facets of the historian's task serve as enabling counterpoints to the social functionalism of mainstream historical writing. Most explicitly, such an argument chimes with McCann's vision of the respective roles of the literary writer and the historian, and the role of the writer as historian: 'The writer desires to see inside the dark corners in order to make sense of the room that has already been swept clean (or clean-ish) by historians, critics and journalists.'[12] McCann's endeavours in *Dancer* are a project of creative reclamation and of imaginative resuscitation. It is a project that pays tribute to the enabling force of creativity in dealing with the past, and one that recognizes the disabling distance of time and space in approaching those past personalities, places and events. The importance of 'ordering' in historical writing is laid bare by McCann in his repeated acknowledgement of his text's fictionality. In addition, in alighting on the lives and stories of a cast of disposable historical characters, McCann emphasizes the ways in which historical 'ordering' can be both redemptive (in his narrative) and exclusionary.

Through its appropriation of the life of Rudolf Nureyev, one of the twentieth century's stellar artists and politico-cultural icons, *Dancer* tantalizes the reader with the 'truth' value of biographical record. Yet as McCann's paratextual materials impress, the novel simply utilizes

Nureyev's existence as a means of re-imagining the latter half of the century, and in order to interrogate the nature of art and storytelling. Rather than focus on, and ratify again, the publicly accepted mythologies of Nureyev's biography, McCann is more concerned with the impacts of genius, of unrestrained celebrity and of the egotism of the supreme artist upon those that mingle around Nureyev over the course of his life, and the consequences of his vocation for his exiled family. In a sense, *Dancer* confronts the discourse of biographical life writing by trying to imagine everything that could not be included in an official biographical narrative. In McCann's view, he never intended 'it to be a book about Nureyev...it's about stories, other people telling stories and accidentally (almost) revealing a life'.[13] For McCann, biographies are points of imaginative departure and suggestiveness, rather than acts of textual confirmations or closure. Out of the officially recorded events and personalities of Nureyev's life, McCann appropriates, re-invents and transforms people, places and details to his own speculative aesthetic ends. Rather than adhere to the autocratic politics of consummate biographical testimony, *Dancer* effectively disturbs the factual historical anchorage of the field of biographical life writing.

Biographical life writing can be read as a sub-set of the larger field of historical writing discussed above. And *Dancer*, as McCann attests, functions as a lyrical and democratic deconstruction of the principles of narrative veracity, which are more often than not indexical of these two historical fields. In terms of biography, specifically, one of the key intentions of McCann's novel is evident in Hermione Lee's recent diagnosis on biographical life writing. An accomplished biographer in her own right, Lee gestures to one of the fundamental problems of biography when she argues 'that it can tend to sound too knowing and firm about the shape of its subject's life, to make it read too smoothly, to be too selective'.[14] Lee's argument bears affinities to the criticisms voiced earlier about contemporary historiography – both sets of criticisms seem underwritten by an equivalent urge for inclusivity, or, at least, regret the exclusionary limits of the respective forms of historical writing. 'Alternatives,' Lee continues, 'missed chances, roads not taken, accidents and hesitations, the whole "swarm of possibilities" that hums around our every experience, too often disappears in the smoothing biographical process.'[15] These latter possibilities are precisely the details McCann gathers in his narrative and they are, again, crucial to the democratic and utopian politics that undergird his entire aesthetic enterprise. Lee's self-reflexive comments, then, reflect the problems and the expectations that adhere to the field of biography. And her intimation of the value of the creative and the currency of the marginal within biography are affirmations of the viability of McCann's metafictional usurpation of Nureyev's life stories. Both McCann's novel and Lee's critical commentaries on biography highlight the extent to which biography traverses fields of writing, learning and criticism. In any given biography: 'History, politics, sociology, gossip, fiction, literary criticism, psychoanalysis, documentary, journalism, ethics, and philosophy are all scrambled up inside the genre.'[16] Such a melange of discourses plays to the creative impetus of McCann's project, facilitating his fictional permissiveness with the past. In addition, the disparity of discourses explains the necessary autocracy of biographical representation – it is simply required to tame and to display this variety in a digestible, legible form. In *Dancer*, we witness the revolt of the former against the authority of the latter, and one of the key ways in which this representational disobedience is accomplished is through McCann's privileging of the body.

The mobile, sexual vigour of Rudi's body, in dance most explicitly, is a muscular refutation of the boundaries of biographical textual record. Again, Lee is instructive on this issue: 'What makes biography so endlessly absorbing is that through all the documents and letters and witnesses, the conflicting opinions and partial memories and fictionalized versions, we keep catching sight of a real body, a physical life…The life of the body plays much more of a part in contemporary biographical narratives.'[17] Herein we reveal the proximity of McCann's text to the field of biographical writing in its most explicit form. It is not just the novel's thematic attention to sexuality and ballet that presses the 'body' into centre-stage, but it is equally *Dancer*'s orbit around biographical writing that brings the 'body' into focus. The violence and the energy of Rudi's body confounds the subjugative intentions of the biographer's will; his visceral magnetism resonates beyond the signifying codes of the written word, as well as leaving lingering traces on the anonymous historical persons who came within his circle and his family life. Official biography cannot capture the physical pains, exhilarations or transient grace of his dancing body, nor can it do justice to its affectiveness in those moments of bodily expression. Like any textual representation, biographies aspire to completion, but 'like lives, are made up of contested objects – relics, testimonies, versions, correspondences, the unverifiable'.[18] Biographies are also replete with gaps, silences and absent details, and all of the foregoing are seized upon and exploited by McCann in *Dancer*. Yet despite the relevance of discussing *Dancer* in relation to biography, it is emphatically not a biography. What it achieves is an implied critique of the genre, as well as employing accepted principles of the field of biography as a means of contesting the self-evidence of historical representation. Biography, then, is another weave in McCann's self-reflexive engagement with the art and act of storytelling. It is another mode through which he explores the politics of historical representation and reveals the elision of subaltern historical narratives.

In his hyper-sensual, free-wheeling narrative, Rudi's friend, Victor Pareci, a fictionalized homosexual *bon-vivant* in 1970s New York, distils one of many perspectives on Rudi's lifestyle. But Victor also exhibits a critical self-awareness about the narrative production of Rudi as a cultural and sexual icon: 'everyone with a Rudi story and each one more outrageous than the next – probably untrue – so that Rudi is a living myth' (*Dancer*, 199). Rudi's notoriety and accessibility as a celebrity fosters an economy of gossip and semi-attachment via rumour and hearsay. His life, in Victor's eyes, becomes an industry of speculation, projection and misrepresentation, and this is precisely McCann's point. In so far as *Dancer* approximates to biography, it too partakes of this narrative industry. The lure to create a fictionalized biographical portrait of Rudi is parasitical on the earlier, persistent economy of myths that crowd around Rudi and his memory. Victor provides a key metacritical pause in the midst of his own relentless, insatiable narrative arc. The remainder of the novel, its structure, voices and textual forms are referenced in Victor's conclusion above. But while he seems to be superficially concerned with the truth quotient of these batteries of stories about Rudi, McCann's real focus is the fact that deliberating over truth and falsity is futile anyway. The formal variety and the chorus of disparate voices afforded narrative space in *Dancer* highlight the author's ambiguous attitude to the claims of historical or biographical verisimilitude: 'for, as Rudi says, remaining unknowable is the only true way to be known' (*Dancer*, 200).[19]

Part of McCann's methodology in preparing *Dancer* takes us back to the field of biographical life writing and the impulse to unearth facts or shards of truth on the personality, the life story under consideration. In interview McCann describes visiting Nureyev's hometown of Ufa on a research sortie, but this ostensible return to origins yielded scant concrete information on his subject: 'Amazingly, very few people there knew him. He was sort of like a rumour. That, in itself, helped contribute to the novel.'[20] The dearth of information gleaned by McCann in the home place is, firstly, a form of licence to imagine the character and the life that appears in *Dancer*. Rudi's insubstantial existence for the residents of Ufa acts as a catalyst for McCann to wrestle with the conventions of biographical form. Equally, the suggestion that Rudi survives as a kind of spectral figure fleshed out only in rumour actually becomes a key way of understanding the formal structure of the novel. The open-endedness implied by McCann's comments on his fictional subject feeds into his thematic concentration of the art of storytelling in *Dancer*. Similarly, the structure displayed is not univocal biographical storytelling, but multi-formal and multi-perspectival. The novel is a confection of textual forms, historical characters and events, invented characters and events, and semi-fictionalized versions of historical characters. Outlining the relative veracity of the novel, as well as justifying the factual liberties taken in the narrative, McCann remarks:

> On the broad canvas it's fair but it's an abstract fairness, if you will. It's an abstract portrait, concentrating on lines and brush-strokes and traditionally neglected parts of the canvass...Is it factual? No...But facts are mercenary things: they can be used and exploited in so many ways. I wanted to create a texture that was true. I also wanted to question the idea of storytelling. Who owns a story? Who has a right to tell a story? Who and what legislates what becomes a supposed fact?[21]

The catholicity of McCann's narrative forum in *Dancer* means that in responding to his own questions above, the solution seems to be that almost anyone, however peripheral to Rudi's life and legacy, is afforded an occasion to contribute to the tapestry of the larger story. The disparate cast-list includes Rudi's disaffected sister, Tamara; the husband and daughter of his first dance teacher; Margot Fonteyn; Andy Warhol; a young female Chilean dancer at the Kirov Ballet in Leningrad; a bachelor cobbler in London; Rudi's French housemaid, Odile; an anonymous rival at the Kirov; a further anonymous male who frequented homosexual meeting spots in Leningrad; Victor Pareci, Rudi's close friend and fellow-traveller among homosexual gatherings in New York; and the wife of his dance teacher in Leningrad. The copiousness of the voices does not unfurl the coherence of the narrative; Rudi, though elusive and enigmatic, provides a magnetic core to the brachiating narrative vectors. But it is not simply that McCann shepherds a diffuse cast of voices and characters into *Dancer*, there is also a plenitude of textual forms through which these 'versions' of Rudi are articulated. Again, among the textual registers that punctuate the novel, we note diary entries, letters, magazine headlines, state surveillance reports, private journals, an aviation incident report form, and brief interpersonal notes. In addition to these forms of textual representation, McCann includes telephone conversations and radio broadcasts, as well as the ubiquitous communications of rumour and innuendo. Naturally some of these modes of representation and communication are more prominent than others, and they all vie with an occasional omniscient historical narration for narrative prominence, perhaps even authenticity. Thus the range of people and representational codes that clamour within *Dancer* evoke the vertiginous resonances of Rudi's life in other lives, yet none manage to secure a definitive version of Rudi. Neither individually nor in aggregate do the textual fragments adequately begin to know or to manage Rudi's character. Just as Rudi the exile remains unbounded by geographical borders, the textualized Rudi constantly evades final signification; in equal measure, Rudi's balletic body transcends the parameters of socialized corporeality. In each of these formal respects, McCann assents to Rudi's own belief in his precious unknowability.

DANCING BODIES

If, as we briefly noted, and as Susan Cahill maintains, 'Nureyev's life is used to engage with questions concerning storytelling, the creation of iconic figures, the relationship between individuals and historical discourses, and the place of the corporeal in such discourses', then it is worth accounting for the relations that exist between dance, the dancing body and history.[22] Rudi's balletic agency constitutes a somatic excess, which, following Derrida's theoretical figuration, harbours a specific liberating, deconstructive force.[23] The physical possibilities of dance are a further symptom of McCann's utopian politics, and balletic dance is another aesthetic field in which these hopeful politics are manifest.

Indeed, the utopian energies of dance form part of Ernst Bloch's utopian ur-text, *The Principle of Hope*. In this multi-volume philosophical-political survey, Bloch declares: 'The dance allows us to move in a completely different way to the way we move in the day, at least in the everyday, it imitates something which the latter has lost or never even possessed. It paces out the wish for more beautifully moved being, fixes it in the eye, ear, the whole body, just as if it already existed now.'[24] Bloch's argument envisions the seeds of a better existence in the refined expressive physicality of the dancing body; this operates in sharp contrast to the socialized contours of the labouring or consuming everyday body. The performed 'becomings' of dance transcend the oppressive gravity of the stilted or static body, and such politics are present in McCann's efforts to present the impacts and the possibilities of Rudi's balletic genius. Dance, then, becomes a presiding aesthetic and political agent within the novel, intersecting with the deconstructive re-imaginations of both historical writing and biographical life writing.

Within the discourse of dance studies, sentiments such as those expressed by Bloch, and represented by McCann, abound and cohere around a general 'philosophy that understands the body not as a self-contained and closed entity but as an open and dynamic system of exchange, constantly producing modes of subjection and control, as well as resistance and becoming'.[25] Lepecki's transgressive vision of the dancing body is endorsed in a feminist context by Elizabeth Dempster, who argues that: 'the body, dancing, can challenge and deconstruct cultural inscription...In moments of dancing the edges of things blur and terms such as mind/body, flesh/spirit, carnal/divine, male/female become labile and unmoored, breaking loose from the fixings of their pairings.'[26] In broaching the affective violence and discipline of balletic dance through Nureyev, McCann, then, faces a problematic as author. The arguments of Lepecki and Dempster affirm the empowering contingency of dance as an affront to the embalming grasp of signification. Yet, as an author, McCann must remain conscious of the ultimate failure he faces in his efforts to represent, in text, the affective force of Rudi's balletic performances. The danger of metaphorizing dance as a critical tool is that one (either critic or novelist) reduces the art form to a function of an abstract idea. So, it is true that 'Derrida theorises dance as a conceptual movement that disrupts and reorients spaces through which it moves', but one must retain a perspective on the non-conceptual aspects of dance.[27] In other words, as dance critic Susan Leigh Foster counters: 'these writings…move quickly past arms, legs, torso and head on their way to a theoretical agenda that requires something unknowable or unknown as an initial premise. The body remains mysterious and ephemeral, a convenient receptacle for their new theoretical positions.'[28] Foster's is a polemical caveat, but it is worth recalling as we discuss the somatic articulations of McCann's Nureyev, and as we consider the service to which McCann puts this bodily incarnation of freedom and beauty. Nevertheless, there is a sense in which McCann's narrative, firstly, remains conscious of and loyal to the bodily functions of the art of dance, as Foster demands. And, secondly, there is a continuous awareness of the transformative agency of dance as an art form voiced by Rudi and others in the narrative. Thus, McCann certainly exploits both the metaphorical possibilities of dance, following Derrida, and the physically affective after-effects of dance on performers and audiences.

From a critical perspective, and drawing on Derrida's essay 'Choreographies', Cahill pursues the deconstructive dimensions of Rudi's balletic performances in relation to the framing of historical and memorial time. Put simply, she concludes that: 'Dance seems to evade and resist any attempt to freeze it in representation', a problematic that McCann is boundaried by, but is eager to display in his inevitable failure.[29] Despite the significations and figurations of choreography, the dancing body overcomes such idealizing and conventional codes to become 'an experiment, all of its impulses going to the creation of an adventure and the end of each adventure being a new impulse towards further creation' (*Dancer*, 209). The performative cannot be contained within signification; it is resistant to documentation or to archivization and thereby hints at a vital utopian impulse. The body in balletic movement is visceral, toned, sexual, desired and violent, and is the site of intense utopian creativity. The body in performance cannot be held or stilled; as Peggy Phelan argues, performance is its own annihilation and performance becomes through its own disappearance.[30] Part of Rudi's elusiveness as a person, which is crucial to McCann's allusions to biography, is conditioned by his life as a performer. Rudi's career, his entire life and lifestyle, are deeply performative; his talent, celebrity and political notoriety demand the cultivations of personae, so that, in the end, we are left querying where or who or what is Rudolf Nureyev.

And, perhaps, this is one of McCann's key speculations. If, as Phelan contends, 'in the plenitude of its [performance] apparent visibility and availability, the performer actually disappears and represents something else', then where are we ever likely to locate Rudi?[31] McCann's deliberate engagement with historiography and biography, together with dance theory and the politics of performance, cohere around the impossibility of representation. Rudi's body and his life provoke mystery, desire and rumour, all of which have been domesticated by the publication of biographies; his enlistment to political causes; and his absorption into dance history. Yet his stories are those of others in McCann's treatment, and Rudi's meaning is always elsewhere and diffused; it is as unlikely to be captured in *Dancer* as in any other textual representation. Primary among the tensions in *Dancer* is that between the arresting, explosive performances of Rudi as dancer and the choreographic structure of balletic dance. Rudi abides by the firm hands of disciplined practice and exertion, yet his onstage performances travel beyond the received conventions of the art. As C.J.C. Bull notes: 'ballet...represents ideals of exquisitely controlled technical precision and emotional expressions combined with a classical (traditional) framework.'[32] In other words, traditionally there is a scripted form to the balletic performance, as Bull stresses terms such as 'ideals', 'controlled', 'classical' and 'framework'. But throughout the novel, Rudi seems to possess an intuition that disavows any unquestioning allegiance to the ideals of traditional balletic tradition. Helen Thomas re-iterates Bull's argument on the primacy of structure to the successful realization of balletic beauty. She suggests that: 'the mastery of the *codified* positions, shapes, and "steps" constitute the core of the ballet student's training in pursuit of the idealised body based on the aesthetic ideals of classical beauty [my emphasis].'[33] Again, Thomas's language accentuates the importance of abstracted ideals to the dancer's body, and emphasizes the necessary subjugation of that body to the traditional codes of the discipline. In a sense, both Bull and Thomas underline the foundational forms of balletic dance, pressing the key role played by rigour and structure in dance as a bodily vocation. And there is evidence in *Dancer* of the extremities to which the young Rudi extended his body to achieve the stature, proportions and malleability of the accomplished balletic artist. In training and rehearsal, Rudi shows commitment and subservience to the formal structure of his art; however, in public performance the

heightened levels of affectiveness that his dancing engenders are suggestive of an artist that has transcended such formal codification. Rudi is
an artist who is expressing a vibrancy that extends beyond the nota-
tions of classical balletic beauty. Diagnosing this potency in the young
Rudi, his first dance teacher, Anna, believes 'that he was somehow born
within dance, that he was unlettered in it, yet he knew it intimately, it
was a grammar for him, deep and untutored' (*Dancer*, 44). Rudi's relationship with his vocation, then, is, at one level, a confrontation with
history and with artistic form; his excessive performances are
affronts to conventional concepts of both. Thus both body and textual
forms are thrown into the centre of the narrative by this problematic
crux at the core of Rudi's artistic career. Rudi's body is one of the
dynamic agents across the narrative – indeed the somatic is a pivotal
symbolic locus for McCann's novel as a whole. But of similar relevance
is the overt concern for textual form and the mosaic-like fragments that
are corralled to form McCann's fractured narrative. The co-location
of the body and of narrative as key thematics, thus, operates in terms
of form and content.

In a scene that bears more than a passing resemblance to Ursula
Andress's sensual exit from the sea in the James Bond film *Dr. No*, Margot Fonteyn describes Rudi's emergence after a swim: 'She watches
Rudi's slow rise from the water, head first, then shoulders, then chest,
his tiny waist, his penis large even after the chill of the water, his giant
thighs, the tough calves, the Michelangelo of him' (*Dancer*, 160–1).
This first part of her meditation on Rudi's drenched, muscular anatomy
asserts the rippling physical prowess of Rudi. His body is detailed, even
objectified, in Fonteyn's systematic representation of its parts. Rudi's
hyper-masculine physique is, in Fonteyn's view, historical, even epochal,
in its stature; in her description Rudi's body becomes an object of art,
a sculptural emergence from the sea. This is a body that she is
acquainted with through their years of dance partnership: 'She has, in
dance, touched every part of him. His clavicle, his elbow, the lobe of his
ear, his groin, the small of his back, his feet. Still, she raises her hand
formally to her lips, as if to compensate for her lack of surprise'
(*Dancer*, 161). Not only does her account re-affirm the intimate physicality of the discipline and the art of dance, but these outlines of Rudi's
body are objective lists of external features and appendages. The
aggregation of these bodily parts in balletic motion is, as we shall

discuss below, vigorously affective across a range of characters and audiences. But at this point, it seems that despite the affectiveness of Rudi's bodily exertions, there remains something remote about the body. In this regard, McCann suggests its fragility and its isolated humanity in Fonteyn's portrait. What we get, in essence, is a description of a biological body – beautiful in its proportions but one that is vulnerable to ageing and to objectification. At the same time, this body in balletic movement is capable of transcending such simple objectification and, as such, the body, Rudi's body, becomes a site of contestation. Rudi's body becomes a site onto which competing desires and motives are inscribed. But it also becomes a volatile medium through which, potentially, concretized notions of time, history and identity are challenged.

Immediately succeeding Fonteyn's portrait of Rudi's body, there is a change in narrative focalization, as we move to a first-person narrative in Rudi's voice. Invoking one of the many extra-diegetic texts in the novel, this section opens with Rudi reflecting on the contemporary global monumentalization of his body:

> *Cosmopolitan: The world's most beautiful man.* One must confront the fact that the face will change and the body is vulnerable. But so what? Enjoy the moment. The *world's* most beautiful man! When I'm seventy and sitting by the fire, I will take the photos out and weep, ha! Somebody stuck the cover on my mirror and added devil's horns. I wouldn't mind but the bastards ruined my eye-liner pen – it is probably the fat cleaning bitch who left in tears yesterday. (*Dancer*, 161)

Having moved from Fonteyn's intimate appreciation of Rudi's beauty, his physical allure is trumpeted on an international scale through a mass-media publication. Rudi is firmly ratified as a rarefied object of aesthetic value by this high-circulation magazine. The headline underscores Rudi's achievement of popular fame, and of the fact that his body has entered global circulation as an object of high aesthetic currency. The first-person narration betrays the momentary consciousness of inevitable mortality and decline, but quickly re-establishes the current and future worth of this media celebration of his physique. Yet the final sentences of the extract reveal the subcutaneous sides of Rudi's volatile character. The superficial celebrity bestowed by this brand-defining image is complicated by implications about Rudi's interpersonal behaviour. Nevertheless, *Cosmopolitan*, and this episode, represents a triumphant moment in Rudi's narrative; the bold headline is a brief, but telling, 'version' of Rudi and it exposes the centrality of his body and its beauty, to who and what he is and will become. Rudi's physical prowess is core to the narrative of celebrity, of objectification and of commodification, which provides one of the strands through which the body is explored by McCann. Celebrity and commodification, and the ways in which the body is forced to perform, are parts of the debilitating logic of progressive history. They become means by which Rudi and his body are tamed and rendered marketable, and appear knowable. But these are limits that Rudi's life and his body transcend and escape in other crucial ways. There is a profoundly delimiting and conservative orientation to Rudi's exposition as an ideal of physical beauty. But it is within his means, his bodily means, to defy these limits through the sheer force and ambition of his balletic performances.

In a letter to his sister Tamara dated June 1964, having heard of his father's death, Rudi lays bare many of the travails of his career. In this missive he details his travels, his emotional condition, his fears, his political opinions, and his deep regret and sorrow at his father's passing. The narrative form is one of the few occasions we gain access to Rudi's first-person testimony, and while there is certainly an intimacy and a physical dedication in the act of letter writing, it equally implies distance and physical separation. Whereas the selected diary entries we read of Rudi's progress are private, veering from impressionistic to intense in tone, this letter forms part of a familial rapprochement, or at the very least an effort at détente across the European mainland. The letter is not especially lengthy, but compacted into its frame are insights into Rudi's public and private lives. The passing of his father, with whom he had a remote and fractious relationship, initiates a burst of textual self-reckoning for Rudi. The formal composition of the letter represents a disciplining of the body and mind, a process of focused reflection and expression, but, as above, its very necessity betrays the incessant motion of Rudi's life away from his family and his homeland. Given his political defection from the Soviet Union, both his family and his homeland are not only distant, but are effectively sealed from his return. Indeed, the letter is likely to be the object of censorious scrutiny over the course of its journey from West to East. Nevertheless, we find a stress on the importance of dance for Rudi and an effort by him to separate fact from fiction about his life condensed into the letter. He is keen to address the distortions that abound about his lifestyle to his sister, maintaining that these are political in their motivations. The letter is significant, then, in that it is an attempt to humanize Rudi, as he tries to strip away the fabulous mythologies and ideological propaganda, which form so much of his perceived persona. Yet, through all of his exiled travel, the patronage and the wanton rumours, dance is a palliative outlet for Rudi; ballet retains a non-judgemental purity for him as an escape from the demands of his political and cultural objectification.

On the night following the belated news of his father's death, Rudi takes to the stage in Milan, but this dedication to performance is not based on a sense of professional duty. Again gesturing to the almost preternatural qualities of dance, Rudi writes to Tamara that: 'dance to me, as you know, is every emotion perfectly crystallised, not just celebration, but death, futility and loneliness too. Even love must pass through loneliness. So I danced him alive. When I went on stage I was released. You may choose not to believe this, but it is the truth' (*Dancer*, 139). With the demise of one body, his father's, Rudi's excessive physical talent assumes a kind of spiritual function. Despite the protracted tension of this father–son relationship, Rudi submits a charged and emotive performance as an act of resurrection for his father. The burden of emotional distance that obtained between Rudi and his father, particularly due to Rudi's choice of career, is assuaged by the balletic performance. The physical bounds of the body, which inevitably include decrepitude, pain and death, are overcome for Rudi by this performative restitution. If death is the telos of human life, the unavoidable terminus of linear time, as Cahill argues in her Derridean reading of *Dancer*, 'Rudi's body operate[s] within the narrative as a codification of alternate modes and paradigms of conceptualising time and memory.'[34] The past, his father, their life together are resurrected through Rudi's balletic dance, through his body's dynamic and transcendent performance, which obliterates the staid uniformity of linear history. The dancing body, and Rudi's life, interrogate the boundaries of both historical time and historical narration. In the same letter, Rudi further attempts to disaggregate his art from its imbrication in the politics of the Cold War. And again, his argument is a moment of self-legitimation to his absent sister: 'Politics is for fat men with cigars. It is not for me, I am a dancer, I live to dance.

That is all...I go from country to country. I am a non-person where I became a person. I am stateless where I exist. So it is. And so it has been, even I suppose since our days in Ufa. It is dance, and dance only, that keeps me alive' (*Dancer*, 140). Of course, it is naïve of Rudi to think that his celebrity and his talent can remain aloof from political exploitation, but is also legitimate for him to imagine beyond the grim polarities of Soviet–American *realpolitik*.

Dance is, as he confirms, essential to his very being; its performance is the kernel of the performance of his identity. As we have seen, dance is redemptive and transgressive at the same time; its somatic articulations and gestures reach beyond the edges of the daily physicality of life and achieve substantial spiritual dimensions for Rudi. As his travelogue essays, his itinerant professional and personal lives may offer opportunities to take 'tea in the White House with President Kennedy...[to dance] at the inauguration of Johnson. At the Vienna State Opera House...' (*Dancer*, 140), but there is a counter-current in Rudi that has 'no desire to be served up as a sensation, a nine-day wonder' (*Dancer*, 140). These examples intersect with his visual objectification via the mass media, but it is here in his letter that he summarily acknowledges how such treatment is managing to hollow out his identity. He touches upon the fact that his life is manufactured as a succession of triumphant spectacles. But, again, he returns to the sanctuary and the vitality offered by and through dance; it is the art that sustains him and that harbours the possibility of retreat from his glamorous rootlessness. Rudi is welcomed and feted everywhere he performs and visits, but it is only in the act of dancing that he really feels a sense of belonging. Only in performance can he elude the superficial roles and identities that have been granted to him, that have begun to stand in for any degree of authenticity. In all of these ways dance, the performative enunciations of his balletic body, possesses vital utopian impulses. His art is a liberating aesthetic of the body, with which he seeks to flee the stasis of Cold War politics and the superficialities of rootless celebrity. And such dynamism is most expressly verbalized by Rudi in the second to last line of his letter when, referring to his mother, he implores Tamara to 'inform her that her son dances to improve the world' (*Dancer*, 142). Rudi's ambition may be overstated but there is no denying the lateral and durable impact of his balletic art across the globe; and his aspiration as a dancer chimes with that attributed to the art by Bloch. But the broader point centres on the utopian possibilities of art: the viability, even responsibility, of creative art to intervene, and to articulate utopian visions. This does not necessarily equate to polemical or instrumental political art but, in McCann's view, a recognition of the historicity of the artist and their art, all of which bring responsibility and opportunity. The hubris of Rudi's statement suggests, on the one hand, a defensive posture from a son exiled from his mother; but, on the other, is indicative of Rudi's ferocious self-belief, which we witness via the novel's other voices. These concluding remarks reveal a burgeoning consciousness of his position as a world-historical figure, but the letter also exposes his ambiguous feelings about assuming such a status. Attaining this status invites celebrity in tandem with vulnerability to misrepresentation, both of which McCann exploits in his re-imagination of this celebrated life and career. But what is crucial about this letter is the centrality it reveals about dance in Rudi's life, and just how dependent he is on his art. The body in motion as exile and as performer operate at different levels in the novel: Rudi as exiled, international performer is confined to a form of corporate incarceration, while Rudi the *avant garde* dancer experiences exhilarating freedom through balletic expression.

The body in history is not only represented by Rudi's life and art in the novel – McCann opens *Dancer* with a graphic account of the brutalizing experiences of Russian soldiers during the Second World War. Delivered by an omniscient narrative voice, the first five pages of the novel, subtitled 'Soviet Union 1941–56', recount the visceral sufferings of these exposed military bodies under the most severe conditions. McCann provides micro- and macro-details of the dehumanizing bodily endurances of this military campaign. The anonymous soldiery undergo punishing exertions and the effects of the war are indelibly scripted onto the surfaces and the dismembered appendages of their bodies. These bodies are described without any of the soldiers being identified, none is allowed to become our primary focalizer, and, consequently, the opening section becomes representative of 'the body in history', and the inscription of politics onto the human body. By opening in this manner, McCann foregrounds the extreme violences that are complacently, and willingly, committed on mass scales under the pressure of political expediency. In image after image, McCann details the exacting carceral toll of history on millions of undocumented historical individuals: 'When they touched bare metal the flesh tore away from their hands...if they shat, which was not often, they had to shit in their pants...To piss, they hitched oilskin sacks under their trousers so they didn't expose themselves to the weather and they learned to cradle the warmth of the pissbag between their legs' (*Dancer*, 7–8). The privacies of bodily functions become ordeals, as the war conditions subvert the normalcy of bodily evacuation. Yet these simplicities, while unhygienic, pale in comparison to the mortal forces of the military equipment that assaults these abject bodies: 'Pieces of shrapnel caught beneath their eyes. Bullets whipped clean through their calf muscles. Splinters of shells lodged in their necks. Mortars cracked their backbones. Phosphorus bombs set them aflame' (*Dancer*, 9). The technology of conflict mutilates and disables the body, and the history of technological invention runs its course parallel to history's violent assault on the human body. And this notion of the violence of history sedimenting dead bodies in the landscape is expressed by McCann: 'The dead were heaped onto horse cars and laid in mass graves blown out of the ground with dynamite...Yet more dead were heaped upon the dead, and frozen bones were heard to crack, and the bodies lay there in their hideous contortions' (*Dancer*, 9). In this opening section, the body is presented as tactile, as vulnerable, as partial, as organic and as disposable. This initial panorama of deformations, then, alerts us to the implication of history, politics and the body, but does so in a torrent of violence. The nightmare scenario depicted by McCann points to the callous choreography of warfare under which the anonymized, militarized body is stripped of humanity as a purely functional entity. But it is at the very end of this section that we catch a glimpse of the future, of a hopeful germ that will enliven the remainder of the novel: 'each winter afternoon a six-year-old boy, hungry and narrow and keen, sat on a cliff above the river, looking down at the trains, wondering when his own father would be coming home and whether he would be broken just like the ones they were lifting from beneath the steam and the bugles' (*Dancer*, 12–13). In retrospect we know this to be Rudi, captured in tense expectancy, imagining and hoping beyond the carnage of the immediate. The dismal toll of bodies up to this point is soon to have a redemptive counterpoint in the shape of Rudi's dancing body.

This boy re-enters the narrative through the first-person voice of a female volunteer at the military hospital at Ufa. As part of the recuperative programme for the wounded soldiers, a troupe of local children visit and dance in the hospital wards. Initially the troupe performs as a group under the stern eye of their female instructor, but 'just when we thought they were finished, a small blond boy stepped out of the line. He was about five or six years old. He extended his leg, placed his hands firmly on his hips and hitched his thumbs at his back. He bent his neck slightly forward, stretched his elbows out and began' (*Dancer*, 20). Amid the bodily ruination of the hospital, Rudi makes his first balletic appearance in the narrative. There is a practised assurance to the preparatory routine that Rudi performs, and McCann presents the young dancer beginning to assert mastery over his body as a performer. His talent, his youth and his blossoming skill as a dancer bestow respite to the exhausted soldiers, and his childish dancing body speaks of the future. The dance troupe represent the endurance of art, but equally the contrary actuation of the body in history as a site of redemption and as an instrument of aesthetic beauty. In this anonymous sight of Rudi the boy-performer, we begin to appreciate the affective agency of dance and, in particular, the affective agency that Rudi will wield over so many in the ensuing years of his career. At this juncture, however, the dystopian terrains that assail the bodies of the Russian soldiers, that dismember them as sacrifices to politics, are countered by the utopian energies of Rudi's boyish grace in dance.

DESIRE AND DANCE

But as Rudi develops as a dancer, with Anna's tuition and, subsequently, at the Kirov Ballet in Leningrad, it becomes apparent that his performances, indeed his whole bodily carriage, are transfused with much more than simple grace. Gradually, dance becomes the dominant articulation of his body; it is as if it was the precise reason that his body was created. As Yulia, Anna's daughter, remarks: 'He stood stately in the centre of the room, feet together, and it struck me that his body had now accepted dance as its only strategy' (*Dancer*, 80). The measured routine of the boy in Ufa has evolved into a holistic bodily performance – dance is the only energy that circulates in Rudi's body at this point. And such total immersion manifests in Rudi's dexterous balletic performances, even at this formative stage of his career. At his first showcase performance at the Leningrad Choreographic, attended by Yulia and Anna, Rudi's achievement is breathtaking. Transcending the logic of scripted choreography, Rudi's rendition of *Notre-Dame de Paris* is perfect, in Anna's view: 'he danced perfectly, light and quick, pliant, his line controlled and composed, but more than that he was using something beyond his body – not just his face, his fingers, his long neck, his hips, but something intangible, beyond thought, some kinetic fury and spirit' (*Dancer*, 81). So while Rudi remains faithful to the postures and gestures of his balletic education – he assimilates the foundational codes of the tradition – Yulia intuits an extra-bodily power at work in Rudi's performance. Her intuition suggests that there is, indeed, an 'excessive' quality to Rudi's dance, which if it is 'beyond thought', may well lead to desire and spirituality. Yulia does not, at this stage, fully apprehend the affectiveness of Rudi's performance, nor does McCann fully develop the effects of his dancing body on his audiences. For the moment, the singular parts of Rudi's body, as listed by Yulia, far exceed their prosaic physicality. The bare biology of Rudi's body, in stark contrast to that of the Russian soldiers at the beginning of the novel, is broiling with potential, and it is intimated that this corporeality houses an anticipatory aesthetic promise. This same sense of a vivifying extra-physical performer is apparent shortly after, when Rudi's mother and sister attend a performance at the Tchaikovsky Concert Hall, again in Leningrad. The opulence of the hall's decorative trappings is far removed from the provincial material poverty of the lives of these two women, but, again, Rudi's dancing entrances and uplifts. McCann's description focuses on the combined physicalities of both dancer and his family members: 'As the dance begins their hands are clenched tight in their laps, but soon the women are gripping each other, amazed to see Rudi, not just the dance, but what he has become, whole and full and fleshed, patrolling the stage, devouring space, graceful and angry' (*Dancer*, 91). But it is his mother's response to witnessing her son perform for the first time that ends this section: 'His mother leans forward in her plush velvet seat, awed and slightly frightened. This is my flesh and blood, she thinks. This is what I have made' (*Dancer*, 91). The nervous energy of Rudi's family is dissipated by the vision of his balletic achievement; the mother and daughter are drawn together in an enthralled embrace at the sight of his performance. In contrast to Yulia's description, there is less focus on the individual parts of Rudi's body, as now we begin to appreciate the emotional and somatic affect-iveness of his body, as well as to understand the creative and destructive vitalities that exist within that body. Rudi's mother's reflection on her biological production of this phenomenon, this nubile, artistic body on stage, reminds us of the base physicality of the ballet dancer. But, more importantly, this stresses the gap that Rudi has opened between that brute physicality and the transcendent balletic motion of his art. Rudi may well be Farida's 'flesh and blood', but in his artistic expressiveness he possesses the capacity to awe and to frighten her.

As Rudi's fame spreads and his talent matures, the provocative abilities of his performances become more apparent, and his artistic flourishes become more closely entwined with expressions of sexuality and desire. In this register Rudi's performance is mediated by Yulia; we receive a highly charged first-person account of her exposure to Rudi's dancing body. Though experienced in crowded venues, though they are communal events, the dancing body of Rudi provokes the audience in private, individual ways. Yulia's account of Rudi's entrance in *Giselle* at the Kirov captures the incendiary force of his performance: 'The lights were dimmed. When Rudi entered, exploding from the wings to a round of applause, he tore the role open, not so much by how he danced, but by the manner in which he presented himself, a sort of hunger turned human' (*Dancer*, 125). The allusion to 'hunger' naturally suggests a lack of satiety and a striving after fulfilment. Rudi's dance is not complete in itself as a classical masterpiece, rather it unfolds as a 'becoming' – there is a simultaneous feeling of rapture in the presence of the dance, and regret at its immediate disappearance in performance. The balletic performance is an instantiation of creation and obliteration, a consummate expression of desire, and it is the idea of desire that is crucial to Yulia's response to Rudi's performance. As Rudi's performance crescendos, so too does Yulia's emotional and visceral response; she returns to describing the contours of Rudi's body as 'a thing of the most captivating beauty – hard lines at his shoulders, his neck striated with muscle, enormous thighs, his calf muscles twitching' (*Dancer*, 126). But while Yulia may be able to rationalize and to catalogue the individual parts of Rudi's body, she is not in control of the affectiveness that his body exercises on her body. These portraits of Rudi are superficial, but the ensuing effects on Yulia excite deep carnal desires. Watching this dancing body in motion, she 'tried to quell whatever emotion was overcoming me. I was holding the edge of the chair far too tightly, nails gripping the wood' (*Dancer* 126). Rudi's dancing evokes an unconscious and frenzied response from Yulia, which is ultimately expressed in fumbled sexual intercourse with the husband she scarcely loves. The beauty and the artistry of the performance that catalyzes Yulia's desire could not be more removed from the stilted choreography of the sexual act that follows:

> When I entered the room Iosif was sitting at the table, drunk. I put my hands on his shoulders and kissed him. Shocked, Iosif pushed me aside, filled his glass, downed it quickly, then stumbled across the room and kissed me back. I tried to guide him into making love to me against the wall, but he was hardly able to hold me, drunk as he was. Instead he pulled me to the floor. (*Dancer*, 126)

Yulia's sexual assertion is a positive assertion of her repressed sexual self under a grim marital regime. This is enabled by her experience of the sublimity of Rudi's dancing body, which, as she reveals, 'still spun in me – Rudi had stood upon that stage like an exhausted explorer who had arrived in some unimagined country and, despite the joy of the discovery, was immediately looking for another unimagined place, and I felt perhaps that place was me' (*Dancer*, 126). Still further, as she confesses, she harbours a lingering sexual desire for Rudi – the young provincial who arrived and lodged with her several years before his becoming a dazzling object of sexual desire for her. His performance is a spur to the memory of her sexuality, which has been dormant in her marital years. Her figuration of Rudi's posture on stage encapsulates the inherent utopian dynamic of his art, and is connotative of the desire and the hunger that are at the heart of Rudi as dancer. Through his embodiment of desire in dance, Rudi provokes the appetites of his audiences. Some desire him; to others he just awakens the memory of desire. As Cahill argues: 'The novel details the impact dancing makes on the corporeal but throughout the text, the body dancing, that is, the body moving through space and time, is figured as exerting an influence over the audience. Rudi while dancing seems to possess the ability to lend his physical potential to the viewer.'[35]

The virtuosity of Rudi's talent is not only narrated by first-hand experiences such as Yulia's, but McCann also provides lyrical omniscient descriptions of his balletic athleticism. While the first-person narratives reveal the individual effects of the dancing body, the latter sections of the novel allow McCann the author to revel in language.

McCann attempts to represent the actualities of Rudi's performances in highly descriptive passages, trying to seize the somatic articulacy in words. In one such elongated passage, he writes:

> Music reaches into his muscles, the lights spin, he glares at the conductor, the tempo is corrected, and he continues, controlled at first, each more careful and precise, the pieces beginning to fit, his body elastic, three *jetes en tournant*, careful of the landing, he extends his line, beautiful movement ah cello go. The lights merge, the shirtfronts blur. A series of pirouettes. He is at ease, his body sculpted to the music, his shoulder searching the other shoulder, his right toe knowing the left knee, the height, the depth, the form, the control, the twist of the wrist, the bend of his elbow, the tilt of his neck, notes digging into his arteries, and he is in the air now, forcing his legs up beyond muscular memory, one last press of the thighs, an elongation of form, a loosening of human contour, he goes higher and is skyheld. (*Dancer*, 168)

In this key passage, McCann strives to 'write' performance as a physical enactment; the passage chases Rudi's dancing body in its efforts to represent the balletic exertion of this body. There is an effort here to convey the sinewy muscularity and the supreme virtuosity of Rudi's performance, yet there is always a gap, a loss and an absence in the author's endeavour to represent the performative. McCann employs language in order to grasp the dynamic, ethereal qualities of Rudi's dancing body. Rudi is 'a blur of unbroken energy' (*Dancer*, 168); with the audience in stunned, silent rapture, he is 'a thing of wonder...no body anymore no thought no awareness this must be the moment the others call god as if all the doors are open everywhere leading to all other open doors no thing but open doors forever...this is my soul in flight born weightless born timeless' (*Dancer*, 168–9). McCann's Joycean idiom in the latter quotation connotes a sensation of unfettered freedom in balletic expression for Rudi. Yet McCann's syntax, diction and figuration can only deliver a belated approximation of this quasi-religious experience. It is possible to import the technical language of classical ballet into the narrative – '*jetes en tournant*'; '*entrechats-dix*' (*Dancer*, 168) – but the enactment of these abstractions belongs to a different level of somatic and spiritual experience.

McCann's self-evident failure to seize the aggregated rapture of performer and audience is, of course, symptomatic of all negotiations between performance and representation. And it is this enabling excess or elusiveness that constitutes one of the key concerns of McCann's authorial intent. In focusing on this one particular performance by Rudi, with Margot Fonteyn, McCann gestures, in fictional form, to the impossibilities faced by the novel. This one performance can be rhapsodized in lyrical language, it can be figurated in poetic prose, but there is always a loss at the heart of the representation. Similarly, the multifaceted character of the focal point of the novel, Rudi, is equally elusive and deferred. We gain snapshots, vignettes of his life, its impacts and tragedies, and of world history, but, ultimately, all are as provisional and insubstantial as the attempt to textualize the achievements of Rudi's body in balletic motion. In this sense, we can read both this portrait of Rudi in performance and McCann's narrative more generally in terms of Peggy Phelan's comments on the relationship between performance and representation: 'Performance's only life is in the present. Performance cannot be saved, recorded, documented, or otherwise participate in the circulation of representations of representations: once it does so, it becomes something other than performance' (*Dancer*, 146). There is, then, an inevitable failure to McCann's attempts to seize the balletic in prose form; but, equally, all forms of narration, including history and biography, fail to subdue and to contain Rudi's stories. But this inevitable failure is infused with utopian impulses, which defy, or contradict, the certainties of narrow representational boundaries. In accenting polyphony, McCann conducts a self-reflexive critique of authorial autonomy in relation to the fields of historical and biographical life writing. He employs the idea of performance, both in terms of dance and, more generally, as a social concept, to confront these discursive issues. *Dancer* provides a welter of memorial accounts of varying lengths and degrees of familiarity in a cross-section of textual forms as a means of highlighting the provisionality of its own bases. The novel is partly, then, a metafictional narrative that raises questions about the complacent attitudes to historical writing and biographical life writing. In these ways, McCann's narrative possesses deconstructive and utopian energies, as it deploys imaginative and critical-creative strategies in its construction. In utopian vein, *Dancer* asserts the viability of a more democratic attitude to historical representation; McCann produces a narrative that tackles the politics of performance as well as the performative nature of the historical subject.

The concluding section of *Dancer* narrates, via his sister, Tamara, and Yulia, his long-postponed returns to Leningrad and Ufa. After over twenty years of self-inflicted political and personal exile, Rudi makes a typically fleeting return visit to two sites of origin for him as a person and as an artist. For much of the novel, one of the submerged themes of Rudi's adult life was the impossibility of returning to his home, and this is suggested by his difficulty in never securing a sense of rootedness or homeliness across these years of exile and across these geographies of celebrity. Rudi locates a sanctuary, though, in his art, in the balletic performances detailed above. Indeed as we recall Rudi's final encounter with Ufa and with his mother, his condition bears more resemblance to Edward Said's characterization of exile. Said writes that exile is 'restlessness, movement, constantly being unsettled and unsettling others. You cannot go back to some earlier or perhaps more stable condition of being at home; and, alas, you can never fully arrive, be at one with your new home or situation.'[36] As Rudi is driven through the streets of Ufa before he is reunited with his elderly mother, we get a picture of how disconnected the present is from Rudi's memories of this town. In Pierre Nora's terms, Rudi is deprived of *lieux de memoire* on his return: 'The Opera House was closed; our old house on Zentsov Street had been knocked down long ago; the hall on Karl Marx Street was locked up; and the road to the Tatar graveyard was impassable' (*Dancer*, 277). The mark of history is legible on the geography of Ufa, but the intimacies of personal history and memory are only signalled by their absence for Rudi. Ufa, Rudi's Ufa, lives on in his memory through its very disappearance. This feeling of dislocation retreats from the public spaces of Ufa into the privacies of Rudi's family home when he visits his mother on her sick-bed. By returning to see his mother, it is possible that Rudi is searching after some form of redemption, or pursuing a level of security that has been denied in his current life. If he is looking for either he does not find them in Ufa. Having spent several hours in vigil by her bedside, he emerges to the communal area of her home resigned to the fact that: 'She didn't recognise me' (*Dancer*, 281). Both the physical and familial coordinates of his earlier life have altered irrevocably, and Rudi's ultimate exilic condition is, perhaps, confirmed by this final meeting with his ailing mother. Naturally her declining health impairs her senses, but it is the symbolic qualities of the mother–son exchange that are most relevant to the overall thematic scheme of the novel. Rudi alludes to the inauthentic versions of his identity that proliferate globally in his later, and final, meeting with Yulia in Leningrad. As they reminisce and inquire after each other's lives, Rudi admits that 'everyone hears about me, they always get it wrong...nobody knows me' (*Dancer*, 284). While earlier in Victor's narrative, this seemed to be part of Rudi's aura, in the aftermath of his failed reunion with his mother, Rudi's unknowability takes on a more tragic nature. Over the course of the novel, then, McCann alerts us to the enabling and vivifying opportunities of Rudi's unknowability, but, here, at the end, he reminds us of the less energizing consequences of Rudi's identity.

Rudi departs Yulia's apartment, her life and the novel in characteristically performative guise by transforming the space of the apartment block stairwell into a space of artistic creativity. He ...

> ... threw his scarf over his shoulder and performed a perfect pirouette on the concrete slab...He stepped slowly to the next landing, through the rubbish and broken bottles, stepped once again in the arc of light and his shoes sounded against the concrete as he spun a second time...and I thought to myself [Yulia]: Let this joy extend itself into the morning. In the lobby Rudi pirouetted one final time and then he was gone. (*Dancer*, 287–8)

McCann's narrative does not follow the conventional time-line of biography in its resolution; Rudi exits in balletic flight and is not pursued to his death. McCann allows the memory of Rudi in performance to resonate beyond the completion of his narrative, and it is Rudi's dancing body, his balletic artistry that are permitted to triumph at the end. In Yulia's description of this theatrical departure, Rudi's dancing body is in full affective form, transforming the dour functional space of Yulia's home into a stage of joyfulness. This final performance by Rudi is a generous, utopian act, which kindles pleasure and hope out of a separation of friends. Despite the ostensible failure of his return to his origins, Rudi is capable of this concluding act of grace and beauty. Amid the poverty and utilitarian geography of his homeland, Rudi delivers a hopeful gesture towards something or sometime better through this aesthetic performance. With his astonishing physical beauty together with the litany of his hyper-athletic balletic and sexual performances,

Rudi embodies and also provokes intensities of desire. As Yulia concludes: 'Something about him released people from the world, tempted them out' (*Dancer*, 286). Rudi is an object of global temptation, but even more he incarnates the transgressive forces of human desire, and not just sexual, in his provocative physicality. And this is another reason why McCann refuses to adhere to the life-cycle structure of biographical life-writing. Unlike the codes of that genre, in this version of biography the subject lives on in the imaginations and the desires of those that encountered him and those that desired him. In fact the novel does not strictly end with Rudi's dramatic exit from Yulia's life. The narrative reaches its conclusion with a catalogue of lots from 'The Rudolf Nureyev Collection' sold in 1995 in New York and London. The material objects auctioned include 'Six pairs of Ballet Boots'; 'Costume for Swan Lake Act III. Prince Siegfried 1963'; 'A French Walnut Refectory Table'; and 'Pre-Revolutionary Russian China Dish in oak box' (*Dancer*, 289–90), among several others of Rudi's accumulated possessions. The auctioned inventory, as a textual document, stands in for an historical account of his physical death. The sundry items represent different times, locations and relationships from Rudi's life, but they are all infused with the magnetic afterglow of his life, performances and personality. The success of the auction is a testimony to the durability of desire that surrounds Rudi. The listed artefacts touch upon his balletic performances, his material wealth and accumulation of exotic possessions, and, specifically, the china dish is a simple token of continuity with Anna and Yulia. The china dish was an heirloom in their family, which Yulia gave to Rudi on the evening of their final meeting. Among the glamorous costumes and expensive consumer purchases, this 'damaged' box evokes the endurance of the past in the present; it is an unadorned symbol of the chorus of minor voices that have spoken throughout the novel. But, in the end, each of the auctioned items coheres around McCann's core thematics: storytelling and desire. Each of the auctioned fragments of Rudi's life tells part of the story, and they are, differentially, symbolic of desires: sexual, consumer and the desire to be remembered.

NOTES

1. Harold Bloom, *Where Shall Wisdom Be Found?* (New York: Riverhead Books, 2004).
2. Derek Hand, *Irish University Review – Special Issue – John Banville*, 36, 1 (Spring/Summer 2006), p.x.
3. Ibid.

4. 'Interview with Colum McCann', *The Stinging Fly*, Summer (2003). http://www.stingingfly. org/issue9/mccann.html.
5. All further references to *Dancer* (London: Weidenfeld & Nicolson, 2003) will appear in parenthesis as *(Dancer)*.
6. Linda Hutcheon, *The Politics of Postmodernism* (London and New York: Routledge, 1989), p.49.
7. Ibid., p.50.
8. Ibid.
9. Ibid., p.73.
10. Ibid., p.78.
11. Richard Jenkins, *Refiguring History: New Thoughts on an Old Discipline* (London and New York: Routledge, 2003), p.5.
12. Colum McCann and Aleksandar Hemon, 'The Writer Sees in the Dark Corners Swept Clean by Historians', *Guardian* (30 June 2003). http://www.guardian.co.uk/ books/2003/jun/30/fiction.
13. Joseph Lennon, 'An Interview with Fiction Writer Colum McCann', *Poets & Writers* (2003). http://www.pw.org/content/interview_fiction_writer_colum_mccann.
14. Hermione Lee, *Virginia Woolf's Nose: Essays on Biography* (Princeton, NJ and Oxford: Princeton University Press, 2005), p.1.
15. Ibid.
16. Ibid., p.2.
17. Ibid., pp.2–3.
18. Ibid., p.5.
19. On this theme see Edward A. Hagan, *Goodbye Yeats and O'Neill: Farce in Contemporary Irish and Irish-American Narratives* (New York and Amsterdam: Rodopi, 2010).
20. 'Interview with Colum McCann', *The Stinging Fly* (Summer 2003). http://www.stingingfly.org/ issue9/mccann.html.
21. Ibid.
22. Susan Cahill, 'Choreographing Memory: The Dancing Body and Temporality in *Dancer*', in Susan Cahill and Eóin Flannery (eds), *This Side of Brightness: Essays on the Fiction of Colum McCann* (Bern: Peter Lang, 2011).
23. See Jacques Derrida, 'Choreographies', *Points: Interviews, 1974–1994* (Stanford, CA: Stanford University Press, 1995), pp.89–108.
24. Ernst Bloch, *The Principle of Hope* (Oxford: Blackwell, 1986), p.394.
25. André Lepecki, *Exhausting Dance: Performance and the Politics of Movement* (New York and Abingdon: Routledge, 2006), p.5.
26. Elizabeth Dempster, 'Women Writing the Body: Let's Watch a Little How She Dances', in Susan Sheridan (ed.), *Grafts: Feminist Cultural Criticism* (London: Verso, 1988), pp.50–2.
27. Cahill, 'Choreographing Memory: The Dancing Body and Temporality in *Dancer*'.
28. Susan Leigh Foster, 'Dancing Bodies', in Jonathan Cary and Sandford Kwinter (eds), *Incorporations* (New York: Urzone, 1992), p.480.
29. Cahill, 'Choreographing Memory: The Dancing Body and Temporality in *Dancer*'.
30. Peggy Phelan, *Unmarked: The Politics of Performance* (New York and London: Routledge, 1993).
31. Ibid., p.150.
32. C.J.C. Bull, 'Sense, Meaning, and Perception in Three Dance Cultures', in J.C. Desmond (ed.), *Meaning in Motion: New Cultural Studies of Dance* (Durham, NC and London: Duke University Press, 1997), p.272.
33. Helen Thomas, *The Body, Dance and Cultural Theory* (Basingstoke: Palgrave, 2003), p.97.
34. Cahill, 'Choreographing Memory: The Dancing Body and Temporality in *Dancer*'.
35. Ibid.
36. Edward W. Said, *Representations of the Intellectual: The 1993 Reith Lectures* (New York: Pantheon Books, 1994), p.39.

6

Embracing the 'Other':
Zoli (2006)

ROMA GYPSIES AND THE IMAGINATION OF THE 'OTHER'

Though clearly not a literary polemicist, McCann can, as we have seen, be read as a politically engaged author. And, certainly in interview, he regularly alludes to his consciousness of political and social inequalities during the creative process. As is readily evidenced in a novel such as *This Side of Brightness*, there are elements of the social novel in McCann's corpus of works. The latter novel is, perhaps, most closely allied in his oeuvre to his 2006 work, *Zoli*, the subject of this chapter's discussion. Both novels deal with extreme cases and conditions of social and historical ostracization, but in radically different geographical and political contexts. Both *This Side of Brightness* and *Zoli* seem to embody the spirit of McCann's response when asked in interview by the *Financial Times* in 2009: 'What does it mean to be a writer?' In reply McCann re-affirms his political consciousness and his imaginative utopianism as an artist: 'I would hope that it means embracing empathy. Imagining the life of the "other" is the greatest privilege of all.'[1] Crucially McCann accents empathy rather than sympathy, permitting a level of egalitarian agency to the 'other' in an empathetic rather than a sympathetic relationship. He places a premium on recognizing and valuing the common humanity of the marginalized, and often vilified, social constituencies that populate his fictions. In combining the empathetic impulse of the writer with the privilege the author receives in engaging creatively with the 'other', McCann disestablishes the 'authoritative' position of the artist. Empathetic feeling is designed to re-enforce the democratic potential of storytelling; storytelling is not an autocratic process but a series of negotiations. Likewise, in imagining the 'other', the author is granted a privilege, but a privilege that comes with duties and a responsibility to remain sensitive to cultural difference. The 'other', in McCann's view, is approached imaginatively not as an anthropological object, but as an autonomous, acculturated historical subject. And in turning our attention to the subject matter at hand in *Zoli*, we encounter one of the most consistently persecuted 'others' of modern European history: the Roma gypsy populations of eastern Europe.

In her seminal *Bury Me Standing: The Gypsies and their Journey*, Isabel Fonseca documents the accepted excoriation of gypsies within Europe. Through a confection of myth and warped historical recollection, gypsies 'had remained quintessential outsiders of the European imagination: sinister, separate, literally dark and synonymous with sorcery and crime'.[2] Europe's gypsy populations were, and still are, pathologized according to a battery of indices that emphasize their emphatic 'otherness' to the received social and moral mores of enlightened, settled civility. Historically, the lived realities of their material cultures were abstracted into idioms of racial typologization, romantic fetishization, criminal profiling, and mythological distortion. Rather than participating as agents in their own histories, gypsy populations became props in legends not of their own making. In common with Europe's Jewish population, gypsy communities had their cultural identities ratified as 'other' by Europe's majority communities. The term 'gypsy' became a cultural and social descriptor around which a limited range of static 'roles' were assigned to historically changing gypsy individuals and groups. The gypsies became transhistorical and immutable in their behaviours and intentions in the eyes of majority settled populations. As the Roma gypsy expert, Ian Hancock, suggests:

> People who never met a Gypsy in their lives are nevertheless able to provide a fairly detailed picture of how they think Gypsies look and how they live. Their mental image, partly negative and partly romantic but mostly inaccurate, is the result of the response to a Roma identity which has become institutionalized in the Western tradition to the extent that it has become part of its cultural heritage.[3]

Hancock's characterization of the complacent stereotyping of gypsies by settled communities signals an economy of unreflective racism, and his language echoes that of Edward Said in his explication of the cultural politics of Orientalism under Western imperial regimes.[4] The cultural, political and social mechanisms that Said laid bare in his early work of colonial discourse analysis seem readily apparent in the relations that obtain between gypsies and non-gypsies in Europe. Easy racism is facilitated and legitimized by a cultural architecture of objectification and, in consonance with the processes of 'orientalizing' under Western colonialism, gypsies have no input into the formulation of their representation. It is a point noted by Mary Burke in her recent study of cultural representations of Irish 'Tinkers': 'those who wish to write of the culture concerned decide long in advance of contact what it is that the tradition "symbolises", and will iterate this vision regardless of any contradiction presented by actual association.'[5] Burke's, Hancock's and Said's adjacent arguments intimate how the imagination of the lives of the 'other' can operate as a means of demonization and disempowerment. What is of note in each of these arguments is that the group assumes an irrefutable cultural identity, while individuals are subsumed under this fabricated identity. The individual as historical actor and as political subject is displaced by historical actant and political object. Disempowerment, then, through romantic sanitization or moral pathologization became means of discursively 'locating' and legally containing the roaming communities of Europe. Their racial 'otherness', their linguistic incommensurability, their temperamental inscrutability, and their physical mobility became, and remain, reasons to fear itinerant gypsy groups. As Jean-Pierre Liegois concludes, the gypsies, 'moving about in their nomadic groups, were seen as physically threatening and ideologically disruptive. Their very existence constituted dissidence.'[6] At the very least, the fear generated by the innate 'dissidence' of gypsies is managed under the discursive 'orientalism' mentioned above, but very often discourse becomes the underwriter of extreme legal, political and cultural violence against gypsies.

The orientalizing formation of understandings of gypsy culture in Europe furnishes a textual monumentalization of an internally diverse and historically changing series of gypsy communities. Because of this sanctioned 'typing', gypsies have actually lived, in Paul Carter's resonant phrase, beyond 'the horizon of writing'.[7] Their textual incarnations persist as counterfeits, while historical and contemporary material realities remain outside of history. And it is precisely these confrontations between textuality and orality, between gypsy and settled (or gadže) communities,[8] and between art and politics, which McCann explores in

Zoli. The novel is replete with political idealism, even utopianism, of different hues, each of which impact upon the central protagonist, Zoli Novotna, and her community with disastrous consequences. McCann illustrates how received ideas about gypsy culture have been differentially mobilized for political projects without requisite consideration for the effects on gypsies. The tyranny of excessive political idealism betrays the subtle complexity of gypsy cultural mores repeatedly across *Zoli*. McCann's task in *Zoli*, then, is complicated by all of these factors, and is, itself, implicated in the textualization of a predominantly oral culture and history. One of the dangers faced by McCann was how to avoid becoming complicit in the 'orientalizing' narrative of Europe's gypsy populations. Avoiding the repetition of these disabling portraits of gypsies, *Zoli* is an effort to redeem and to dignify gypsy culture through the semi-historical life story of one member of that community. Writing on the ethics of engaging with 'otherness', Richard Kearney alights on several key philosophical points that are germane to the cultural politics of *Zoli*. *Zoli* narrates the story of a female member of the Roma community across the twentieth century, and while it highlights the intensity and protraction of oppression undergone by that particular community, in more general ways the novel alerts us to the persistence of physical and epistemic violence endured by all 'othered' peoples. Kearney draws attention to the manner in which, latterly, the nation-state has become a discrete imagined edifice that must be inoculated against the intrusion of undesirable 'others'. The institution of borders and legislation – contrary to those who speak easily of a borderless, global geography – perpetuate a discriminating historical discourse of 'self' and 'other', insider and outsider, and them and us. In Kearney's assessment: 'Most nation-states bent on preserving their body politic from "alien viruses" seek to pathologise their adversaries. Faced with a threatening outside the best mode of defence is attack. Again and again the national *We* is defined over and against the foreign *Them*. Borders are policed to keep nationals in and aliens out.'[9] The historically sanctioned cultural strangeness of gypsies, then, provides discursive persuasiveness to the relative 'othering' of this population. The internal normalcy of the settled populations is confirmed by the unyielding transhistorical difference of gypsy communities. In deconstructive and psychoanalytical terms, the self is, however, defined and haunted by repressed 'otherness'. And as such, the historical and contemporary demonization of European Roma can be diagnosed as basic symptoms of cultural anxiety. Scapegoating of gypsy populations becomes a means of generating calm, as well as solidarity, within settled communities. A racially bigoted political consensus is arrived at that, in turn, continues to serve the marginalization of gypsies. These 'strangers, gods and monsters', as Kearney christens them, 'threaten the known with the unknown – they are often set apart in fear and trembling. Exiled to hell or heaven; or simply ostracized from the human community into a land of aliens.'[10]

Kearney's ethical response to these enduring trends in the self/other dyad is designed to offer what he terms 'a hermeneutic pluralism of otherness, a sort of "polysemy of alterity"'.[11] In other words, Kearney's framework is based on the mutual implication of all selves and others – not on the infinite iteration of difference and deferral of deconstruction, but in terms of a mutual recognition of self-hood between relative 'others'. As we shall see with McCann's text, Kearney's ethical code is strongly empathetic in quality. In proposing to de-alienate the 'other', 'ethics rightly requires me to recognise the other as another self bearing universal rights and responsibilities, that is, as someone capable of recognising me in turn as a self capable of recognition and esteem.'[12] This latter ethical perspective emphatically runs counter to the tone of historical and contemporary cultural and political exchanges between settled and gypsy populations. What Kearney calls for is an acknowledgement and an apprehension of the subjecthood of alienated 'others'; an egalitarian tolerance of cultural difference that is uncoupled from fear, suspicion and persecution. Kearney's ethical project is marked by its utopian credentials, and its inclusive democratic aspirations are explicit when he concludes that there 'is no otherness so exterior or so unconscious…that is cannot be at least minimally interpreted by a self, and interpreted in a variety of different ways'.[13] This vision chimes with McCann's in authoring a novel such as *Zoli*, which provides a forum through which 'otherness' can be explored as an historical and contemporary epiphenomenon in Europe. *Zoli* is not another romantic rendering of Roma exoticism, nor does it trade on easy stereotypes about these communities. In *Zoli*, McCann partakes of Kearney's ethical impulse towards 'recognition and esteem' and attempts to assert the selfhood of one of European history's persecuted 'others'.

ZOLI

Zoli opens in 2003 with a Slovakian journalist, David Smolenak, entering a Roma settlement in Slovakia intent on procuring information about the whereabouts of Zoli Novotna. The vivid details of the natural and man-made disarray of the camp are, firstly, reminiscent of Conradian or Naipaulian versions of Africa's inner recesses. The manner in which the landscape looms and broods over the tremulous interloper evokes a return to an earlier historical period or, at least, signposts the individual's removal from the comforting coordinates of organized civilization. Yet, clearly, McCann's motivation is not of a piece with either Conrad or Naipaul. Instead, McCann's rigorous description of the squalid settlement emphasizes the extent to which Roma gypsies have become and remain dehumanized within the broader European political imagination. The unkempt camp may be remote from our lives, but it is not unimaginably alien from our world; this abject poverty is not divorced from our society but thrives within, and because of, our society. In a scene recollective of Treefrog's Hadean home in *This Side of Brightness*, Smolenak's careful navigation of the settlement is detailed by McCann in all of its graphic decrepitude: 'He drives alongside the small streambed and the terrible shitscape looms up by increments – upturned buckets by the bend in the river, a broken baby carriage in the weeds, a petrol drum leaking out a dried tongue of rust, the carcass of a fridge in the bramble.'[14] Steering his way through this symbolic terrain of impoverishment, Smolenak at last reaches his destination: 'there, across a rickety little joke of a bridge, is the grey Gypsy settlement, marooned on an island in the middle of the river' (*Zoli*, 4). The islanded settlement could be disappearing into or emerging from the waters of the river. Its precarious, suspended location here is a forceful imagistic correlative of the political animus of McCann's broader narrative. Yet as suggestive as this figuration of the island camp is, this opening section delivers a grim portrait of the destitution of the gypsy community in almost social realistic description. McCann details the unruliness of the poverty and the sentiments of defamiliarization felt by the visiting gadže journalist as he approaches and enters the settlement. Smolenak is physically and aurally discommoded by these surroundings, and his reactions are consistent with the longer-term 'othering' of the Roma gypsies:

He feels the weight of what he carries: two bottles, notepad, pencil, cigarettes, instamatic camera, and tiny recorder, all away deep in his clothes…He looks up, takes a deep breath, but it's as if a thousand chords have been struck in his blood all at once, his ribcage is thumping, he shouldn't have come here alone, a Slovakian journalist, forty-four years old, comfortably fat, a husband, a father, about to step into the heart of a gypsy camp. He takes a step forward through a puddle, thinking how stupid it was to wear soft leather shoes for this trip, not even good for a quick retreat. (*Zoli*, 5)

Fear conditions Smolenak's response to his immersion in the visual and aural clamour of the gypsy settlement. Burdened with his arsenal of gifts and documentary devices, the journalist is both aggressor and victim in this alien context. His visit is part of an historical continuum of surveillance and attempted documentation of the gypsies – operations that we see at other junctures across *Zoli*. The technologies of record he possesses are viewed with violent suspicion by the Roma, as they are freighted with the history of repression undergone by previous generations of their community. Smolenak enters the camp on his terms, as a journalist seeking nothing more than an erstwhile gypsy poet: Zoli Novotna. But on the terms of the Roma such an investigative intrusion is inseparable from previous violent and, ostensibly, benevolent gadže interventions. There is a level of authorial self-consciousness to Smolenak's incursion into the private sphere of gypsy culture. His investigations re-visit the interfaces between gadže and gypsy, literary and oral cultures, and sedentary and mobile traditions. His efforts to redeem and reclaim the forgotten poet are, of course, consistent with McCann's own authorial task. In a novel that is pervaded by guilt and betrayal, and by lapses in personal responsibility to others, opening with this self-conscious scene of authorial/journalistic intrusion is a gesture by McCann to his own implication in the textual narrativization of this unremembered Roma artist. Yet before she can be found, before there is speech and Zoli's story, silence resounds around her absence and her discarded memory. As Smolenak cautiously negotiates the subtleties of gypsy hospitality, he hesitantly mentions Zoli's name and reveals the purpose of his visit: 'But when he mentions her name – leaning forward to say, "Have you ever heard of Zoli Novotna?" – the air stalls, the drinking stops, the cigarettes are held at mouth level, and a silence descends' (*Zoli*, 9). The first section of the novel concludes with a glimpse of the banished poet and her name reverberates through history to foment a tense silence, again, between gypsy and gadže. The mention of her name is enough to shut down the narrative and to seal off communication between the two groups. Smolenak's inquiry anticipates later narrative revelations about how previous gypsy and gadže interaction actually led to Zoli's expulsion from her tribe. The narrative of Zoli's life as a poet, then, is initiated by silence and by a refusal to acknowledge her existence.

If *Zoli* is primarily concerned with the politics of 'otherness', we are again confronted with issues of basic human dignity. In this regard, and as we have seen in Chapter 3, Wole Soyinka twins dignity and freedom as 'the obverse of power and domination, that axis of human relationship that is equally sustained by fear'.[15] Fear, in its turn, emasculates, deracinates and incarcerates individuals and communities, depriving them of volition and access to self-representation. And in attending to the relations that exist between various institutional bodies of the state in *Zoli*, Soyinka's attention to the tension between dignity and empowerment versus fear and disempowerment seems axiomatic to our discussion. As we have noted, the transhistorical rafts of measures to contain vagrant communities, in particular Roma gypsies, have consistently denied such dignity and freedom to these 'othered' groups. As Robbie McVeigh reiterates: 'The idea of a travelling underworld has been a source of concern to European states for centuries. And the efforts of the state apparatus to "deal with" this supposed threat have always constituted a brutal and undemocratic project.'[16] In McCann's novel, Zoli's life and journeys, as well as those of her kinsmen, are forever pursued by the macrostructural and microstructural machinations of an anxious, and therefore repressive, state. The projects to assimilate forcibly or to ostracize resolutely are an obsessive concern for the state regimes under which Zoli's life plays out.

Smolenak's visit to the contemporary gypsy settlement may open the novel onto a provocative scene of physical impoverishment and abandonment but, equally, the episode is suggestive of the fractious terms on which the gypsy and gadže relationship was, and is, founded. The solitary journalist's investigation is but one instance in the novel of the prevailing friction that fuels exchanges between the two communities. As we shall see, Smolenak returns at the end of the novel, and his impact is at a deeply personal level for Zoli. But we also need to consider the larger-scale incursions into traditional gypsy culture by gadže society in the form of

the state and its institutions. The ways in which the state and its ideological apparatuses intervene in gypsy society are by no means uniform
in *Zoli*, and range from idealistic celebrations of their culture to more
cynical manipulations of that culture. We see Stalinist rationalizations
and re-settlements of nomadic gypsies as well as systematic murders of
their population. And each of these is refracted through Zoli's life; in
fact, at times she becomes a central figure in the workings of the state's
politico-cultural programmes. Indeed, her relative intimacy with the
ways of gadže politics and society allow her, late in the novel, to
reflect on the pervasive ignorance of gadže on the true nature of gypsy
culture. Her comment that: 'they are so fearful, sometimes, of their
own invented fears' (*Zoli*, 213), not only reminds us of the Saidian
'orientalizing' of gypsies, but suggests that settled society is paralyzed
in a blind cycle of terror and hatred, which repeatedly justifies its own
excesses. In such an environment where fear dominates and manifests
as repression, there is, in Soyinka's terms, no real freedom available to
anyone.

ART AND POLITICS

Zoli's narrative opens with her account of the tragic, and murderous,
scene of her parents' death at the hands of Hlinka guards. The troupe
of gypsies was herded onto a frozen lake, fires lit and they drowned
when the ice melted. Only Zoli and her grandfather, fortuitously,
survived, having been away from the camp on that day. Thus both Zoli's
orphanage and her victimization at the hands of racialized political
ideology are signalled as conditioning aspects of her biography and of
the narrative at large. But these distorted racial perceptions of gypsies
are not simply evident in extreme acts of violence; rather they are
witnessed in the incremental pathologization of this community. In the
pre-Second World War period, Zoli's narrative meanders across the
crucible in which she experiences the stubborn incommensurabilites
that persist between gadže and gypsy. From Zoli's medical documentation and examination, to her abortive attendance at formal education and
onto the introduction of new repressive legislation on gypsy freedom of
movement, Zoli's lifestyle is prey to the state's codification of her
innate 'otherness' to its referents of normality. Each of these arenas
of state management raises one of the key tensions of the narrative,

discussed below: gypsy suspicion of textuality and of the written word, which is pitted against their dependence upon the somatic commitment of an oral culture. Zoli's time under formal educational structures is not solely an example of statist conformity, but showcases the endemic nature of anti-gypsy sentiment, as she is repeatedly victimized by her fellow school children. Random police searches of gypsy camps, in Kafkan fashion, promote guilt without reference to any crime, and there is a naturalization of guilt and criminality attached to the Roma. McCann's narration of the episodic but persistent scenes of major and minor bigotry against gypsies in the pre-Second World War context progresses into the extremities of the wartime period and in the early sections of the novel we see, and hear second-hand about, the weight of history burdening the Roma across Europe. In a series of passages, the sufferings of the gypsies move from the locality of our protagonists to the stories of international repression. There is a combination of rumour and of conjecture on the extent of persecution and of daily experiences of legally enshrined racial prejudice: 'They were quiet days in the Yellow Farmer's field but bit by bit we began to hear that terrible things were afoot in the country. The Germans didn't take over as they had in the Czech lands, but Grandfather said it hardly mattered, the Hlinkas were just like Gestapo, except they wore different badges. The war was coming our way' (*Zoli*, 34). Zoli might begin to hear stories of repression in the present, but these stories, in the broader context, are warnings from history. The atrocities are not unique to the wartime period of Zoli's life, but are representative of the history of sys-temized gypsy persecution. In fact, her grandfather's comment suggests as much, as he realizes that it does not actually matter what colour the uniform, what the nationality of the aggressor may be – violence remains violence. And Zoli relays the practicalities of this daily violence under the new regimen of anti-gypsy legislation:

> We were only allowed in the cities and villages for two hours a day, noon until two…After these hours, no Roma man or woman was allowed in public places. Sometimes even the purest woman was charged with spreading infections and was thrown in prison. If a man was on a bus or a train, he was beaten until he couldn't even crawl…We learned the sound of military vehicles the way we'd learned the sound of animals…And yet we still thought ourselves to be among the lucky ones. (*Zoli*, 34)

The legal measures are designed to inoculate settled public space from the contagion of gypsy presence, and their extremity of violence is an index of anxiety in the face of cultural strangeness. But throughout *Zoli* there is a more lateral historical context alluded to by McCann, and there are core ethical issues he wishes to alert the reader about in the contemporary moment. Zoli's group may be prey to the kinds of legal exertions detailed above, but 'many of our Czech brothers streamed south with terrible stories about being marched down the many-cornered road' (*Zoli*, 35). Europe is on the cusp of a frenzied period of warfare and ethnic genocide. Industrial modernity, which contrasts itself so favourably with the benighted ignorance of the Roma, is embarking upon a campaign of unfettered blood-letting, and it is, in Zoli's case, the always already marginalized that will be among those who suffer most acutely. The Roma experience, which includes the Holocaust, is symbolic for McCann of the ease with which received idioms and abstractions of prejudice can be digested and acted upon.

Physical violence is partnered by symbolic violence during the Second World War, as we see a concerted coordination of repressive tactics. In a tragically resonant series of acts, the Roma are coerced into burying their favoured musical instrument, the harp: 'there was a new law out that said we needed licences for any type of musical instrument...the harps were buried in huge wooden containers that the men made out of maple trees' (*Zoli*, 36). The new law is a comprehensive denial of cultural expression to the Roma, as in an orally based culture such as they live in, music and lyricism were of paramount importance. The harp was, then, of practical and symbolic value; the instrument was a means of preserving and transmitting history and traditions. But it was also a practical tool in generating income through public musical performance. Proscribing musical instruments is at once a further conflagration between textual legality and oral musicality and, simultaneously, a firm deprivation of cultural legacy to the Roma community. Not only does it represent a severing of means of communing with the past, it represents the proscription of a means of creativity towards the future. In this sense, the law constitutes a profoundly anti-utopian measure in its intended consequences, and its denial of an interest in the future for the Roma. Yet out of this instance of repression we witness the blossoming of another form of creative expression. Despite the symbolic violence of the enforced interment of their harps, the episode concludes with the first stirrings of a new utopian energy in the shape of Zoli's emergence as a creator of original poetic lyrics: 'Conka and I ran to the place of the burial and she started a game where she jumped up and down on the ground and we pretended that music was coming out from the earth and that's when I put together a song in my mind, about down in the ground where the strings vibrate' (*Zoli*, 37). However, Zoli's burgeoning talent as an accomplished poet and singer is not permitted to remain as an unproblematic utopian energy within Roma culture by McCann. In general terms, her talent raises matters related to the relationship between the artist and his/her community, and questions the responsibilities that the artist may have to that indigenous group. Likewise in the heavily politicized context of the novel, McCann also allows us to view Zoli as an artist whose work becomes entwined in the workings of idealistic political campaigning, ultimately against her better judgement. In the end, we see the conflicting loyalties and vulnerabilities of the artist in the face of communal tradition and political opportunism.

The image of 'the harps listening to the grass growing above them, and the grass listening back to the sounds two metres below' (*Zoli*, 37) speaks of an organicism inherent to the music and the landscape. In common with many of the descriptions in the novel, there is deep ecopoetical sensibility in evidence in McCann's writing. Out of interment comes a vibrant lyric of rebirth and renewal, even the possibility of a future redemption. It is with these utopian impulses that Zoli's lyrics and vocal music are infused; her lyric does not perceive a death burial but the plantation of future creative yields. Under the duress of 'new laws...it was really only song that held me, kept my feet to the ground' (*Zoli*, 45). Zoli's creative resources are the imaginative birthplace of future prospects for the Roma, as well as a preservative agent for their cultural traditions. Furthermore, song itself is understood as qualitatively redemptive for Zoli; song is a respite from and a countercurrent against the excoriating procedures of Fascist legality. However, in the aftermath of the war, her private votive dedication to the cultural weight of her Roma heritage is transformed into a public and political crusade of Communist egalitarian principles by the new government. In these post-war years a programmatic left-wing utopianism tracks Roma society, periodically celebrating and rationalising their practices. The private, vernacular utopian energy of Zoli's lyrical prowess, which was catalyzed by the burial of the harps, is subsequently co-opted by a campaign that lauds the Roma as first among equals in post-war Slovakia: 'the gadže tugged our elbows and said, Come sing for us, Gypsies, come sing. Tell us of the forest, they said. I never thought of the forest as a special place, it was just as ordinary as any other…We were given identity cards, tinned meat, white flour, jars of condensed milk. We burned our old armbands' (*Zoli*, 49). As part of the new utopian programme, Roma are embraced as Comrades and their cultural 'otherness' is adjudicated as a resource to be sought after and cherished rather than buried and harassed. This new utopian political horizon is announced as: 'Cargo planes flew over the city. Manned by the parachute regiment, dropping leaflets: *The new tomorrow has arrived* [original italics]' (*Zoli*, 49). For the Slovakian lands, and for the Roma, the 'revolution' has arrived, and as the most marginal of social underclasses, the Roma are feted as exemplars of economic and political discrimination. The Roma are urged to join and are welcomed into the egalitarian mix of the newly configured political mainstream. To this end, their songs and music are broadcast on radio, they are no longer regarded as vermin, and their culture is valued in song and in visual representation. And for the young Zoli, this utopian vision is too much to resist: 'We waved the red flag, looked down the road to the future. I had hope right up until the end. It was the old Roma habit of hoping. Perhaps I have never lost it' (*Zoli*, 50).

Zoli's contribution to the new political dispensation can be read at two levels: firstly, she is incarnated as the public face and voice of Roma culture. And secondly, she is idealized personally, and politically, by two male writers and activists: Martin Stransky and Stephen Swann. If the novel is centrally concerned with both hope and betrayal, then each of these groups, the state, Stransky and Swann, view Zoli as crucial to the anticipatory utopian politics of the Left. However, in the end, she is ruthlessly betrayed by each of them in actions that finally destroy her life. Not only is Zoli embraced by the state as the voice of the Roma as she performs before bureaucrats and Party apparatchiks, but she becomes a potential bridge between gadže and Roma communities. Her literacy gives her uncharted access to the gadže world of administration, and marks her, ultimately, as resident in both communities, and, paradoxically, alien in both communities at the same time. Zoli is paraded at strategic cultural venues such as 'the Ministry of Culture, the National Theatre, the Carlton, the Socialist Academy…the Stalingrad

Hotel, conferences on literature' (*Zoli*, 81), as the gradual emptying out of Roma culture by means of 'romantic' authentification proceeds at a daily level by Stransky and Swann. While the macro-political opportunism of the state seems impersonal, her relationship with these two activists becomes deeply affective. Zoli, Swann and Stransky become a closely allied threesome, each pursuing differential idealized ends. And it is in the durations and denouements of these relationships that the ideas of hope and betrayal are most acutely dramatized.

Swann's first-person narrative reveals the extent, and the consequences, of his and Stransky's championing of Zoli's work. Having arrived in Slovakia brimming with radical political idealism, Swann is soon under the wing of the seasoned poet activist. Slovakia is a homeland for Swann, as it is his father's birthplace, and his return is as much a nostalgic return to familial origins as it is a pursuit of Marxist revolution. The raw pliability of Swann's unquestioning political idealism becomes a dutiful companion to Stransky's literary editorship of Zoli's lyrics. With this unlikely trio, McCann explores the passionate energies of political and cultural hope, the perils of forced marriage between politics and art, and the tragic tensions between intellectual idealism and emotional commitment. In this small politico-literary circle, Stransky is the *eminence-grise*, as Swann recalls:

> Stransky ran a journal, *Credo*, in which he was always trying to push the limits: he was known for publishing daring young Socialist playwrights and obscure intellectuals and anyone else who vaguely amplified his beliefs…He himself wrote in Slovak against the idea that a smaller language was useless. And now, with Zoli, he thought he'd come upon the perfect proletarian poet. (*Zoli*, 62)

Swann's portrait of Stransky exposes the autocratic character of the older writer. His editorial vision is guided by well-honed political convictions and Zoli becomes the object of this uncompromising editorial process. From an aural viewpoint, the insistent plosiveness of 'perfect proletarian poet' only serves to suggest her role as an *object* of inflexible political ambitions. In Stransky's aesthetic, the political is the primary motor of artistic creation and of aesthetic judgement. In similar manner to the broader state operation, Zoli's art is evacuated of its affective and historical resonances. And, finally, we are reminded of the work of Deleuze and Guattari in Stransky's insistence that a minor language can be a viable vehicle for autonomous cultural and political articulation.[17] But it is Stransky's subservience of art, and of Zoli's lyrics, that is most remarkable about Swann's recollective narrative.

In the vibrancy of these new revolutionary times, Swann's political idealism is energized and trained by that of his master. Stransky's utopian cultural politics propose equality for the Roma, but it is only later that the terms and costs of this benevolent egalitarianism can be accurately gauged. For now Swann is intoxicated by 'the high idealism of an older man', and Stransky is 'sure that having a Gypsy poet would be a coup for him, for *Credo*, and that the Gypsies, as a revolutionary class, if properly guided, could claim and use the written word' (*Zoli*, 70). Even at this point there are intimations of the terms on which gypsy culture, the Roma voice, can be registered. It seems as if their oral tradition will have to be textualized, and modernized, if it is to have a genuine purchase within the gadže world. In Stransky's mind, the Roma are a malleable underclass, amenable to the idealistic abstractions of his Marxist doxology. What, on the surface, appears as acceptance is laced with the prospects of assimilation and manipulation. Stransky's 'revolutionary' cultural politics is, in fact, a retreat to another form of cultural fetishism. Part of his anticipatory vision may involve elevating the Roma, creating 'a literate proletariat', and have 'People reading Gypsy literature' (*Zoli*, 70). But this will only arise after considerable 'management' of that artistic output, and, in particular, the 'creation' of Zoli as poet. Stransky might have been 'convinced that Zoli was creating a poetry from the roots up, but he still wanted to put manners on it' (*Zoli*, 74). Swann and Stransky use a tape recorder to document Zoli's lyrics and proceed to transcribe them in preparation for publication. Thus, her voice and the content of Roma orality are doubly processed and estranged through the disembodying form of technology and on towards textual reproduction. And it is this distancing of the oral through textual form that forms one of the bases for Roma suspicion of the gadže, and foments one of the principal crises of the novel. Both of these technologies, sound recording and textual printing, are symbolic of the gadže world, and as Zoli participates with increasing frequency in this milieu in the months prior to the publication of her poetry, her people become hostile towards her liminal position between the two communities. The determination of Swann's and Stransky's political idealism is summed up succinctly in Swann's admission that: 'We were convinced it went beyond that [Roma gratitude]. We were building a van-guard, there'd never been a poetry like it before, we were preserving and shaping their world while the world changed around them' (*Zoli*, 75). The hubris of Swann's declaration conflicts sharply with the anxieties of the Roma elders, and has grievous results for Zoli. Swann's idiom here returns us to the rhetoric of colonial 'orientalizing', or, in another register, quasi-romanticism. This high political idealism is profoundly compromised as it mutates into a species of exoticization, rendering Zoli and her community into colourful museum pieces. The bond of faith, even trust, which existed between the gadže and the gypsy worlds becomes frayed, and the hope that bound the two communities begins to dissipate as the real power relations materialize.

While Stransky's implacable editorial control of Zoli's poetry might be viewed as a symptom of a broader political betrayal and exploitation, the sexual relationship that develops between Swann and Zoli intensifies the consequences of what becomes a deeply felt personal betrayal later in the novel. Listening to Zoli as he records her voice for Stransky, Swann becomes enraptured by her: 'the thought of her held me fast. Each word she came up with sent a thrill along me…She touched my arm, looked my way. I knew it. We had begun to cross that hollow that had come between us' (*Zoli*, 77). The beginnings of a mutual attraction between Swann and Zoli parallel the putative reconciliation between gadže and gypsy. Their romantic coupling is symbolic of the larger revolutionary affiliation between the communities. But, though the macro-political rapprochement is temporarily accepted, Swann and Zoli's relationship is taboo, and breaks the sexual limits of history and tradition. Theirs is an 'across the barricades' relationship, and, conse-quently, has the potential to unleash great violence. Thus in her literacy, her literary talent, exposure to gadže, and, now, most subversive of all, her liaison with Swann, Zoli consistently tests the boundaries of her Roma traditions. Indeed the extent to which she transcends received cultural boundaries in her personal life is, again, resonant of her later cross-border journeying across the European mainland. Such is the taboo nature of her relationship with Swann that it is always shadowed by risk, but it is Zoli who has assumed the most acute risks. The origin of their relationship is, of course, Swann's attachment to Stransky's political and cultural reclamation of the Roma. But soon the sincerity of Swann's romantic commitment and that of his political idealism are forced into conflict. At the same time that Stransky is 'taming [sic] her line length, structuring [sic] the work into verses' (*Zoli*, 93), the Czechoslovakian state introduces Law 74. This new law is intended to settle the Roma and to, benevolently, provide 'schools and houses and clinics' (*Zoli*, 93). Forces of cultural conformity, then, are converging on the Roma in both Zoli's poetic work and in the re-configured public sphere. It is apparent that the atmosphere of unqualified celebration of the Roma has given way to a heavily qualified assertion of autocratic social welfare. And it is during this period in the early 1950s that Swann is implored by Zoli: 'Stephen, she said, You'll fight with us if we have to, right?' to which Swann replies: 'Of course' (*Zoli*, 93). Tragically, it is a promise that Swann cannot keep.

In the wake of the Hungarian uprising, and its quelling, in 1956, Stransky, Swann and Zoli begin to experience the pressure of new reactionary legislation. The new national tone is mordant, and for Swann the revolutionary ideals that had charged through the country, that had fashioned the embrace of the Roma, were withering: 'the country had changed, turned sour, lost its edge' (*Zoli*, 95). Not only is Stransky soon ostracized, but Zoli and her community return to the status of scapegoat under the burden of this new legislation. The erstwhile idealistic trio are sundered: Stransky is politically outcast and eventually executed, while Swann and Zoli are placed under surveillance. Indeed, the latter are bordered by threats from the state and from Roma tradition. Zoli's refusal to settle or to compromise, as part of the statutes of Law 74, in her affair with Swann in defiance of Roma tenets, or her efforts to escape the 'Gypsy jam-jar' (*Zoli*, 99) mean that there are inevitable punishments awaiting her and the Roma. For the Roma, Zoli is implicated in the state's so-called 'Great Halt' and its legal assault on their way of life. The broadcast and dissemination of her poetry and image become signs of her incremental betrayal of her community. Once the locus of cross-community détente, Zoli is now vulnerable as political object and as ethnic traitor. The final act that will see her banished from her people is the publication of her poetic work. The symbolic and actual textualization of her Roma lyrics will prove to be the gravest transgression in the eyes of her elders. To this end, again, she pleads with Swann not to proceed with the publication; in a sense she is asking him to fulfil his earlier promise of support to her. In the pivotal scene in the novel, Zoli tests Swann's loyalty to her: 'If you print this book they'll blame me...They'll have a trial. They'll make judgement...The blame will come down on me...burn them. Please' (*Zoli*, 106). At this point Swann's commitment to either Zoli or his political convictions is under scrutiny, as the abstraction of his dissipating political ideals are pitted against a forbidden yet real emotional attachment to Zoli. But Swann cannot extricate himself from the bogus arguments in favour of proceeding with the publication. He presents a barrage of arguments that do little but dissimulate and cloud the truth:

> ...the book could not be shelved, the Union of Slovak Writers wouldn't allow it. Kysely and I were under strict instructions. The government could arrest us, there were darker things afoot. They needed the poems to continue resettlement. Zoli was their poster girl. She was their justification. They needed her. Nothing else could be done. They'd soon change their minds. All she had to do was wait. (*Zoli*, 106)

These false professions of compulsion and duty, Swann's insincere promise of a positive future resolution, eventually yield to his under-standing of what his stubborn publication would actually mean. As the technology of print reproduction heaves into motion, he reflects: 'The metal began to roll. Its dark and constant rhyme. I couldn't give it a meaning now even if I wanted to, the cogs caught and the rollers spun, and I betrayed her' (*Zoli*, 107). In the shadow of technology, Swann confesses to his betrayal of Zoli. Though cognizant of the widespread actions of the state's betrayal of Roma trust, and the demise of the country's once vigorous revolutionary zeal, Swann lacks the courage to abandon his political idealism. With his redundant promises and justifications to Zoli and to himself ringing in his head and aching his conscience, Swann touches upon another of the primary thematics of McCann's literary ethical project. In a moment of clarity, he concludes: 'It is astounding how terrifying words can be. No act is too shallow so long as we give it a decent name' (*Zoli*, 107). This concise reflection carries beyond Swann and *Zoli*, across McCann's fiction. It raises ques-tions relative to the proximity of language and violence, and politics and morality. Swann's betrayal of Zoli destroys their relationship and leads to her permanent exile from her community. As Anne Fogarty astutely observes: 'Swann in effect turns Zoli into a symbol to suit his needs. The view of Zoli as the quintessence of solitude is a Romantic projection that bypasses her and ignores her actual dilemmas. She is seen in this manner by all of the men in the novel and turned into an embodiment of absolute difference.'[18] Though Zoli is betrayed by Swann, the publication of her poetry is, in fact, adjudged as continued complicity with the gadže by her fellow Roma and, consequently, she undergoes a purity trial. Despite her long and spirited defence during the ritualized staging of her judgement, Zoli is deemed to be guilty and faces the most severe punishment: 'the congress said that she was weak, that she did not have the strength of body or mind, and they sentenced her to Pollution for Life in the Category of Infamy for the Betrayal of Roma Affairs to the Outsiders' (*Zoli*, 114–15). The sharp lines of division between gypsy and gadže are highlighted in the verdict and Zoli is convicted of the most heinous betrayal. At this stage she has lost her trust in Swann and the state, and she has lost the trust of her entire community: 'she can see nothing before her that she wishes to enjoy, and little behind that she cares to remember' (*Zoli*, 115). From a position within a marginalized community to a choreographed status within the state armoury, Zoli is now utterly abandoned and placeless. She can make no claim on her communal past, as she is banished from participating in that culture. Equally she has no role in the future of her community. Her Roma origins dictated that she was part of a mobile, nomadic community, but there was structure and solidarity to that nomadism. On foot of her expulsion, Zoli remains mobile and transient in her physical movements, but these are now conducted as a universal outcast. There are no communal structures of kinship to protect her and she becomes a ghostly and abject itinerant presence on the European landscape.

ORALITY AND TEXTUALITY

At one point in her epistolary narrative, Zoli reminds her daughter that: 'You can die of madness, daughter, but you can also die of silence' (*Zoli*, 195). The latter association of death with silence is a keynote of the novel, as well as being a defining preoccupation of McCann's fiction. Just as Kearney asserts that 'stories make possible the ethical sharing of a common world with others', access to representation is a means of sustaining cultural life into the future.[19] Zoli's equation of silence with death recalls the subaltern status of the Roma gypsies in the narrative and in narratives of European history. As Roma scholars like Hancock correctly argue, Roma gypsy identity has more often been the product of non-gypsy politicians, historians and sociologists.[20] Thus, McCann's novel focuses on the struggles for representative space undergone by Roma gypsies. The state-sanctioned physical and cultural violences evident in *Zoli* are effects of the bigoted and ventriloquized histories produced about Roma gypsies. Zoli's community are typically taxonomized as 'traditional' or 'archaic', and as preceding modernity, and, consequently, out of joint with the demand of modernization. But what McCann's novel urges is that Roma life and values should not be viewed as anti-modern or regressive, but are, in Johannes Fabian's terms, coeval with modernity.[21] The state-led efforts to domesticate Roma itinerancy and orality misrecognize coevality for anteriority; they assume anachronism instead of alternative simultaneity. In fact, McCann's narrative, and the political point inherent to the novel, accords with Dipesh Chakrabarty's contention that 'the writing of history must implicitly assume a plurality of times existing together, a disjuncture of the present with itself'.[22] Chakrabarty's subalternist historiographical argument is fuelled by the same ethical animus as Kearney's reading of 'otherness', and both are at the kernel of McCann's ethical and political agenda in *Zoli*.

As McCann acknowledges, *Zoli* is loosely inspired by the life of Papusza, a Polish poet who lived between 1910 and 1987, and, in that sense, we can draw a tentative line of comparison between this novel and his previous work, *Dancer*. Both *Zoli* and *Dancer* are works that appropriate the formal masks of biography – in divergent and limited ways – and both centre on the lives of artist-performers. Theoretically, then, these two recent novels are metacritical reflections on the lives of artists and on notions of narration and historical representation. *Zoli* and *Dancer* explore the utopian possibilities of art, but are aware of how programmatic utopian politics can burden and disfigure the life of the artist and the work of art. In addition, McCann telescopes the ideas of art and embodiment in performance, as in both novels aesthetic pleasure issues from the somatic articulacy of the central characters, but again in discrepant forms. In *Zoli*, one of the foremost tensions is between the embodied artistry of oral lyricism, and oral culture generally, and attempts to 'preserve' its artefacts through technological reproduction. At various junctures in *Zoli*, it seems that orality is only prized when it can be rendered into a textual version of itself. It is important, then, to recall that the novel draws on the life of a celebrated Roma poet, who was steeped in an oral lyrical tradition, as we begin to consider the tensile relations between orality and textuality. In discussing the orality of Roma in *Zoli* we might view it as yet another agent in the arsenal that is employed to define the Roma as cultural 'other' in the novel, and in the contemporary historical context.

Emphasizing the historical gap that exists between the text-centric gadže world and the orally transmitted Roma culture, Fonseca states: 'there are no words in Romani proper for "to write" or "to read". Gypsies borrow from other languages to describe these activities.'[23] If language is what we use to create our world, then textuality is effectively non-existent in the culture described by Fonseca. Such a fundamental incommensurability at the level of communicative forms becomes central to cross-communal discord that surfaces in *Zoli*. In foregrounding the tensions between orality and textuality, McCann does not idealize orality over the textual; it is not a question of undoing a naturalized hierarchy of value by fetishizing the authentic purity of an orally communicated system of knowledge transfer. What is of concern, however, is exposing the illegitimate superiority of text over orality; in *Zoli* orality is not an exotic refuge of archaism but a dynamic and living cultural system on which an entire communal and ethnic legacy is founded and reproduced. Orality is not portrayed as a kind of original cultural salve, which can remedy the functional excesses of ideological textual record and documentation – though these imposing textual exertions are in evidence in the novel. In other respects, Zoli's oral heritage is analogous to the mobility of her and of her community's physical lives. At different stages in the novel both their linguistic and physical mobility are preyed upon by the textual and physical stasis of the state. Just as she becomes a mediator between gadže and gypsy communities as a literary cult figure in the 1940s and 1950s, Zoli is equally the embodiment of difficult and, in the end, destructive negotiations between oral and textual cultures.

In his work on memory and oral tradition, Jan Vansina underscores the collectiveness of oral cultures. In his view, 'oral traditions are sources of exceptional value since they convey not only the interpretation of the witnesses to an event but those of the minds who transmitted it.'[24] Oral traditions permit a more generous historical accessibility to the historian, but, more importantly, Vansina's point indicates a greater degree of democratic participation and record is possible through oral transmission. Bypassing the singularity of textual authorship, oral cultures represent collective assertions of democratic articulation. Through the registration of a polyphony of voices and minds, orality seems to be both more inclusive and, therefore, more elusive than the textually enshrined document. In terms of *Zoli*, Fonseca argues for an equivalent collective value in her précis of Papusza's oral folk songs: 'Many of Papusza's song-poems fit into this tradition: through hundreds of refinements and retellings, they are mostly faceless, highly stylized distillations of collective experience...It is impossible to tell the origin or era of most songs by their words, because they speak of the universal and unchanging *cacinos* – truth – of a people living as best they can outside history.'[25] In *Zoli*, her songs belong to this tradition. Though she sings both inherited and her own original compositions, Zoli's lyrics are all firmly rooted in the kinds of heritage outlined by Fonseca. Additive to the collective pedigree of oral culture, Fonseca signals another notable feature of orality in her allusion to the practices of 'refinement', 'retelling', and 'stylized distillation'. Because these lyrics are inherited, there is a drama of negotiation, compromise and re-invention involved between successive singers. As we noted with respect to Rudi's role as performer in *Dancer*, each new [oral] performance of these songs is a renewal of the song, whether it is performed by the same artist or by different artists and different times. Oral art forms remain important sites of reference, and performance and are not exclusively reserved for the purposes of aesthetic pleasure or leisure. As Angela Bourke explains, there is an aggregation of use to which oral art forms are put: 'Oral cultures have therefore developed elaborate verbal art forms through which to arrange knowledge and ideas in patterns, partly in order to conserve and transmit them with maximum efficiency; partly for the intellectual and aesthetic pleasure of such patterning. Much of what an oral culture has to teach is packaged and conveyed in stories.'[26] From pedagogy to aesthetic pleasure, and acting as a mnemonic structure of recollection, orality is densely layered and is critical to the cultural scaffolding of any given oral community. Thus, when we witness the opportunistic enlistment of Zoli's oral songs for politically strategic publication by Stransky and Swann, it is not merely a matter of committing a series of lyrics to textual form. The underlying tension arises from the fact that the entire project is a fundamental re-shaping of how these oral songs were created and how they can, and will, undergo repeated re-invention into the future. The drama between orality and textuality in *Zoli* stems from the fact that orality is not just a *facet* of culture, but is elemental to that culture's *weltanschauung*.

In formal terms, Zoli's narrative is relayed in the first person and is framed as a direct address to her absent daughter. Again, the novel mimics, or re-asserts, the intimacy of oral storytelling form. The first-person focalization also re-visits the territory of biography, in this case gendered and ethnically marginalized. And all of these points gesture towards the inventiveness of oral narrative, and the possibility for inventive self-fashioning present in biographical representation. The mother–daughter narrative frame is not accidental, as Zoli's own deceased mother is the apparent source for her own singing and poetic talent. Her childhood and adolescence are conditioned by a culture of oral performance, and her beautiful voice and proficiency for remembering old songs singles Zoli out among her peers. In another vein, this talent also prepares the way for her future isolation, as her genius is exploited and betrayed in future years. The songs and stories of her early years are relayed in late-evening and late-night rituals and the Roma stories are populated by 'twelve-legged horses and dragons and demons and virgins and cruel aristocrats, about how the gadže blacksmiths tricked us with their molten buttons' (*Zoli*, 34). While the songs that Zoli performs range from 'They broke, they broke my little brown arm, now my father cries like the rain', to 'I have two husbands, one of them sober, one of them drunk, but each one I love the same', and 'I want no shadow to fall upon your shadow, your shadow is dark enough for me' (*Zoli*, 26), the latter lyrics are deceptively simple and are preoccupied with personal pain, love and sorrow, themes that, as Fonseca argues, are predominant in Roma folk songs. It is this raw, emotive simplicity that appeals to Stransky in his appropriation of Zoli as iconic gypsy poet.

MOBILITY AND EXILE

In a recent essay on postcolonial European cinema, Rikki Morgan-Tamosunas and Guido Rings argue: 'The idea of Europe is increasingly

recognized as a highly mobile and provisional concept and configuration
for a variety of reasons including the ambiguity of political and geographical definitions, the constantly evolving membership of Europe as a
federation of states, and its operation within an increasingly global
context.'[27] Europe's provisional identity might well strike these critics
as an emergent phenomenon, but what is missing from their analysis is
the sense that the ambiguity mentioned engenders anxiety among
sections of Europe's population. For many, especially Roma gypsies,
there is little that is ambiguous about 'geographical definitions', as
border controls and immigration legislation are enforced with ever-
increasing impunity and violence. As Europe's internal 'other', the
Roma cannot savour the newly hewn liberties of a borderless and globalized continent. In many ways, this newly configured European polity
only heightens the voltage of panic and suspicion among settled populations and their governments about Roma movements. Zoli's banished
wandering across the European mainland is, of course, prior to the
re-imagination of Europe as we understand it in the contemporary. But
her experiences throw into relief the physical rigidity of imagined
national and political frontiers; and her clandestine journey is symbolic,
for McCann, of continued contemporary displacements, which
are conditioned by stealth, fear, and disorientation. Contrary to the
argument cited above, there is never a universal experience of political
or geographical borders. As *Zoli* makes clear and Roma experience
illustrates, these are contingent on ethnic origin and prevailing patterns
of cultural 'othering'.

The stasis of her political objectification under Stransky's editorial
optic is an explicit counterpoint to Zoli's protracted march across
Europe. Stasis meant co-option and a degree of tolerance for her,
but at an extreme price, while her mainly pedestrian movement is a
symptom of irrevocable expulsion and 'otherness'. Yet the impulse to
move has been integral to Zoli and her lifestyle throughout the novel,
and this is not just evident in her community's nomadic tradition, but
is figurated by McCann through his repeated use of fluvial movement
in the narrative. As we have seen in his earlier novels, the river is a
recurring symbolic device for McCann, and, in *Zoli* the central protagonist is once more closely linked to the perpetual movement of the
river. Even at an early stage, prior to her exile, Zoli's bodily affinities
with moving water were flagged in Swann's narrative: 'I woke in the

morning to find her dozing happily under the floribundas. She washed in the running stream distant from the house. She couldn't fathom someone taking a bath in standing water' (*Zoli*, 91). There is an inscrutable Romantic quality to Swann's portrait of Zoli, she is placed seamlessly in an idyllic, pastoral setting and her habit is an additional function of her appealing cultural difference. But in later exiled years such Romantic framing is redundant, as the geographies of Europe become obstacles and conceal threats to Zoli and her body. Though her extensive travel is precarious and physically painful, the river does not shed its recuperative value to Zoli. In Swann's portrait, the river is part of Zoli's, and gypsy, superstition, but in subsequent years the river becomes a curative for Zoli: 'By early afternoon beads of sweat shone on her forehead and a dizziness propels her. I must find a stream to plunge my head into, some moving water to take this fever away. But she can find no sound of running streams along the road' (*Zoli*, 120). In exile and in physical distress, Zoli manages to retain a somatic link to her Roma heritage; her instinct is to locate moving water as a medicinal relief to her suffering. The river might be an overt symbol of transience and momentum, but it also has lingering affective currency for Zoli as a connective to the past and to the life that she has been exiled from as punishment. As her trek proceeds she does find water, and it is a stream that has iced over, perhaps a compromise between still and moving water. But also a reminder of the iced water that cracked and melted under her family as they were murdered. Nevertheless, Zoli breaks the ice to reveal the moving water below the ice cap:

> With a deep breath she plunges her face into the water, so cold it stuns the bones in her cheeks...The blisters have hardened and none of the cuts have gone septic, but the makeshift bandages have become part of her skin. Zoli inches her feet into the burning cold of the water and tries to peel away the last of the bandages. Skin comes with them. Later, over a small fire, she warms her toes, pushes the flaps of torn skin against raw flesh, attends to her wounds. (*Zoli*, 153)

There are deliberate spiritual overtones, Biblical echoes, in McCann's descriptions of Zoli's dependence on the river water as a physical and psychological analeptic. The exiled impoverishment of her condition is eased by the regenerative properties of the river. So that not only does the river symbolize movement, its healing qualities enable Zoli to tend her wounds in readiness for further, perhaps indefinite, travel.

The curative waters of the river may harbour an ideal figuration of mobility and possess positive redemptive power for Zoli, but the broader realities of her physical movement are dictated by international and ideological boundaries. And borders, analogous to rivers, are both practical and figurative presences in the novel. Zoli repeatedly tests and traverses various boundaries, cultural and political, but now she is confronted with the invested violence of political frontier-zones. Quoting Kundera, Fiona Doloughan touches upon the barriers in prospect for Zoli: 'As long ago as 1971, Kundera bemoaned the fact that "[i]n our society it is counted a greater virtue to guard frontiers than to cross them".'[28] Borders figure, then, as further manifestations of the state's material intrusion on individual and communal movement. At the same time borders are strategies of containment deployed against political and cultural outsiders. As she imagines making her way to Paris, a random yet utopian choice of destination by Zoli, she wonders: 'How many borders is that? How many watchtowers? How many troopers lined along barbed wire? How many roadblocks?' (*Zoli*, 155). The full armoury of the state is engaged as Cold War politics supplement national borders with the barrier of the 'Iron Curtain'. The blind anticipatory gesture of nominating Paris as a speculative endpoint to her travels is tempered by the industrial militarism of gadže surveillance. Roma itinerancy is easily visioned as an absolute 'other' to such intense policing of national contact zones. Borders can be viewed as sites of utopian energies, where cultures can potentially mingle in enriching ways and where new prospects are envisioned. But the co-location of her imagined destination and the insuperable system of barriers to be overcome is suggestive of the fragility of utopian consciousness and of its absolute necessity. McCann suggests how the hopeful geographies of borderlands can be denuded of their vitality by the paranoid politics of the nation-state. In Zoli's case, it is the border between East and West, between competing sides in the Cold War that proves the most daunting. Her situation provides the starkest instance of the vulnerability of the individual in the shadow of programmatic utopian politics and ideology. As a gendered and ethnic migrant, she is helpless in the drama of Cold War politics. Her art has already been hijacked by these politics, and now she must overcome the physical boundaries dictated by these antagonistic versions of political truth. And she is sensitive to the grounds on which political borders are based, and to the importance of fear and hatred to their preservation: 'The other border, East and West, she knows, will begin in a matter of days and it strikes her, as she walks, that borders, like hatred, are exaggerated precisely because otherwise they would cease to exit altogether' (*Zoli*, 165).

Much of the second half of the novel is taken up with Zoli's journey from Bratislava to Compeggio in northern Italy. Her travels are partly fu-elled by her wish to forget the minor and major betrayals of her life in Slovakia, to escape the memories of Swann and of the lateral political manipulation of the Roma. Yet there is nothing to which she is consciously headed, and Paris is, simply, at this stage, a fantasy or an imagined point on the horizon of her travel. In symbolic fashion, she begins her journey by declaring: 'I struck out west' (*Zoli*, 186), and thereby invokes a much longer history of hopeful *westward* travel; the 'west' has always been seen as the trajectory of new prospects and hopes, while the 'east' is more often associated with mystery and the unknown. Indeed, in other works such as *Fishing the Sloe-Black River* and *Songdogs*, McCann presents characters that travel on westward journeys as a means of escape or in pursuit of knowledge. For Zoli, westward travel suggests hope and liberation and it offers the chance of anonymity from the effects of her banishment from the Roma community. To return to both *Songdogs* and *This Side of Brightness*, Zoli's travel is a form of liminal movement. Flensed of her original cultural coordinates and devoid of any structural support from the Roma community, Zoli is cast into a topography of risk but, also, potentially, a terrain of opportunities. She endures savage deprivation during the prolonged period of isolated journeying, to the point of abject dehumanization. Indicative of her struggles, we read: 'Villagers stared at me as I passed. I was sure I looked wretched, all skin and bone and rags…At a deserted farm, I filled my pockets with bonemeal from a feeding trough and later boiled it and ate it without thinking. The paste clove to the top of my mouth and I thought to myself that I was eating the food of animals' (*Zoli*, 186). Her diet, her appearance, the locations where she sleeps, cumulatively suggest the gradual divestment of Zoli's humanity. Her physical decrepitude indexes her increasing remoteness from social propriety of any kind. McCann's description of Zoli's physical decline is another instance where he demurs from presenting an objective and exoticized version of the Roma. Zoli's apparent community with the natural world, part of the gadže's historical stereotype, is absent from the protracted narration of her gruesome liminal trek across Europe. Contrarily, her body is wracked by pain and starvation in these exposed physical conditions. Her journey allegorizes the vulnerabilities – historical and contemporary – of Europe's nomadic communities and undermines belief in the universal virtues of unfettered globalization.

Despite the betrayals she is fleeing and the perils she encounters and imagines during her flight, there are moments of human generosity evident in the narrative. The journey might figure the plight of 'otherness', but McCann implants hopeful acts of solidarity. Though the novel is apparently dominated by repeated acts and programmes of persecution, McCann resists such pessimistic historical evidence by emphasizing the persistence of interpersonal solidarity between gadže and gypsy. In the throes of abjection Zoli receives several gestures of unconditional generosity from strangers during her travels. In one of the first of these, Zoli receives food and drink from a farmer and his mother, having hidden in an out-building of their farm for several days. The act of giving is, of course, physically sustaining for Zoli, and, as above, its significance is amplified by the fact that it is unconditional. Yet there is more to the effects of Zoli's receipt of this sustenance; as she prepares to depart the farm, 'Zoli feels a pulse of strength...As she moves out, across the stone wall, onto the tarmac, she has the sudden feeling that if a truck screams down the roadway now she will undoubtedly be able to stand out of its way' (*Zoli*, 130). Zoli is revivified both physically and spiritually; she is charged with renewed purpose, and this is the real worth of the act of generosity. But not only is this an act of generosity, it is a recognition of Zoli's common humanity and an affirmation of her entitlement to basic human dignity. In its brevity and simplicity, this act restores much of Zoli's dignity, in stark contrast to the prolonged efforts of the state in previous years to thieve this dignity.

This utopian gesture is not isolated in Zoli's narrative, and in the face of naturalized prejudice against Roma gypsies, Zoli benefits from several different kinds of aid. She travels with another farmer and her initial suspicions of this man yield when he offers cigarettes, provides her with apples, empathizes with her in his 'passion for the travelling life' (*Zoli*, 211), but, crucially, counsels her against the threat of the state police. Likewise, she encounters long-distance truck drivers hauling consumer goods across the continent, and she is welcomed into their vehicles. In another instance she is invited to travel with a family in their car and 'to gladden them I began to hum the tune of the old horse song. The man turned in his seat and gave a smile, though the mother kept looking straight ahead. I sat back and hummed some more and he said he liked the humming and I surprised myself with song' (*Zoli*, 216). The confined space of the car becomes a space of dialogue and sharing between gadže and gypsy in this short-lived, and not unqualified, episode. Though not devoid of suspicion, there is a palpable mutuality of respect evident in the sharing of Zoli's music. In another way, her art returns, and through her own volition she brings and offers it to an exterior gadže audience. These differential episodes in Zoli's narrative, then, are aspects of McCann's faith in human redemption, and evidence of the utopian impulses that energize his fictions. This is not to argue that such discrete pockets of solidarity or sharing can preside and can undo the ingrained politics of repression endured by Roma gypsies. Rather, they stress the precariousness of human dignity but also the possibility of its sustenance and redemption in the contemporary world. The last instance is, arguably, the most powerful in this sense, in that it showcases the redemptive agency of art as a bridge between gadže and gypsy histories.

As the novel draws to a close, Zoli comes into further contact with institutional bodies of the gadže world, but in both of these cases they are proposing to aid her and her community's plight against displacement and racism. Having navigated the border between East and West, Zoli wakes to find herself in a Displaced Person's (DP) Camp in Austria. And her initial reaction is entirely conditioned by her prior experiences of institutional benevolence in Slovakia; she violently rejects all promises of help and hygiene. Despite the stated charitable intentions of the DP camp and its staff, the long history of gadže and gypsy relations manifests again in terms of instinctive suspicion. Zoli is so acquainted with the processes and the language of bureaucracy that she is unable to accept the sincerity of their motives towards her. In fact, her stay at the DP camp is another ambiguous location, as it provides sanctuary to Zoli, but it also appears as an extension of state efforts to document and to account for the movements and the origins of displaced peoples. For Zoli, the idiom of the camp and its staff is all too reminiscent of the past she has been striving to escape. In contrast to the random gestures of generosity she receives and welcomes in other contexts above, Zoli is resistant to the pleas of her medical assessor, Doctor Marcus: 'You don't have to suffer, she said, there's no point, why don't you tell me your situation and then I can help, I promise' (*Zoli*, 193). To this medical intervention, Zoli exhibits a well-earned cynicism: 'It was like an old song, a children's rhyme. I had heard it so often, it was as if she had taken the words of a bureaucrat and put them in a child's mouth' (*Zoli*, 193). Her time at the DP camp allows Zoli to commune again, and to assist a family of Roma gypsies in their plans to re-settle to Canada. It is always her intention to leave the camp, as she cannot accept the institutional and bureaucratic mechanics of re-settlement, even in this putatively charitable guise. Unable to abide by the spirit of the camp's administrative systems, she departs the camp and arrives, and settles, in Compeggio in Italy. This location delivers a life that is rooted for Zoli, and here she marries and has a family, a daughter, to whom the narrative is addressed and with whom she will complete the novel.

Zoli finally arrives in Paris in 2003 on a visit to her daughter, Francesca. In this final section of the novel, Zoli's story is no longer relayed through her first-person narration but is related via an omniscient voice. Her arrival in Paris brings a kind of resolution to the imaginative wandering she undertook decades before, and, fittingly, during her time in Paris she is forced into a reckoning with her past and with Swann. But what is of significance also is the convention of an academic conference on the topic of 'From Wheel to Parliament: Romani Memory and Imagination' (*Zoli*, 250). The event is organized and hosted by Francesca, and its inclusion in the novel is another moment of self-reflexiveness by McCann. The conference references contemporary initiatives in the United States and European academia to represent Roma history and culture. In an adjacent manner to the DP camp, the academic conference is a liberal and institutional act of support for the Roma, but as Zoli intuits, it too is not unproblematic. The list of attendees include 'Academics...Social scientists...Romani writers...Some poets', and indicative topics to be covered are 'the Holocaust, the Devouring, Lexical Impoverishment...Police Perception of Belgian Roma' (*Zoli*, 256). Francesca's defiant assertion at the conference opening that 'We will not be made to stay at the margins any longer' (*Zoli*, 256) is a resolute political statement. But the suspicion is that these events are purely academic in nature, and cannot be translated into material ameliorative action. Zoli's instinctive discomfort and her refusal to participate actively must be read as symptoms of, firstly, continuing Roma resistance to gadže initiatives that proposed to improve and to understand Roma life. Secondly, it suggests, again, her well-founded scepticism about institutional endeavours to intervene in her life and her culture. And, finally, it is relevant to the broader critical and ethical issues on how and where academics and writers can and should represent cultural and political 'others'. How can the legacies and endurances of such 'othering' be equably redressed or even addressed at the present time? This does not disqualify the efforts currently being made, but raises justifiable questions. Francesca's conference is, then, centred on furnishing a voice for her Roma heritage within a mainstream discursive context, but it is apparent that, from her life experience, Zoli is attuned to the question of whose terms dictate this participation in the mainstream.

Paris is a city of reunions and reckonings in this final part of *Zoli*. She is reunited with her daughter, she visits a Roma enclave in Parisian tower blocks, and the broad topics at the conference highlight some of the history of her people. But this final section also brings the three focalizing protagonists of the novel together at the conference hotel, as it strives for a resolution to their disparate searches and travels. The Slovakian journalist Smolenak confronts Zoli, informing her of his prolonged investigation into her whereabouts and her work. Smolenak, in effect, breaches the fabric of history, allowing a torrent of memories to engulf Zoli. His investigation into her location had opened the novel, and now it foments an intense crisis for Zoli as the past she had repressed returns in the form of Smolenak's project. What is literary historical research for the journalist is profoundly personal and emotional for Zoli. The betrayals of decades before are invisible to Smolenak, who simply sees Zoli as 'a new voice from old times' (*Zoli*, 263). The scene of the conference is doubly problematic for Zoli because she is confronted with the discursive discussions of liberal academics and the popular historical research of Smolenak. She sees her life and its manifold tragedies, as well as those of her people, mutating into the abstract interests of gadže intellectuals. Having fled her status as cult figure and outcast, Zoli senses history's urge to repeat itself, as Smolenak's work positions Zoli as a resurrected literary figure and is, in some ways, comparable to earlier 'productions' of her work and image. It is Smolenak's unsolicited interventions that promise the reunion between Zoli and Swann in Paris. But a forced reunion would never heal the betrayal by Swann years previously, and though they cursorily converse at the conference hotel, there is no conclusive reconciliation. In fact, McCann does not present an explicit reunion between the former lovers in the novel; instead it is promised at the end of the narrative – it will happen in the future. The reconciliation will, therefore, be on Zoli's terms and not hijacked by Smolenak:

> And then Zoli knows for sure, yes, she will take a taxi to the train station, stop off first at the hotel…call Swann's room, stand in the reception, wait, watch him shamble across toward her, hold his face in her hands for a moment, and kiss him, yes, on the fore-head, kiss him, allow him his sorrow and then she will leave, take the train, alone, home to the valley. (*Zoli*, 273)

The promise of reconciliation between Zoli and Swann is, symbolically, fixed for the future, and she will assume the responsibility. Zoli will indulge in another act of spiritual generosity towards her erstwhile lover. McCann does not end the novel with a conclusive resolution of this fractured relationship but does hint at the prospect of redemption. Having decided to visit Swann the following day, Zoli enters the living room of Francesca's apartment, in which musicians have gathered, and it is this space, with this music, that *Zoli* concludes. The conference centred on hearing the Roma voice, but, as we noted, the danger remained that this voice could become objectified or abstracted. By way of comparison, McCann ends the novel with Zoli and the enunciation of her voice as a Roma poet and singer. In the final scene, Zoli's identity is seen as performative rather than constative; she is an artistic subject rather than a discursive object. The novel concludes with Zoli in the midst of the gadže world, but, tellingly, she is about to sing on her own terms. Zoli's is the final voice that is registered and, herein, McCann once more brings art and politics; art and redemption; and music and hope into focus:

> 'Go on,' she says, 'Play.' The curly-haired one strikes a note on the mandolin, a bad note, too high, though she rinses it out with the rest, and the guitarist joins in, slowly at first, and a wave moves across the gathering, like wind over grass, and the room feels as if

it is opening, one window, then another, and then the walls themselves. The tall musician strikes a chord and nods at Zoli – she smiles, lifts her head, and begins. She begins. (*Zoli*, 274–5)

The general political impulse of *Zoli* is candidly summarized by Fogarty when she argues that: 'McCann constructs an indictment of societies that are intolerant of difference and create Others in order to shore up their corrupt regimes.'[29] This is a contention that we have pinpointed throughout the chapter and one that, clearly, informs much of McCann's fictional output. But the political effectiveness of McCann's novel is not only recognized within literary critical responses such as Fogarty's. Ian Hancock is equally effusive about the sensitivity of McCann's portrait of his community: 'I review a great many Roma-themed manuscripts for publishers, but none has ever moved me as profoundly.'[30] *Zoli* portrays a complex cultural constituency without reducing it and its history to Romantic typologies. There is a sense in which McCann acknowledges the subaltern nature of Roma culture – a culture that is not anterior, archaic, or 'traditonal', but that exists as a vibrant, coterminous culture to mainstream 'modernity'. Indeed David Lloyd's summation of subalternity seems apposite to the Roma experiences narrated by McCann in *Zoli*. Lloyd writes: 'the apparent discontinuity of popular or non-elite history furnishes indications of alternative social formations...the insubordination of such formations is in precise differentiation to the narrative forms of official histories.'[31] Lloyd's suggestive use of the word 'insubordination' is the key to understanding the litany of representation and misrepresentation undergone by the Roma, but it is also crucial to the imagination of a utopian politics. A politics that does not fetishize difference and 'otherness' or subordinate in different ways, but one that recognizes and restores dignity and hope.

NOTES

1. Anna Metcalfe, 'Small Talk: Colum McCann', *Financial Times* (29 August 2009). http://www.ft.com/cms/s/2/7ea126ca-9362-11de-b146 00144feabdc0.html#axzz16NnyntuC.
2. Isabel Fonseca, *Bury Me Standing: The Gypsies and their Journey* (London: Vintage, 1995) p.273.
3. Ian Hancock, 'The Struggle for the Control of Identity', in Michael Hayes (ed.), *Road Memories: Aspects of Migration History* (Newcastle: Cambridge Scholars Publishing, 2007), p.4.
4. Edward W. Said, *Orientalism* (London: Vintage, 1978).
5. Mary Burke, *Tinkers: Synge and the Cultural History of the Irish Traveller* (Oxford: Oxford University Press, 2009), p.271.

6. Jean-Pierre Liegois, *Gypsies: An Illustrated History* (London, 1985), p.104.
7. Paul Carter, *The Road to Botany Bay* (London: Faber, 1987), p.326.
8. The term *gadže* is the Roma term for non-Roma people.
9. Richard Kearney, *Strangers, Gods and Monsters: Interpreting Otherness* (London: Routledge, 2003), p.65.
10. Ibid., p.3.
11. Ibid., p.81.
12. Ibid., p.80.
13. Ibid., p.81.
14. Colum McCann, *Zoli* (London: Weidenfeld & Nicolson, 2006), p.3. All further references to *Zoli* will be in parenthesis as (*Zoli*).
15. Wole Soyinka, *The Climate of Fear* (London: Profile Books, 2004), p.99.
16. Robbie McVeigh, 'Theorising Sedentarism: The Roots of Anti-Nomadism', in Thomas Acton (ed.), *Gypsy Politics and Traveller Identity* (Hatfield: University of Hertfordshire Press, 1997), p.8.
17. Gilles Deleuze and Felix Guattari, *Kafka: Towards a Minor Literature* (Minneapolis and London: University of Minnesota Press, 1986).
18. Anne Fogarty, 'Contemporary Irish Fiction and the Transnational Imaginary', in Eamon Maher (ed.), *Cultural Perspectives on Globalisation and Ireland* (Bern: Peter Lang, 2009), p.139.
19. Richard Kearney, *On Stories* (London: Routledge, 2002), p.150.
20. Hancock, 'The Struggle for the Control of Identity', pp.6–7.
21. Johannes Fabian, *Time and the Other: How Anthropology Makes its Object* (New York: Columbia University Press, 1983).
22. Dipesh Chakrabarty, 'Minority Histories, Subaltern Pasts', *Postcolonial Studies*, 1, 1 (1998), p.25.
23. Fonseca, *Bury Me Standing*, p.11.
24. Jan Vansina, 'Memory and Oral Tradition', in Joseph C. Miller (ed.), *The African Past Speaks: Essays on Oral Tradition and History* (Folkestone: Dawson, 1980), p.276.
25. Fonseca, *Bury Me Standing*, p.5.
26. Angela Bourke, 'The Baby and the Bathwater: Cultural Loss in Nineteenth-Century Ireland', in Tadhg Foley and Seán Ryder (eds), *Ideology and Ireland in the Nineteenth Century* (Dublin: Four Courts Press, 1998), p.81.
27. Rikki Morgan-Tamosounas and Guido Rings, 'Images of the Self and the Other in Postcolonial European Film', in Rikki Morgan-Tamosounas and Guido Rings (eds), *European Cinema: Inside Out* (Heidelberg: Heidelberg Universistatsverlag, 2003), p.15.
28. Fiona Doloughan, 'The Myth of the Great Return: Memory, Longing and Forgetting in Milan Kundera's *Ignorance*', in Michael Hanne (ed.), *Creativity in Exile* (New York and Amsterdam: Rodopi, 2004), p.150.
29. Fogarty, 'Contemporary Irish Fiction and the Transnational Imaginary', p.140.
30. Cited in Carolyn T. Hughes, 'Adventurist: Interview with Colum McCann', *Poets & Writers* (Jan/Feb 2007), p.54.
31. David Lloyd, *Ireland after History* (Cork: Cork University Press/Field Day: 1999), p.84.

7

'Burning from the Inside Out':
Let the Great World Spin (2009)

9/11 – ART AND POLITICS

The encounter between 9/11 and literature brings into focus the triumphs and deformations of language and representation since the acts of criminal terror unfolded almost a decade ago. A symbology and a semiotics all of its own has evolved from 9/11. The term itself has entered linguistic circulation as a universal shorthand for murderous terror and noble resistance to unseen terroristic agencies. But, equally, dissent has arisen about the moralistic mobilizations of 9/11 as a legitimation for surveillance, violent interrogation, and illegal invasion. Heated exchanges have cohered around the ethics of employing 9/11 as a political lodestone and/or as an emotional default in the invocation of national identity in the United States. When we come to consider artistic responses to, or reflections on, 9/11 we enter battle-worn ground on which politics and culture have colluded and competed. And at the epicentre of these debates is language and how it has been competitively utilized as a means of cultivating jingoistic assent, or, less often, non-partisan critical reflection on 9/11 as an act of terror. This is also the case when matters revolving around the performances of a morally endowed national identity in the US are brought into play. In many respects, instead of provoking lateral constructive argumentation on global relations – political, economic and cultural – institutional responses to 9/11 have, more often, recoiled at the prospect of polyphonic debate in lieu of patriotic consensus. Simply put, there has been a degree of 'anti-intellectualism' afoot in the aftermath of the 11 September attacks and the intervening duration of the 'War on Terror'. For Susan Sontag there is 'the suspicion of thought, of words', and 'hiding behind the humbug that the attack of last September 11 was too horrible, too devastating, too painful, too tragic for words, that words could not possibly do justice to our grief and indignation, our leaders have a perfect excuse to drape themselves in borrowed words devoid of content. To say something might be controversial...Not saying anything is best.'[1] There is a passionate political criticism and consciousness to Sontag's diagnosis. But her argument also dovetails with the actions and reactions of writers after the events of 11 September. In Susan Buck-Morss' view, 9/11 might have been a 'mute act' requiring subsequent narrative coding.[2] But the dominant narrative patterning of 9/11 has been univocal, by and large, and has striven to quell critical questioning. The popular call for unity from within the US, and that reached across, and was accepted by, the 'West', is matched and abetted by cultural agents that do not defy, but affirm, simplistic, binary thinking on East/West relations – historical and contemporary. Difference and diversity, long mainstays of American popular culture, are now watchwords of new idioms of paranoid and xenophobic legislation and monitoring. Political and cultural differences are not the basis for pluralist or multicultural inclusiveness, but are now markers of potential menace. Indeed it is not an exaggeration to speculate that the political and cultural climate of the 'West' has entered the frames of dystopian literary history for many of its narrative figurations in the years since 9/11.

In this intensified state of political and cultural sensitivity, it is worth posing the following questions, as Daniel Lea does in his piece on literary responses to 9/11. Lea inquires: 'why are the views of writers, and in particular novelists, deemed so worthy of collation and dissemination? Why, in the aftermath, were novelists sought out to air their opinions on the traumatic character of events? What, in other words, does the novelist have to offer that cannot be provided by reportage or political commentary?'[3] Lea's series of questions centres on the role of the novelist in relation to 9/11 and asks what are the exceptional abilities harboured by the literary artist that might enable them to mediate such shocking events for a general readership. The premium placed on the writer, as opposed to the narrative conventions and content of media and political opinion, is not difficult to explain. There is an assumption that the rhetoric of news coverage and political newspeak are blighted by evasion, slant or outright misinformation, whereas the explanatory fictions of the novelist are deemed to express and to possess truths and consolations for the reader. Clearly, Lea's point coheres with the broader issue of the appetite for narrative and explanation after the 9/11 attacks, but it also touches upon other critical issues. In summoning writers to respond to these catastrophic events, it seems as if there is an explicit acknowledgement of the capacity of the literary artist to provide guidance out of the silence and the clamour attendant to 9/11. Likewise, the possibility that literature itself might be a source of succour or solace is implicit in Lea's speculations. This is not to locate the literary artist as a kind of renovated seer in the light of 11 September, but there has been a renewed weight placed on the literary as a medium of consolation and resolution in many critical interventions since 9/11.

And another series of queries, this time by David Simpson, opens up the discussion of what might be termed a recalibrated utopian function of literature since 9/11. In his *9/11: The Culture of Commemoration*, Simpson asks: 'Does the experience of literature inevitably or even plausibly lead us to a compassionate response to the sufferings of others? Is literature the best means by which we can educate ourselves into an appropriately full engagement with the deaths of others?'[4] Simpson is sceptical about the moral and affective agencies of the literary – in his view repeated textual familiarity with or exposure to the suffering of others can inure one against feelings of empathy. Contrary to the views of critics such as Martha Nussbaum, Simpson expresses doubts regarding the conjunction of literature and empathy.[5] Nevertheless, Simpson's case has been met with distinguished and widespread opinion, which articulates the contrary viewpoint and partakes of Nussbaum's argument. The impacts of 9/11 as physical and symbolic assaults, then, were pinpointed as moments that required not only explanation but redemption, and literature was a cultural medium through which such redemption could, potentially, be found. Out of the elevated reality of the trauma of 9/11, a journey or process of redemption must emerge.

Countering Simpson's suspicion of the necessary redemptive agency of literature are critics including Richard Kearney and Michael Rothberg – whose arguments chime with the logic of Nussbaum's longer-term work. Both Kearney's and Rothberg's contentions underscore the political and critical responsibilities of literature. And there is a call to vigilance evident in each of these cases, and a demand for attention against complacent consumption of divisive and bellicose narratives within the public sphere. In his view, a combination of philosophy and literary criticism, Kearney draws a crucial distinction between popular media outlets and the realms of literary narratives:

> Philosophical and artistic works are…capable of furnishing some extra, because indirect, insights into the enigma of horror. For both proffer an *unnatural* perspective on things – by virtue of style, genre and language. And this unnatural perspective is almost invariably absent from the all-too-naturalistic stance of most entertainment and mass media…The advantage of art and philosophy is that they are critical discourses which underscore the character of such illusion.[6]

Focusing on narrative form, Kearney displays an awareness of the limits of narrative realism when confronted with an event of such sublime proportions as 9/11. The inherent formal flexibility of artistic narratives enables them to respond to such events and such spectacles in more reflective ways than mere information outlets or partisan broadcast channels. There is a utopian impulse embedded within Kearney's appraisal; he displays a consciousness that literature and art are fully sensitive to the artificialities of narrative production and, therefore, bring us closer to truths by exposing the falsities of populist and propagandized narratives. The view espoused by Rothberg is, arguably, more explicit in its alignment of literature with politics and terrorism in the post-9/11 context. Under his critical optic, the literary can act as a riposte to terrorism itself, and can be a voice in analyzing and speaking back to the political contexts out of which terrorism arises. Literary art in this schema is resolutely public and capable of revealing 'the interconnectedness of the public and the private'.[7] The broad concerns of national and international politics that appear to unfold on the stages of the public sphere, of course, impact upon the private lives of individuals, particularly under 'states of emergency' maintained at various levels since 9/11. According to Rothberg: 'the aesthetic has a particular role to play in responding both to acts of extreme violence and to the political process in which they unfold and to which they give rise'; furthermore, 'the aesthetic is neither an apolitical zone closed off from violence nor a realm that can simply be subsumed under the seemingly more urgent activity of politics, even in a moment of perpetual emergency.'[8] Rothberg's conclusion is that 'the aesthetic constitutes a bridging realm that connects subjective experience to larger collectivities'.[9] Literary artists were expeditious in their responses to 9/11 in personal and journalistic pieces, but Rothberg's point is trained on how they did, and can still, react in purely literary terms. Literature, the aesthetic, is a political agent; it is a competent mediator between the geopolitics of the public sphere and the anxieties, the terrors, or discontentments of the private. And in this conceptualization of literary art, Rothberg's case joins Kearney's as one that is energized by a utopian dynamism. Both are significant because they reflect the felt need for a critical reckoning with the narration of 9/11, and literature is a viable vehicle for conducting such a project. The aesthetic, then, in its attentiveness to language and its differential usages; to the mechanics of narration; its facility to critique the contemporary political order; and to re-imagine and to redeem alternative worlds and histories becomes a muscular political and cultural resource after 9/11. And, perhaps, there are some of the reasons, to answer Lea's series of questions above, that artists, novelists in particular, were enlisted as respondents to the terror of 11 September. And it is why their artistic works that reflect on 9/11 and its resonances are important contemporary cultural and political touchstones.

If the question of empathy is crucial to understanding McCann's work, then the relationship between empathy and narrative is essential to any engagement with his fiction. As we discussed above, the possibilities of evoking empathetic feeling through literary reading is a highly contentious field of critical debate. But it is a suite of arguments that was thrown into focus again in the light of literary responses to 11 September. In his short piece published in *The Guardian* on 15 September 2001, Ian McEwan draws empathy and the power of the imagination together in his polemic against the cruelties of the 9/11 hijackers. McEwan cleaves to the conviction that: 'If the hijackers had been able to imagine themselves into the thoughts and feelings of the passengers, they would have been unable to proceed.'[10] In his view, empathetic feeling is rooted in the imagination – in one's ability to place one's self in the situation of another, the 'other'. In pairing empathy and imagination, McEwan asserts that this facility to imagine in such compassionate ways is 'at the core of our humanity. It is the essence of compassion, and it is the beginning of morality.'[11] A failure of imagination leads to charges of mass murder; a failure of empathy is an index of the abandonment of human fellow feeling. Indeed, McEwan's essay 'Only Love and the Oblivion' is endorsed by Kearney in his own writing on 9/11. And Kearney's agreement with McEwan again underscores the privileged position of writers as respondents to scenes of immense trauma – scenes which seem to confound our narrative perceptions of reality and our apprehensions of what constitutes our external realities. For Kearney, 'it is not insignificant that some of the most insightful responses to 9/11 came from thinkers and artists...The contribution by McEwan to *The Guardian* a few days after the event is to my mind one of the most cogent testimonies to the power of *narrative understanding*.'[12]

LET THE GREAT WORLD SPIN AND 9/11

Again the 'narrative' labour and expertise of writers, together with their 'imaginative' range are signalled as a means of fashioning and relating understanding to dazed readers. Returning to Lea, in the wake of Rothberg's and Kearney's arguments, is there an inevitability to the prominence of writerly responses to 9/11, and other such extreme public events of violence and spectacle? McEwan's location of empathy in the imagination, and his belief that this is where morality begins, centres literature as a primary political agent after 9/11. There was little that was empathetic or imaginative about many institutional political responses to the attacks of 11 September. But it seems from these combined reactions that literature houses utopian possibilities towards political and cultural critique, and towards the cultivation of empathetic feeling beyond the local. Post-9/11, novels and other works of art are not solely concerned with eliciting sympathy or empathy for the victims of the hijacked planes – though this is important – this sub-genre of contemporary fiction is also cognizant of the need for narratives that complicate our understandings of the 'other'. These 9/11 fictions can help us to see hope in place of an insistent rhetoric of vilification and retribution; and they can impress the possibilities of redemption through empathy rather than through violent purging. The brachiated and democratic structure of *Let the Great World Spin*, in tandem with one of its central themes, creative daring, allow McCann to address these questions. McCann's literary intervention is a 9/11 novel, and it attempts to loosen the grip of the 9/11 grief industry, which tries to stage-manage the cultural digestion of 9/11. *Let the Great World Spin* is a political and social novel that looks aslant at the attacks of 9/11; McCann suggests that it is an allegory on human suffering, which partially speaks to 11 September. Nevertheless, the novel de-monumentalizes the suffering of the victims of 9/11, without denigrating their memory. Instead, McCann showcases the longevity and the breadth of human suffering and resilience across races, classes and nationalities in New York City. It is a novel that is stalked by menace and violence, but one that rises to moments of grace and hopeful anticipation. And in this latter point, it coheres with Rothberg's and Kearney's faith in art after 9/11.

Speaking in interview after the publication of *Let the Great World Spin*, McCann admitted to a certain confusion as an author dealing with 9/11, particularly as a resident of New York City. He confessed that he 'began to wonder, Who's going to write about this?' and that as responses of various forms and political persuasions began to proliferate, he remarked that 'every piece was poignant...And everything had meaning: it was like the whole city was infused with meaning.'[13] The everyday is transformed into the sacred, as figuration and suggestion engulf the brute realities of a debris-strewn and ash-thickened atmosphere. As the force of the reality of 9/11 manifested itself, understandings of its 'meaning' only became admissible through figuration – symbols and metaphors were drafted in as explanatory buffers: 'You couldn't help thinking that everything had importance. Even the child's painting of the two buildings holding hands was a powerful image.'[14] McCann's point re-iterates the fact that even this event, perhaps especially this event, cannot escape 'the reach of symbol and metaphor'.[15] Whereas many saw recourse to narrative and figuration as routes out of aphasia and grief, towards a semblance of healing, it is equally true that 9/11 became a part of a dominant semiotics in the geopolitical imagination. In other words, 9/11 became a symbolic agent of neo-conservative politics and acted as a guarantor of moral legitimacy for physical and cultural violence across the globe. Its cultivated mythology has seen it conscripted into narrow and heavily politicized commemoration. As Simpson avers: 'The event has been and will be made to mark a new epoch, and as such it is already generating a mythology and a set of practices of its own.'[16]

The attacks of 11 September were entirely without public warning or, apparently, precedent. Yet as Slavoj Žizek argues, the forms the attacks assumed are familiar features of our visual fantasy worlds.[17] But the sheer spectacular qualities of the World Trade Centre attacks take us back to Lea's series of questions: were writers summoned in order to verbalize some meaningful explanation of the silent spectacle of the terror attacks? The mute eloquence of the events can be adjudged to confer a level of uniqueness on 9/11, as Buck-Morss concedes: 'The staging of violence as a global spectacle separates September 11 from previous acts of terror.'[18] Nevertheless, the lethal visibility of 9/11 reminds us of the relative invisibility of other acts of terror, often committed in its wake and on our behalf. But the spectacular nature of the event brings into tension the viewers' sense of what is real and what is fictive; and occasions a blurring between the real and the cinematic. There is, in other words, a clash of communicative or narrative codes, and at the moments of the attacks there is no mediation to untangle this confusion. The perpetrators of the crime well understood both the symbolism of the twin towers and the centrality of the visual to the West's cultural economy, as well as the intimacy of remembrance and images. In differential modes – remembrance, cinema, information – the visual is crucial to understanding 9/11, and is a key motif in McCann's 9/11 novel. To return to one of the early novelist respondents, Martin Amis, we see this exact point concisely articulated: 'But no visionary cinematic genius could hope to create the majestic abjection of that double surrender, with the scale of the buildings conferring its own slow motion. It was well understood that an edifice so demonstrably comprised of concrete and steel would also become an unforgettable metaphor. This moment was the apotheosis of the postmodern era – the era of the image and perceptions.'[19]

9/11 can be located in a specific set of geographical locations, and the abbreviated nomination indicates the calendar date of the attacks in 2001. Through the labours of policymakers and media agenda-setters, 9/11 has outgrown any sense of itself as a mere temporal marker; the event has transcended historical time and has entered epochal time. As other literary critical volumes amply illustrate, literature and, in particular, the novel, has responded variously to 9/11, though much of the literary output and pursuant literary criticism has tended to reflect on American legacies and experiences of 9/11.[20] In a recent literary critical survey, Catherine Morley notes a suite of trends in 9/11 fiction: 'While many of the initial reactions to the events of 11 September were notable for their uniquely subjective emphasis, with writers discussing what the attacks meant to them, to their art and to their writing, what many writers have also been integrating into their fiction has been the American response to the attacks.'[21] The current discussion strives to depart from domestic, subjective reactions to 9/11 in literary fiction and essays by looking at the National Book Award-winning *Let the Great World Spin*, which deals with 9/11 in an elliptical way. McCann's novel is set, like much of his previous fiction, in New York, but principally unfolds in 1974, and deals with, in figurative fashion, themes of trauma, loss, and redemption. *Let the Great World Spin* is initiated by the narration of a high-wire walk between the towers of the World Trade Centre on 7 August 1974, and this imaginative performance reverberates forward in time to 11 September 2001, as a utopian act of creation. But rather than re-create a world-historical universe in 1974, McCann prefers to navigate the margins of a profoundly troubled metropolis. *Let the Great World Spin* gestures to the accumulated grief of 9/11 and to the symbolism of the attacks by way of Philippe Petit's walk, and McCann spotlights the possibility of redemption and recovery in the recessed spaces of New York's cityscape. Grief is not confined to this date and this event, and neither is hope; the novel is, then, an allegory about all human suffering and how that suffering can be alleviated or endured.

Let the Great World Spin cannot but be considered a political and social novel given its embrace of criminality, destitution, addiction, and class division. Set in 1974 in New York, the narrative primarily spans downtown and uptown Manhattan, as well as the South Bronx, with interludes in Ireland and upstate New York. Gathered within its plotlines are characters of different nationalities, races and class locations: the anonymous high-wire walker; the Irish monk, John Corrigan and his brother Ciaran; Tillie and Jazzlyn Henderson, mother and daughter prostitutes, who are friends with John Corrigan; a wealthy couple grieving for the son lost in Vietnam, Claire and Solomon Soderberg; and Gloria, who lost three of her sons in the same war; a teenage photographer on the hunt for new subway graffiti; and a young artist, Lara, who is involved in John Corrigan's death and begins a long-term relationship with his brother after that accident. From the outset, *Let the Great World Spin* clamours with diversity, and pulses with the tensions and insecurities of its cast. The novel acknowledges both the material and the symbolic as forces within daily life, and traces how, as McCann puts it 'the accidental meets the sacred'.[22] And a fraction of its political engagement is, of course, its concern with 9/11 as a material and a symbolic event. McCann accepts the immense symbolic trauma of 9/11, but he is equally keen to stress the lateral material sufferings that nourish, and are often subordinated to, the public emphasis on symbolic victimhood or symbolic violence. *Let the Great World Spin* is, in this way, a politically engaged narrative, which speaks from an equivalent critical position to that outlined by Rothberg and Kearney above. It is a forceful, though tangential, artistic-political response to 9/11, but there is more to the work than this neat summary may suggest: '9/11 was the initial impetus for the book...But I am aware of the pitfalls of labelling it a "9/11" novel...9/11 is certainly part of the book's construction, but it is not limited to that...I really wanted to lift it out of the 9/11 "grief machine".'[23] While he acknowledges the symbolic threads that link *Let the Great World Spin* to 9/11, it would be reductive to define McCann's novel as one that is exclusively trained on these events. It is a novel that responds to 9/11 without ever becoming obsessed by the immediate repercussions in 2001 in any direct way. McCann does not 'enter' the world of 9/11 or post-9/11 in a sustained fashion, nor does he imagine characters or events implicated directly in this contemporary tragedy. Tellingly, he implies that 9/11 might actually compromise his work, that 9/11 as a 'cultivated' event could contract the interpretive scope of his narrative. In this there are echoes of Jacques Derrida's argument that works of literature might themselves become objects within the commemorative industry of 9/11.[24] All of these issues, though, cannot disavow the fact that 9/11 is a thematic and ethical point of departure for *Let the Great World Spin*. But it is equally the case that the novel's visions outstrip the political and cultural agons surrounding the 2001 attacks. As McCann stresses: 'it's a novel that tries to uncover joy and hope and a small glimmer of grace...a novel about creation, maybe even a novel about healing in the face of all the evidence.'[25]

RE-IMAGINING SPACE AND PERFORMING HOPE

Mobility and exile are defining preoccupations of McCann's previous two novels, and this makes them much more obviously 'spatial' in their concerns. Yet *Let the Great World Spin* asserts the locality of spatial politics; its topographies are, principally, those of New York City, but exile and mobility remain prominent. There are other geographies present: Ireland figures at the outset and at the conclusion, and California enters the narrative via telephonic communication. Allusions are made to Guatemala; Cleveland, Ohio; England; Brussels; Naples; New Orleans; Little Rock, Arkansas; Vietnam; and Genoa, but New York City is the spatial main stage. New York City is the localized global space and it is the endpoint of all of these vectors of travel and displacement. Within the city, and the novel, McCann juxtaposes terrestrial and airborne spaces, which are figurations of hope and despair as well as reminders that life at ground level can be as precarious as life on an elevated tightrope: both demand balance that is often threatened and uncertain. And this is one of the possible interpretations of the wire walker's funambulism, as an acrobatic correlative of the fragile precariousness of daily living. At the same time, his act is an outrageous seizure of urban space, an act, apparently, with no constructive end other than the outstanding beauty of the act itself. The twin towers and the references to the Vietnam War unfolding at this time are affronted by the vision of the wire walker's spatial creativity. Both the war and the buildings are parts of the same capitalistic continuum and are complicit in the spatial appropriation of the globe. Empire building was, and is, founded on the basic contestation of, and appropriation of, space, and both the towers and the war are internal and external signs of this politics. As Edward Soja summarizes: 'The production of ideas (and ideologies) is thus an important component of the production of spatiality but this relationship is rooted in social origins.'[26]

Though he is never named in the novel, *Let the Great World Spin* opens on the morning of Philippe Petit's tightrope walk between the twin towers of the World Trade Centre on 7 August 1974. Immediately McCann gestures to the agency of the visual as both a universal cultural medium and as a core motif of the novel. Vision, spectacle and sightings provide a link between the opening act of funambulism in *Let the Great World Spin* and the brute spectacular of 9/11. Indeed the 'walker's', as he is referred to, preparation to step out onto his high wire is met with similar silent awe and trepidation by the congregation of confused viewers on the streets of Manhattan below: 'Those who saw him hushed…Others figured it might be the perfect city joke – stand around and point upward, until people gathered, tilted their heads, nodded, affirmed, until all were staring upward at nothing at all.'[27] The grouped crowds may be witnesses to the 'walker's' actions, but there is nothing besides suspicion and uncertainty in the accumulated speculations. There seems to be a disjuncture between vision and comprehension in the presence of this acrobatic feat, yet curiosity persists among the viewers:

> He could only be seen at certain angles so that the watchers had to pause at street corners, find a gap between buildings, or meander from the shadows to get a view unobstructed by cornice work, gargoyles, balustrades, roof edges…It was the dilemma of the watchers: they didn't want to wait around for nothing at all…but they didn't want to miss the moment either…Around the watchers, the city still made its everyday noises. (*LGWS*, 3)

In this opening set-piece, McCann corrals fantasy, illusion and reality; the expectant silence of the watchers and the commotion of the city morning; and the minute vulnerability of the human body amid the domineering concreted scale of the city. The repetitions, the habits of the everyday, are intruded upon by 'a dark toy against the cloudy sky' (*LGWS*, 3) – the 'walker'.

The build-up to the moment when the 'walker' steps off the edge of the tower captures the heteronomy of sounds and sights as the working day in Manhattan commences. McCann's description evokes the mobility, even the transience, of the city: 'Ferry whistles. The thrum of the subway. The M22 bus pulled in against the sidewalk, sighed down into a pot-hole. A flying chocolate wrapper touched against a fire hydrant. Taxi doors slammed…Revolving doors pushed quarters of conversation out into the street' (*LGWS*, 4). Snatches of urban sensuousness form the backdrop to the 'walker's' defiant artistic performance high above the street level bustle. Yet the fragmented sensory chaos of Manhattan is somehow nullified by the 'walker's' gesture; his presence on the skyline unifies the disparate lives into an integrated audience. His brazen act is received with reverent silence as the watchers mingle and convene in pockets on the pavements: 'Doctors. Cleaners. Prep chefs. Diamond merchants. Fish Sellers. Sad-jeaned whores. All of them reassured by the presence of one another' (LGWS, 4). The improbability of the sight and the rumours that it generates – 'he was some sort of cat burglar, that he'd been taken hostage, he was an Arab, a Cypriot, an IRA man, that he was really just a publicity stunt, a corporate scam' (LGWS, 5) – creates a tangible level of community between the gathered watchers. The slow, methodical preparations of the 'walker' allow time for the pedestrian audience to intrigue about his motivations, but more importantly, this period of silent viewing must be and is filled with expectancy and mystery. For those at street level, 'the waiting had been made magical…shared. The man above was a word they seemed to know, though they had not heard it before. Out he went' (LGWS, 7). Given the historical context in which the novel is set, a period during which New York City was rife with violent crime and drug addiction, as well as facing the prospect of financial bankruptcy, the image of the 'walker' perched on the highest building in the world is a signal utopian moment. And the significance of using Petit's daring in this fashion, and in a 9/11 novel, is touched upon in these exact terms by McCann. The moment of physical transcendence became a powerful symbolic act for McCann in the wake of 9/11, what he calls 'a spectacular act of creation'.[28] The private sufferings and griefs of ordinary people, which exist side by side with faith in possible recovery, are primary thematics of the novel, and Petit's walk catalyzes this possibility of redemption. Equally this emboldened creative act assembles disparate individuals in Manhattan, however briefly, and allows them to share a unique spectacle. In this sense, the 'walker's' gesture facilitates an instance of belonging and restores faith in the possibility of solidarity; it is suggestive of the numinous touching upon the banalities of the everyday. The 'walker' is apparitional on the Manhattan skyline, a spectre on the horizons of the visible and of the possible. But he is, most importantly, an agent of hope in the allegorical structure of the novel. His decision to step out onto the high wire is the ultimate act of faith: faith in oneself. And it is an inspirational, generous act offered to those who stop, wait and watch his sky-borne performance.

The wire walker's feat is an imaginative re-calibration of spatiality;

it is an unforeseen subversion of the logic of capitalist space. The hubris and the rational architecture of the World Trade Centre are challenged by the wire walker's re-casting of the twin towers as objects of acrobatic beauty. And the implications of the wire walker's actions are consummately expressed in the novel by the grieving Claire Soderberg: 'And an attempt at beauty. The intersection of a man with the city, the abruptly reformed, the newly appropriated public space, the city art. Walk up there and make it new. Making it a different space' (*LGWS*, 103). Claire's description has implicit references to Ezra Pound's Modernist injunction 'to make new', and to Karl Heinz Stockhausen's provocative statement that the World Trade Centre attacks were pieces of high art. Her reaction on hearing of the wire walker combines space as art, the redefinition of urban utility, and the aesthetics of violence, in particular in relation to 9/11. In this emotional processing of the wire walk, McCann touches upon: 9/11; the pursuit of arresting innovation in art; and the rousing utopian dynamism of the spatial re-conceptualization of iconic capitalist edifices. The twin towers were the concreted and glazed embodiment of a set of economic, political and cultural abstractions, and there is no gainsaying the symbolic violence of their destruction. But rather than dwell on the destructive levelling of the towers in 2001 as an act of incommensurable violence, McCann urges us to appreciate the imaginative spatial assault on the towers in 1974. The wire walk is, of course, a temporary performance, but no less affective for its brevity; it is a jolting act of faith and creativity. And the achievement, with its possibilities, are apprehended by Claire's husband, Solomon, who is the judge assigned to try and to sentence the wire walker after his arrest. For Solomon Soderberg:

> The tightrope walker was such a stroke of genius. A monument in himself. He had made himself into a statue, but a perfect New York one, a temporary one, up in the air, high above the city…He had gone to the World Trade Center and had strung his rope across the biggest towers in the world. The Two Towers. Of all places. So brash. So glassy. So forward-looking…The glass reflected the sky, the night, the colors: progress, beauty, capitalism. (*LGWS*, 248)

The wire walker not only stills and silences the gathered urban crowds, but he carves a monument out of thin air. The spectacle of the walker undermining rationality as he draws his audience skyward, re-imagines the potential use of the twin towers. These other monuments, to financial functionalism, are alternatively deployed by the wire walker's performance. His act and his art are highly impractical, and they are, in fact, treated as criminal. But the brazen creativity displayed infects the lives of those that witness the walk first hand, and those that hear of it subsequently. The walk may not change the ways in which spatiality is conceived of and produced in New York City, and it does not alter the spatial employment of the twin towers. But the wire walker's gesture opposes 9/11 in pre-emptive fashion with an act of daring creation. The tightrope walk defies belief, but is equally motored by the belief and the faith of the walker, and, again, flags the roles of faith and belief in the overall narrative. The wire walker, then, performs a utopian spatial act that strikes one of the thematic keynotes of *Let the Great World Spin*.

The wire walker's sky-borne theatre anticipates, but creatively contradicts, the spectacular spatial violence of 9/11. And the realms of the visual and the creative are not confined to this astounding air-borne act – the novel sees creativity constantly jousting with destructive impulses. If we bracket *Let the Great World Spin* as a 9/11 novel, then part of its distinctiveness within this subgenre of fictions is not only its authorship by a non-American-born novelist, but also its anachronicity to the events and its emphasis on differential acts and forms of creativity, from the wire walker to graffiti art and failed mainstream painters. Corrigan may be the most explicit embodiment of lived redemption and faith in the novel, and the wire walker does suggest hope in his physical and imaginative performance, but there are less prominent but telling exercises of creative imagination and redemptive grace across the narrative. And it is the tenacity of creativity that McCann offers as a respite to even the most acute of grief and tragedy. *Let the Great World Spin* clings to the belief that in the wake of extreme loss, in the gloom of catastrophe, life must and can proceed. Basic human faith, generosity of spirit, and fertile creativity are constants in human history, in the same way that violent tragedy persists across history. The wire walker is not the only 'visual' artist in the novel: Lara is a painter, but more interestingly, McCann takes us into the underground and to the world of urban graffiti in 'Book Two'.

At the beginning of 'Book Two' we move to the New York subway system – a retreat, again, to the landscape of *This Side of Brightness*. The 'Tag' chapter is a fleeting but revealing third-person narration of a teenager's obsession with the 'Zoo York' culture of urban graffiti. The boy, Fernando, rides precariously in the crook of the subway carriages hoping to discover new graffiti tags and to capture them in photographs. McCann's account of the clandestine cataloguing of a guerrilla art form has overtones of a subterranean wire walker: 'He surfs the thin metal platform as the train jags south out of Grand Central. At times he gets dizzy, just anticipating the next corner. That speed. That wild noise in his ears. The truth is, it frightens him. The steel thrumming through him. It's like he has the whole train in his sneakers. Control and oblivion' (*LGWS*, 167). The visceral intensity and potential violence of this pursuit of art has a parallel in the exertions of the wire walker, who is preparing for his first sky-borne step at the very moment that this boy is scavenging the underground for illicit art. In much the same way that Corrigan and the wire walker are embodiments of spatial and hopeful extremes, this boy is one end of the spectrum of beauty and, again, the wire walker the other. Yet both are linked by their faith and by the riskiness of their search for beauty in what are marginal aesthetic forms. But not only does the boy find beauty in the darkest corners of the New York subway, he locates the hope that sustains his everyday life. Seeking out new, distinctive graffiti tags is 'the only thing that oils the hinges of his day'. For this disaffected teenager, 'everything else crawls, but the tags climb up into eyeballs' (*LGWS*, 167). What we see is quite literally an underground art, which retains an enlivening and enabling energy because the search for the artistic artefact is as important as the piece of art. Of equal significance is the doubly visual emphasis at this point. The illicit visual register of the urban graffiti is recorded and unearthed by the boy's photographic seizures, so that the power of the visual is accented again by McCann. Affective visions that inspire, provoke, and shock are commonplace across *Let the Great World Spin*, and this is another of the thematic strands that foreshadows the spectacular atrocity of 9/11. McCann's novel encompasses the most public spectacle as well as the least accessible visual media, pointing towards the saturation of modern culture by visual agents. Its omnipresence is not necessarily retrograde; certainly its gross commercialism is suffocating, but in this novel, the visual is frequently a register of insight, respite, desire, and silent rapture.

In other ways, by foregrounding the visual, McCann reminds us of its basic sensuality; visual culture often lets us forget its rootedness in the human body as a sensory experience. Both the wire walker and the graffiti hunter are figured in terms of the visual, but also as performing potentially fatal physical actions. Each of their pursuits of beauty is dependent upon carceral danger and stress and, thus, the achievement of aesthetic beauty, its visual record, are essentially bodily experiences. The wire walker compels his watchers to stop and look up, and in this action he demands an alternative use of the body in space, an alternative orientation of the body in public space. Public space is re-fashioned on this morning, the conveyor belt pavements of Manhattan are transformed into muted viewing galleries. And this is central to the utopian imagining of the novel. *Let the Great World Spin*, therefore, refuses to accept the inability of the ordinary to inspire and to accept only despair without the possibility of recovery from grief. The underground, as in *This Side of Brightness*, might be assumed to be the horizon of dejection and vagrancy, but even here, art is produced despite physical risk and the proximity of death. The 'Zoo York' graffiti is arduously created and recorded, and this difficulty is part of the fascination for the young boy:

> It's a mystery to him if the writers ever get to see their own tags, except maybe one step back in the tunnel after it's finished and not even dry. Back over the third rail for a quick glance. Careful, or it's a couple of thousand volts. And even then there's the possibility that a train will come. Or the cops make it down with a spray of flashlights and billy clubs. Or some long-haired puto will step out of the shadows, white eyes shining, knife blade ready, to empty out their pockets, crush and gut. Slam that shit on quick, and out you go before you get busted. (*LGWS*, 170)

All three, then, the wire walker, the graffiti artists, and the young photographic chronicler are interconnected by the physical risk of their aesthetic expressions. Just as the wire walker's tense balancing act is a physical and figurative evocation of the idea of the volatility of equilibrium in our daily lives, these latter underground artists perform their own funambulist feats. This is a continuation of McCann's interest in the notion of balance, which, again, sends us back to *This Side of Brightness*. Balance as a psychological state, as a physical action, and as a figural device unites these two New York novels. But in spotlighting equilibrium in *Let the Great World Spin*, McCann moves from an opening performance of acrobatic balance to the vulnerabilities of ordinary, earth-bound and buffeted lives on the streets. All of his characters are funambulists, they all are forced to take risks and are all delicately perched between life and death, and hope and despair. Fernando's brief appearance in the novel is resonant in a number of directions, not least for its reminder that the tedium of the mundane is often the source of the beautiful and the inspirational. As he mulls on the nature of art while sweeping the floor of his stepfather's barbershop: 'There was a guy he saw once on television who made his money knocking bricks out of buildings. It was funny but he understood it in a way. The way the light came through. Making people see differently. Making them think twice. You have to look on the world with a shine like no one else has' (*LGWS*, 173). This is precisely the role that Corrigan and the wire walker play in the novel, and it is the aspiration of the young boy. The wire walker halts his watchers, Corrigan forces others to reflect on the value of the most worthless of discarded lives, and Fernando wants to disinter, and to acclaim, the aesthetic charge of the subterranean graffiti. It is in these unlikely corners that the utopian aesthetic of McCann's work is apparent. The redemptive possibilities of art and the locations of this art are in scenes of everyday functionality *and* everyday dysfunctionality.

FAITH, DESPAIR AND REDEMPTION

Despite the resolutely American locale of the novel, it is book-ended by the landscape of Ireland – not the fantastical topographies of the west of Ireland, but the dour urban vistas of Dublin in the 1950s and, later, 2006. Ireland's presence registers the umbilical link that existed between the two countries via emigration during the twentieth century. But the insertion of an Irish character, John Corrigan, as one of the protagonists, arguably the central personality, permits the introduction of religious faith into the narrative. Corrigan's religious vocation, rooted in Catholicism, but gradually receding from its institutional forms, is key to the enactment of redemption in the story. He is a 'character who's in conflict...[and] I wanted to embrace the expansiveness, the beauty of spirit, the generosity, the decency that actually is embedded in the faith and in the Church'.[29] Corrigan's devotion to the sufferings of others compels him to leave Ireland and to abandon Europe entirely – he is constantly in search of ever greater abjection to which he can devote his spiritual and physical labour. In thinking about the worldview of this character, McCann concludes: 'So you force yourself into a position of difficulty, because it seems to me that we have forgotten...the excellence of difficulty...But there's something really beautiful in the notion of difficulty.'[30] Both the beauty and the excellence of difficulty are evident in Corrigan and the 'walker' – both challenge themselves and test their respective faiths, and both, in the end, offer some hope of redemption to those lives that are affected by their actions. Difficulty, trauma, despair – these seem to have been the primary responses to 9/11 that soon mutated into anger and an appetite for recompense. But for McCann these emotions, these apparent obstacles, are not necessarily devoid of or removed from hope and renewal.

From the outset Corrigan is marked as a unique personality and throughout the novel he is mediated second-hand – apart from one brief confessional interlude. We learn most about Corrigan through his brother's first-person narrative, a narrative that wrestles with one brother's efforts to comprehend the other's excessive immersion in poverty and human misery. As relayed by his brother, Corrigan's entire life from childhood was animated by a compulsion to seek out and to aid those in destitution. Corrigan's life is dictated by an ongoing series of personal sacrifices to physical suffering in the hope of furnishing spiritual succour. As a child Corrigan 'had no idea that his presence sustained people, made them happy, drew out their improbable yearnings' (*LGWS*, 14), and one of the issues raised by Corrigan's early death in the novel is: how can his family, lover and friends sustain themselves in his absence? In these formative years, 'Corrigan liked those places where light was drained. The docklands. The flophouses...He often sat with drunks in Frenchman's lane and Spencer Row...It was a ritual he couldn't give up. The down-and-outs needed him, or at least wanted him – he was, to them, a mad, impossible angel' (*LGWS*, 15–17). Recalling the 'walker', Corrigan is intermittently portrayed as, and might easily be read as, a character with supernatural capabilities. Certainly Corrigan's brother casts him in the role of spiritual healer or saintly seer, and his untimely death in a motor accident has the aura of a martyred demise. Again, in his youth, the drunks of Dublin's inner city might well have viewed Corrigan as an angel, but in later life, as his brother habituates himself to the privations of Corrigan's routine in the Bronx, he is figured in sacrificial and saintly terms. For his brother, Corrigan is one of 'thirty-six hidden saints in the world, all of them doing the work of humble men, carpenters, cobblers, shepherds' (*LGWS*, 44). Corrigan's selfless and anonymous vocation among the drug-addled prostitutes and abandoned elderly of the Bronx is part of the difficulty detailed by McCann. He is one of the hidden saints that 'bore the sorrows of the earth and…had a line of communication with God, all except one…who was forgotten…Corrigan had lost his line with God: he bore the sorrows on his own, the story of stories' (*LGWS*, 44). The naked sacrifice of Corrigan's life is just as suggestive of a Christ-like existence – a martyred redeemer of the wretched of the earth. And here there is a further symmetry to the figure of the wire walker as a transcendent or resurrected cruciform figure on the skyline. However, it is Corrigan's plight that is, in the end, more important to McCann. While he may be figured as a symbolic and religious icon, Corrigan's work is materially and grossly earthbound. From the docile drunks of Dublin, Corrigan's faith-bound mission takes him to larger-scale geographies of decrepitude. It is an American landscape alien to his visiting brother from popular culture, one that is oppressive and ransacked:

> Corrigan drove me through the South Bronx under the flared-up sky…Arson…Gangs of kids hung out on the street corners. Traffic lights were stuck on permanent red…A building on Willis had half collapsed into the street. A couple of wild dogs picked their way through the ruin…Every now and then a figure emerged from the shadows, homeless men pushing shopping trolleys piled high with copper wire. (*LGWS*, 48)

The lived context of Corrigan's vocation is prostitution and drug addiction; he effectively dwells among a group of black prostitutes providing basic physical and emotional supports as they trade under the Major Deegan expressway bridge in the South Bronx. His dedication to these harassed women is absolute and is tested by repeated physical assaults by pimps, as well as the proximity of the prostitutes' semi-clad, sexualized bodies. Corrigan, the sexual innocent, is engaged in a mission to stretch the limits of his faith in the service of those most exposed to physical and sexual exploitation. In lives wracked by fear, Corrigan's minor gestures of humility and tolerance are occasional stays against overwhelming despair. The vocation pursued by Corrigan identifies him as an edifice of altruistic humanity and hope in the novel – a conduit of generosity to which many of the other characters in *Let the Great World Spin* are drawn and become dependent. But there is remoteness to Corrigan at the same time, which again is suggestive of his presence as an angelic or Christ-like figure. The excess of his faith and his unyielding commitment to alleviating pain are, at times, incomprehensible to his family. Again his brother, Ciaran, at first cannot fathom a vocation that embraces the ruins of New York City and of humanity. But it is precisely within the ruins that Corrigan divines everyday beauty, and it is out of such ruination that his faith gains its strength and legitimacy. Only with the benefit of hindsight can Ciaran apprehend the bases of his brother's faith, a faith that is Christian but ecumenical, that is spiritual but rooted in material privations of the banal, and that inhabits despair but is un-quenchably hopeful. Corrigan's God is 'one you could find in the grime of the everyday' and his conviction 'was that life could be capable of small beauties' (*LGWS*, 20). Corrigan is a pillar of faith and hope in *Let the Great World Spin*, and his death is a figuration of the felling of one of the twin towers in 2001. His life, though enigmatic, is a moral compass to those in his life. Though the wire walker opens the novel and his feat awes and stills early-morning Manhattan, his performance becomes less important as the novel progresses. The twin poles of extreme height at the World Trade Centre and the lows of ghetto life in the South Bronx are symbolic of the proximity of hope and hopelessness, of looking up in wonder and living life at ground level. But for McCann it is the beauty of the terrestrial and the unre-markable that becomes more significant in the end. Indeed, this is a thematic constant throughout his fiction; there are moments of elevated aesthetic beauty, but, more often, McCann endorses the agency of the marginal voice.

On his arrival in the South Bronx, Ciaran Corrigan is dazed by the mouldering vistas of his brother's neighbourhood. As he scans his surroundings, the Major Deegan expressway catches his attention with its 'light-streak of cars zipping above' *(LGWS,* 24). But in another juxtaposition of elevation and interment, it is what is below the bridge of the expressway that proves most distracting:

> Below, by the underpass, a long line of women. Cars and trucks were pulling into the shadows. The women struck poses. They wore hotpants and bikini tops and swimsuits, a bizarre city beach. An angled arm, in the shadowlight, reached the top of the expressway. A stiletto climbed up the top of a barbed-wire fence. A leg stretched half the length of a city block. *(LGWS,* 24)

In this gloomy snapshot, several key motifs and themes of the novel are in evidence: the body, spectacle, performance, incongruous sightings, urban netherworlds, and the proximity of predation. The cabal of prostitutes is introduced as a faceless litany of erotic objects, out of which two emerge over the duration of the novel: the mother and daughter, Tillie and Jazzlyn Henderson. But in this glimpse, they are all Hadean figures, and objects of coarse sexual desires; the scene takes us back to Treefrog's milieu in *This Side of Brightness* and the existence of sites of New York City's 'unconscious'. The latter half of the description expresses the uncanny nature of this sight for Ciaran: an urban beach image, which is distorted by the play of light and shadow. Ciaran's obscured observation of this scene of sexual exploitation is consistent with his initial failure to grasp the gravity of his brother's vocation. Similarly, this passage is a shadowed dismemberment of female bodies and the prostitutes' bodies are projected objects of male sexual desire. Yet the silhouetted shapes retain a certain beauty, in that there is nothing intrinsically debased about the images that are detailed here. Their bodies, in particular their attire, enforce the idea of hyper-sexualization, but the performances alluded to in their poses do not prohibit their potential beauty. The prostitutes are essentially performing, but their tragedy is that they are compelled into these degrading performances through financial pressure, drug addiction, and preclusion from even the slightest social mobility.

Ciaran is initiated into his brother's 'underground' culture, which is physically remote from the centre of the city's consciousness, is legally proscribed and policed in cynical ways, and is indicative of the broader moral corruption in the city. It is in these circumstances that Ciaran's lessons and his ultimate redemption through understanding his brother's devotional labour are located. Continuing with the motifs of balance and performance, the prostitutes that Ciaran is confronted with, especially Tillie and Jazzlyn, are further instances of the precariousness of walking life's everyday tightropes. The potential for violence that each of these women faces on a daily basis in their profession constitutes another of the novel's 'balancing acts'. As we discover, there is an integrated resilience to the prostitutes, which Corrigan attempts to husband in his charitable actions. And one of McCann's concerns is to show the thin border that separates such ordinary resilience and despair. The excessive posturing and semi-naked presentation of their bodies is underwritten by fear, and these are daily demonstrations of their diminished dignity. Yet still they persist. This, for McCann, is the real triumph of the novel, and, again, it is one of the lessons that Ciaran has to learn. He must learn to see past the scene of his first impression and arrive at an understanding of the vulnerable humanity of these women, a humanity that deserves to be heeded, that needs to be heeded in order to preserve its basic dignity.

The visual and the performative are also evident in the lingering erotics of the body on display throughout the novel. We get repeated omniscient and subjective descriptions of and references to characters' physicality. Just as there is an overt physicality to the wire walker's performance and in the combined artistic outputs from the subway tunnels, the narrative dwells on the intimate details of the prostitutes' somatic features – in privileging the body in motion, under stress and in the midst of urban ruination and moral degeneration. As touched upon above, Ciaran's view of the provocative bodily performances of the prostitutes is, at first, suspicious – the women are anonymous objects:

> I woke later to the parasol hooker slamming through the doorway. She stood mopping her brow, then threw her handbag on the sofa beside me...She walked across the room, hitching off her fur coat as she went, naked but for her boots...Her calf muscles were smooth and curved. She hitched the flesh of her bottom, sighed, then stretched and rubbed her nipples full. (*LGWS*, 25)

Using Corrigan's apartment as a bathroom facility, the prostitutes are part of the domestic traffic of his life, but exist at a distance from his visiting brother. McCann's descriptions, which are numerous, attend to the sensuous physicality of these women. They are specimens of physical prowess that reside in a landscape and culture of menace, exploitation, and violence. This is a physical eroticism that is, however, exposed, cheapened and vulnerable, an erotic that reduces the human dignity of the women. And it is the diminution of this dignity that Corrigan's vocational interventions strive to correct. In two successive impressions delivered by Ciaran of one of the youngest prostitutes, Jazzlyn, we grasp the ambiguity of this base erotic of the streets. His view of Jazzlyn reveals the hollowness of the performative poses that are struck daily underneath the Major Deegan expressway. As she enters Corrigan's apartment, Ciaran describes her presence: 'The tallest, in a white tissue minidress, sat down beside me. She looked half Mexican, half black. She was taut and lithe: She could have been walking down a runway…She was very young…with one green eye, one brown. Her cheekbones were pulled even higher by a line of make-up' (*LGWS*, 28). What is remarkable about this portrait is the confluence of the titillating sartorial exposure of her minidress, and the uncertainty of Jazzlyn's ethnic origins. In addition, the fact that her eyes are of two different colours not only recalls Irish oral folk-lore, but can be wedded to the mystery of her ethnicity and, as we learn, the uncertainty of her paternity. She is, at this point, the mother of two young children, and it is their fate to become the primary focus of Corrigan's project in the South Bronx. Jazzlyn's life and death, and her children's lives, reach outwards across the novel via Corrigan to touch upon Solomon and Claire Soderberg, Gloria, Ciaran, and Lara. With the wire walker, Corrigan and Jazzlyn, *Let the Great World Spin* is a novel of connections. Its structure may appear to partake of a postmodernist fragmentation through its dissonant chorus of lives. But there is an underlying unity of purpose to McCann's plural narrative. Despite Jazzlyn's striking physical beauty, there is an equal measure of vulnerability; her pose might intimate agency, but with each performance a fraction of dignity is squandered. And this tone is captured in Ciaran's simile: 'She looked like some failed sunflower' (*LGWS*, 29).

In her narrative of mourning, Adelita, Corrigan's lover, recalls his thoughts on the idea of faith: 'He told me once that there was no better faith than a wounded faith and sometimes I wonder if that was what he was doing all along – trying to wound his faith in order to test it – and I was just another stone in the way of his God' (*LGWS*, 284). Adelita's sentiments are congruent with Corrigan's wish to aid those in most need and to travel to the most deprived locales in order to seek out destitution. Equally, it is consonant with McCann's reference to the attractiveness of difficulty. Does Corrigan couple faith with one's ability to challenge that faith? Is one's faith only as strong as the capacity to withstand tests of that faith? Adelita's reflections here are, conceivably, informed by her grief at Corrigan's death, but they magnify the kernel of Corrigan's vocation. Corrigan's material life in the South Bronx is spare and impoverished and is, perhaps, the easier test of his faith. What Adelita refers to is, firstly, the romantic relationship that developed between Corrigan and her, and, secondly, the suggestion that Corrigan's work and life among the prostitutes is another way of confronting the celibacy of his vocation. In very different ways, Corrigan is faced with his own sexuality, with sexuality per se, and as a religious, this clearly impinges on one of the fundamentals of his doctrinal duties. The dynamics of both crucibles of sexuality are discrepant, but both, in a sense, manage to humanize Corrigan. He is not left as an inscrutable martyred monk, but develops as a physical masculine character. In other words, he emerges from the realms of the purely spiritual to negotiate the carnal materialities of his humanity.

As the passages from Ciaran's earlier narrative disclose, Corrigan inhabits a terrain of sexual exploitation, commoditized eroticism, and carnal trade. And it is not to suggest that Corrigan is ever likely to indulge in any of this sexual performance; it is the proximity of this naked sub-culture that represents the examination of his faith. The daily depravity, the cruel cynicism, and disposable human sexuality surely weigh on the rigour of Corrigan's religious belief: where can one divine redemption in this squalid urban morass? Yet he insists that it can and that it must be uncovered and cherished. In other ways, the charged sexuality of Jazzlyn is occasionally focused on Corrigan. Again there is no overt clue that this is anything other than playful but, regardless, McCann's scrupulous attention to the visual 'embodiment' of Jazzlyn's performance is a reminder of Corrigan's masculine sexuality.

He may not act his sexuality out in this context but Jazzlyn's sexualized play indirectly alludes to the presence of Corrigan's sexual potentials: 'Jazzlyn wore a one-piece neon swimsuit. She tugged the back, snapped the elastic, edged closer to him a hint of a belly dance against his hip. She was tall, exotic, so very young she seemed to flutter' (*LGWS*, 35). While on another occasion, as Corrigan walks through the throng of prostitutes:

> Jazzlyn stood chatting with him, her thumb under the strap of her swimsuit...She leaned close to him again, her bare skin almost touching his lapel. He did not recoil. She was getting a charge from it all, I could tell. The lean of her young body. The hard snap of the strap. Her nipple against the fabric. Her head tilting closer and closer to him. (*LGWS*, 38)

Not only is there a sexual charge to Jazzlyn's provocative posturing, but it seems that in witnessing and in narrating these episodes, there is a voyeuristic visual pleasure derived by Ciaran.

As Adelita hints, there seems to have been an undercurrent to her relationship with Corrigan that was tied to his spirituality. Adelita is a Lutheran nurse employed at a home for the elderly, where Corrigan provided weekly help. And it is the evolution and potential consummation of this relationship that foments Corrigan's sustained emotional and spiritual crisis. In an extended confession to his brother, Ciaran, Corrigan divulges details of the tension between his profound love for Adelita and the strictures of his vocation. His religious vows of celibacy are not worn lightly and the carnal desires aroused by his devotion to Adelita are sources of intense guilt. The virginal Corrigan even expresses the effects of his first physical contact with Adelita in guilt-ridden language. He comprehends the stimulation of carnal desire in the early phases of this relationship with Adelita as a test and as feelings that must be combated. Their first quasi-sexual encounter, which is nominally physiotherapeutic, becomes a trial for Corrigan. As Adelita massages the inside of his arm, he is assailed by an instinctive guilt: 'And there was a voice inside me saying, "Strengthen yourself against this, this is a test, be ready, be ready." But it's the same voice I don't like. I'm looking behind the veil of it and all I see is this woman, it's a catastrophe, I'm descending, sinking like a hopeless swimmer. And I'm saying, God don't allow this to happen. Don't let it' (*LGWS*, 51). The steady control of Corrigan's religious faith is again under scrutiny at this point – there is yet another loss of equilibrium as his commitment to religious vows is tested. But Adelita and her life with her two young children soon allows Corrigan to calibrate his spiritual fervour and his romantic affections. The difficulty of Adelita's life as an emigrant, a single parent and as a member of the economic under-classes re-focuses Corrigan's view of his relationship with her. Though he never outgrows the bonds of his religious celibacy: 'On Sundays I still feel the old urges, the residual feelings. That's when the guilt hits most. I walk along, the Our Father in my mind. Over and over again. To cut the edge off the guilt' (*LGWS*, 56). Corrigan arrives at a liveable but uneasy reconciliation between his religiosity and his sexuality. And vocalizing his anguished state of mind to his brother is liberating and redemptive for Corrigan. The fear of failing his vocation, of betraying his faith, is matched by his unwillingness to abandon Adelita, as McCann does not offer a facile or unproblematic resolution to Corrigan's balancing act. The tensile equilibrium of Corrigan's life is captured by the series of questions that signal the refusal of his crisis to end: 'What might happen if she tumbled short of his dreams? How much might he hate his God if he left her behind? How might he detest himself if he stuck to his Lord?' (*LG WS*, 58).

CREATING THE FUTURE

Though the wire walker's aerial performance is a singular act, as metaphor it is an act of union with the tightrope stitching the twin towers to each other. As we have seen, it is a radical spatial re-imagining as it utilizes the air-space between the buildings as a bridge rather than as a boundary. The wire walker, then, imagines a link out of nothingness and enacts a precocious feat of courage and balance. Such a resounding figuration necessarily carries throughout the novel, and another of the strands in which the motifs of boundaries and balance materialize is in the braided stories of Claire Soderberg, Gloria, and Jazzlyn's orphaned daughters. Claire and Gloria are members of a group of women who meet regularly as a support network for those who have suffered loss in the Vietnam War. The intrusion of geographical and military aggression in this local context, again, hints at the parallels being drawn by McCann between this historical period and the contemporary moment. The women are from different backgrounds, but none seem further apart than Claire, the Jewish wife of a Manhattan judge, and Gloria, a Southern-born, working-class single-mother of three deceased sons. Their respective geographical locations on Park Avenue and in the South Bronx confirm the social distance between the women, and re-enforces the social fragmentation of New York's urban tapestry along class and ethnic markers. Yet their relationship, though pock-marked by difference, is a testimony to the agency of redemptive solidarity that underpins the politics of the novel.

Claire's material wealth does little to compensate for the loss of her only son, Joshua, and her husband, Solomon, is routinely diffident about Joshua's death. And in the context of her support group, this wealth and apparent privilege are further barriers to genuine and unequivocal acceptance by the remainder of the women. On the day that the wire walker performs in downtown Manhattan, Claire hosts a meeting of the support group at her uptown apartment. At the close of this meeting a potentially irredeemable exchange occurs between Claire and Gloria. Claire pleads with Gloria to stay a while longer, but conflates her desire for company with an earlier thought that she might pay Gloria as a housekeeper, and offers Gloria money to stay. The exchange sets Gloria off on a prolonged walk from Park Avenue to Harlem and back to Claire's apartment. She returns after being mugged, and her decision to return to the scene of social embarrassment is instinctive rather than rational, but it enables a valuable reconciliation. The larger unit of the support group had been a means of talking over the past and of resurrecting the memories of dead children. But on Gloria's return to Park Avenue she intuitively resists dwelling exclusively on her deceased sons. When Claire inquires about her boys, Gloria thinks: 'I didn't want to think about my boys anymore. In a strange way, all I wanted was to be surrounded by another, to be a part of somebody else's room...I guess I wanted another sort of question altogether' (*LGWS*, 312). Without neglecting the memory of her sons, Gloria understands the burden of a melancholic fixation with the past. Levelling social, racial and geographical borders, the companionship that is shared by these two women – across many subsequent years, as we learn – is a connection forged despite difference. Their respective lives may have been assailed by the machinations of global politics, but there is the mutual recognition of humanity in their supportive relationship. The novel's insistent metaphor of the tightrope walk asserts the notion of connection. And despite the fractured structure of the narrative, connection is always possible, though not without difficulty, through imagination and acts of faith.

At the end of this day, 7 August 1974, as Claire drops Gloria at her building in the South Bronx, social workers are escorting Jaslyn and Janice, Jazzlyn's daughters, out of the same building. Throughout her time residing in this environment, Gloria has resolutely ignored the lives of squalor that thrived around her. But Jazzlyn's orphaned girls suddenly enter her life, a life that has been renewed with her new friendship with Claire. Symbolically, she is given a chance to save two lives after seeing three lives taken from her through warfare. Gloria alights from the car and 'saw them come out, two darling little girls coming through the globes of lamplight' (*LGWS*, 321). The lumines-cence prompts her memories of these girls and their deceased mother: 'I knew them. I had seen them before. They were the daughters of a hooker who lived two floors above me. I had kept myself away from all that. Years and years. I hadn't let them near my life. I'd see their mother in the doorway, a child herself, pretty and vicious, and I'd stare straight ahead at the buttons' (*LGWS*, 321). Wrapped in the difficul-ties of her own life, Gloria had previously abjured intervening in the lives of those in the projects. But at this moment, she chooses to extend herself in an act of unsolicited and selfless grace. The only motivation that she can reason for adopting the girls is that: 'It was a deep-down feeling that must've come from long ago' *(LGWS*, 285). Her charity is ineffable, and is, in the end, the culminating act of re-demption and hope in *Let the Great World Spin*. The narrative spools forward to 2006, to Jaslyn's brief contemporary narrative. The adult girls now live in post-9/11, post-Hurricane Katrina America, with international wars also ongoing. In temporal terms, McCann reaches past 9/11, framing a temporal link, instead, between 1974 and 2006. In this he urges us, again, to see connections between the possibility for redemption out of tragedies and conflict in the earlier period and similar opportunities in the current time. Symbolically, Jaslyn and Janice pursue 'political' occupations: Jaslyn works for a small foundation helping working-class victims of Hurricanes Katrina and Rita with tax forms, while Janice is in the US army. In fact Jaslyn's occupation is an oblique recollection of Corrigan's immersion in the plights of the discarded. And part of her vocation, her attentiveness to the practical bureaucratic needs of these people, allows her to appreciate the vulnerable yet passionate humanity of such forgotten communities. As Jaslyn reflects on her daily tasks she provides telling summative words on the structure of *Let the Great World Spin*, on the thematic of the potential healing power of relating one's story, and on the intimacy of dignity and self-representation:

> Sometimes it takes them an age just to sign, since they have something else to say – they are off and chatting about the cars they bought, the loves they loved. They have a deep need just to talk, just to tell a story, however small or reckless. Listening to these people is like listening to tress – sooner or later the tree is sliced open and the watermarks reveal their age. (*LGWS*, 337)

The stories that Jaslyn hears may be wildly divergent in form and content, much like the novel itself, but the driving impulses are the needs to share and to connect, and the desire to be heard. From the dizzying summit of the World Trade Centre towers to the recessed graffiti of the New York subway system and all spaces in between, there are stories and potential tellers of stories waiting to be heeded. Art is seen to embody a redemptive moral value system in contradistinction to the destabilizing values of murderous terrorism. Art facilitates a reflective, even temperate, coming to terms with 9/11; again, in contrast to impulses of rage or blind hostility evidenced elsewhere. And this is the context in which we should, finally, read *Let the Great World Spin*. As a work of art the novel advertises and embodies the durability of human creativity as a utopian resource. This literary fiction is exemplary of what Gilles Deleuze calls 'the realm of the possible'.[31] A realm neatly defined by Susheila Nasta and Elleke Boehmer as 'the visionary territory of the imagination, a world situated between the political and cultural borderlines of national/international struggles, a realm where it is the artist's imperative to keep speaking, to keep writing, to keep interrogating, to keep making art even in the face of terror itself, counter-insurgent or otherwise'.[32] It is a multivocal, democratic text that braids diverse narratives and lives together in varying patterns of unity and empathetic understanding. To the dominant US-centric narratives of post-9/11, McCann tenders a disjunctive counter-narrative that expands the horizons of what can be stabled as 9/11 literary fiction.

NOTES

1. Susan Sontag, *At the Same Time: Essays and Speeches* (London: Hamish Hamilton, 2007), p.121.
2. Susan Buck-Morss, *Thinking Past Terror: Islamism and Cultural Theory on the Left* (London: Verso, 2003), p.23.
3. Daniel Lea, 'Aesthetics and Anaesthetics: Anglo-American Writers' Responses to September 11', *Symbiosis: A Journal of Anglo-American Literary Relations*, 11, 2 (2007), p.4.
4. David Simpson, *9/11: The Culture of Commemoration* (London and Chicago: University of Chicago Press, 2006), p.126.
5. For example see Martha Nussbaum, *Love's Knowledge: Essays on Philosophy and Literature* (New York and Oxford: Oxford University Press, 1990).
6. Richard Kearney, *Strangers, Gods and Monsters: Interpreting Otherness* (London: Routledge, 2003), p.134.
7. Michael Rothberg, 'Seeing Terror, Feeling Art: Public and Private in Post-9/11 Literature', in Ann Keniston and Jeanne Follansbee Quinn (eds), *Literature after 9/11* (London: Routledge, 2008), p.124.
8. Ibid.
9. Ibid.
10. Ian McEwan, 'Only Love and then Oblivion', *Guardian* (15 September 2001).
11. Ibid.
12. Kearney, *Strangers, Gods and Monsters*, p.136.
13. Colum McCann, '*Let the Great World Spin* Interview', Colum McCann offical author website: www.colummccann. com/interviews.
14. Ibid.
15. Kristiaan Versluys, *Out of the Blue: September 11 and the Novel* (New York: Columbia University Press, 2009), p.3.
16. Simpson, *9/11: The Culture of Commemoration*, p.16.
17. See Slavoj Žižek, *Welcome to the Desert of the Real* (London: Verso, 2002).
18. Buck-Morss, *Thinking Past Terror*, p.23.
19. Martin Amis, 'Fear and Loathing', *Guardian* (18 September 2001). http://www.guardian.co. uk/world/2001/sep/18/september11.politicsphilosophyandsociety.
20. See Ann Keniston and Jeanne Follansbee Quinn's *Literature after 9/11*; Kristiaan Versluys' *Out of the Blue: September 11 and the Novel*; Dunja M. Mohr and Sylvia Mayer (eds), *Zeitschrift fur Anglistik und Americanistik – A Quarterly of Language, Literature and Culture – Special Issue: 9/11 as Catalyst: American and British Responses*; Daniel Lea, 'Aesthetics and Anaesthetics: Anglo-American Writers' Responses to September 11'.
21. Catherine Morley, 'The End of Innocence: Tales of Terror after 9/11', *Review of International American Studies*, 3, 3 and 1 (2008/2009), p.83.
22. McCann, '*Let the Great World Spin* Interview'.
23. Ibid.
24. Jacques Derrida argues: 'When you say "September 11" you are already citing…You are inviting me to speak here by recalling, as if in quotation marks, a date or a dating that has taken over our public space and our private lives for five weeks now. Something *fait date*, I would say in a French idiom, something marks a date, a date in history,' 'Autoimmunity: Real and Symbolic Suicides – A Dialogue with Jacques Derrida', in Giovanna Borradori (ed.), *Philosophy in a Time of Terror* (London and Chicago: University of Chicago Press, 2003), p.85.
25. McCann, '*Let the Great World Spin* Interview'.

26. Edward Soja, 'The Spatiality of Social Life: Towards a Transformative Retheorisation', in Derek Gregory and John Urry (eds), *Social Relations and Spatial Structures* (Basingstoke: Macmillan, 1985), p.94.
27. Colum McCann, *Let the Great World Spin* (London: Bloomsbury, 2009), p.3. All further references to *Let the Great World Spin* will appear in parenthesis as (*LGWS*).
28. Bret Anthony Johnston, 'Interview with Colum McCann', *National Book Award Website* www.nationalbook.org/nba2009_f_mccann_interv.html.
29. Chistopher Lydon, 'American Literature and New York's Redemption: An Interview with Colum McCann', *Huffington Post* (7 April 2010). http://www.huffingtonpost.com/ christopher-lydon/colum-mccann-american-lit_b_528881.html.
30. Ibid.
31. Elleke Boehmer and Susheila Nasta, 'Cultures of Terror', *Wasafiri – Special Issue on 'Cultures of Terror'*, 22, 2 (2007), p.1.
32. Ibid.

Bibliography

PRIMARY WORKS

Fishing the Sloe-Black River (London: Phoenix House, 1994).
Songdogs (London: Phoenix House, 1995).
This Side of Brightness (London: Phoenix House, 1998).
Everything in This Country Must (London: Phoenix House, 2000).
Dancer (London:Weidenfeld & Nicolson, 2003).
Zoli (London: Weidenfeld & Nicolson, 2006).
Let the Great World Spin (London: Bloomsbury, 2009).

OTHER PUBLICATIONS

McCann, Colum. 'The Tunnels Under New York City', *Fotoshoot Magazine*, A.1 (5 February 1995). www.fotoshow.com/magazine/ tunnels_ a.html.
McCann, Colum. 'The International Bastards', *Irish Echo Supplement*, (March 1998).
McCann, Colum and Hemon, Aleksandar. 'The Writer Sees in the Dark Corners Swept Clean by Historians', *Guardian* (30 June 2003). http://www.guardian.co.uk/ books/2003/jun/30/fiction.
McCann, Colum. 'The Heavens be his Bed', *Irish University Review – Special Issue – Benedict Kiely*, 38, 1 (2008), pp.64–71.
McCann, Colum. 'But Always Meeting Ourselves', *New York Times*, (16 June 2009). http://www.nytimes.com/2009/06/16/opinion/ 16mccann.html.

FILMS

A Basket Full of Wallpaper (1998) – adapted by Robert J Quinn; directed by Joe Lee.
Fishing the Sloe-Black River (1998) – script by Colum McCann; directed by Brendan Bourke.
When the Sky Falls (2000) – directed by John Mackenzie; co-written by Colum McCann.
Beautiful Kid (2003) – co-directed with Michael McCarthy.
Everything in This Country Must (2005) – script by Colum McCann; directed by Gary McKendry.
Colum McCann – Becoming a New Yorker (2009) – directed by Charlie McCarthy; RTÉ Arts Lives Series.

INTERVIEWS WITH COLUM McCANN

'*This Side of Brightness* Interview', Colum McCann official author website: www.colummccann.com/interviews.

'Interview with Colum McCann', Colum McCann official author website: www. colummccann.com/interviews.

'*Let the Great World Spin* Interview', Colum McCann official author website: www. colummc cann.com/interviews.

'There Goes Colum McCann, Telling His Bonfire Stories Again – An Interview with Colum McCann', http://www.powells.com/authors/ mccann.html.

'Interview with Colum McCann', *The Stinging Fly* (Summer 2003). http://www. stingingfly.org/issue9/mccann.html.

Battersby, Eileen. 'Coming Up for Air: An Interview with Colum McCann', *Irish Times* (15 January 1998).

Birnbaum, Robert. 'Interview with Colum McCann', *The Morning News* (2007). http://www.themorningnews.org/archives/ birnbaum_ v/colum_mccann.php.

Camelio, Stephen V. 'Interview with Colum McCann', *Nua: Studies in Contemporary Irish Writing*, 3, 1 and 3, 2 (2002).

Clancy, Luke. 'Writer and Wanderer: Interview with Colum McCann', *Irish Times* (21 June 1994).

Hughes, Carolyn T. 'Adventurist: Interview with Colum McCann', *Poets & Writers* (Jan/Feb 2007), pp.48–54.

Johnston, Bret Anthony. 'Interview with Colum McCann, *National Book Award Website:* www.nationalbook.org/nba2009_f_mccann_interv.html.

Kaufman, Marjorie. 'An Author Fishing for Souls of Irish Emigres', *Sunday New York Times* (10 November 1996).

Lennon, Joseph. 'An Interview with Fiction Writer Colum McCann', *Poets & Writers*, (2003). http://www.pw.org/content/interview_ fiction _writer_colum_mccann.

Lydon, Christopher. 'American Literature and New York's Redemption: An Interview with Colum McCann', *Huffington Post* (7 April 2010). http://www.huffingtonpost. com/christopher-lydon/colum mccann-american-lit_b_528881.html.

Metcalfe, Anna. 'Small Talk: Colum McCann', *Financial Times* (29 August 2009). http://www.ft.com/cms/s/2/7ea126ca-9362-11de-b146 00144feabdc0. html#axzz 16NnyntuC.

ESSAYS AND ARTICLES ON COLUM McCANN

Arrowsmith, Aidan. 'Photographic Memories: Nostalgia and Irish Diaspora Writing', *Textual Practice*, 19, 2 (2005), pp.297–322.

Brown, James S. 'Things Not Meant To Heal: Irish "National Allegory" in Doyle, McCabe and McCann', *Nua: Studies in Contemporary Irish Writing*, 1, 1 (1997), pp.31–51.

Cahill, Susan. 'Choreographing Memory: The Dancing Body and Temporality in *Dancer*', in Susan Cahill and Eóin Flannery (eds), *This Side of Brightness: Essays on the Fiction of Colum McCann* (Bern: Peter Lang, 2011).

Flack, Jack S. 'Telling Shots: Photography in/as/and Literature in Colum McCann's *Songdogs*', *Nua: Studies in Contemporary Irish Writing*, 4, 1 and 4, 2 (2003), pp.77–88.

Flannery, Eóin. 'Rites of Passage: Migrancy and Liminality in Colum McCann's *Songdogs* and *This Side of Brightness*', *Irish Studies Review*, 16, 1 (2008), pp.1–17.

————— 'Troubling Bodies: Suffering, Resistance and Hope in Colum McCann's "Troubles" Short Fiction', *The Irish Review*, 40 and 41 (2009), pp.33–51.

Fogarty, Anne. 'Contemporary Irish Fiction and the Transnational Imaginary', in Eamon Maher (ed.), *Cultural Perspectives on Globalisation and Ireland* (Bern: Peter Lang, 2009), pp.133–47.

Hand, Derek. 'Living in a Global World: Making Sense of Place in Colum McCann's *This Side of Brightness*', in Susan Cahill and Eóin Flannery (eds), *This Side of Brightness: Essays on the Fiction of Colum McCann* (Bern: Peter Lang, 2011).

Healy, John F. 'Dancing Cranes and Frozen Birds: The Fleeting Resurrections of Colum McCann', *New Hibernia Review* 4, 3 (2000), pp.107–18.

Lennon, Joseph, 'Colum McCann', in Michael R. Molino (ed.), *Dictionary of Literary Biography: Twenty-First-Century British and Irish Novelists* (Farmington Hills, MI: Thomson Gale Publishers, 2003), vol. 267, pp.181–91.

McGovern, Kelly. 'Burying Con O'Leary: New York Cartographies of Identity in Colum McCann's *This Side of Brightness*', in Gerhard Stilz (ed.), *Territorial Terrors: Contested Spaces in Colonial and Postcolonial Writing* (Wurzburg: Verlag Konigshausen & Neumann, 2007), pp.173–87.

Mara, Miriam. 'The Geography of Bodies: Borders in Edna O'Brien's *Down by the River* and Colum McCann's "Sisters"', in Helen Thompson (ed.), *The Current Debate about the Irish Literary Canon: Essays Reassessing* The Field Day Anthology of Irish Writing (Lewiston, NY and Lampeter: Mellen Press, 2006), pp.311–30.

Oates, Joyce Carol. 'An Endangered Species', *New York Review of Books* (29 June 2000), pp.38–41.

Wall, Eamonn. 'Winds Blowing from a Million Directions', in Charles Fanning (ed.), *New Perspectives on the Irish Diaspora* (Carbondale and Edwardsville, IL: Southern Illinois University Press, 2000), pp.281–8.

Willis-McCullough, David. 'Tunnel Vision', *New York Times on the Web* (5 April 1998). www.nytimes.com/pages/readersopinions/ index.html.

SECONDARY CRITICISM

Amis, Martin. 'Fear and Loathing', *Guardian* (18 September 2001). http://www.guardian.co.uk/world/2001/sep/18/september11.politicsphilosophyandsociety.

Aronson, Alex. *Music and the Novel: A Study in Twentieth-Century Fiction* (Totowa, NJ: Rowman & Littlefield, 1980).

Ashcroft, Bill. 'Critical Utopias', *Textual Practice*, 21, 3 (2007), pp.411–31.

Ashley, Kathleen M. (ed.), 'Introduction', in *Victor Turner and the Construction of Cultural Criticism: Between Literature and Anthro-pology* (Indianapolis, IN: Indiana University Press, 1990), pp.ix–xxii.

Balibar, Etienne. 'Foreword', in Nando Sigona and Nidhi Trehan (eds), *Romani Politics in Contemporary Europe: Poverty, Ethnic Mobilization and the Neoliberal Order* (Basingstoke: Palgrave, 2009), pp.viii–xiii.

Barenboim, Daniel. *Everything is Connected: The Power of Music* (London: Weidenfeld & Nicolson, 2008).

Beresford, David. *Ten Men Dead: The Story of the 1981 Irish Hunger Strike* (London: Grafton Books, 1987).

Bloch, Ernst. *The Principle of Hope* (Cambridge and London: MIT Press, 1986).

———— *The Utopian Function of Art and Literature: Selected Essays* (Minneapolis, MN: University of Minnesota Press, 1989).

Bloom, Harold. *Where Shall Wisdom Be Found?* (New York: Riverhead Books, 2004).

Boehmer, Elleke and Nasta, Susheila. 'Cultures of Terror', *Wasafiri – Special Issue on 'Cultures of Terror'*, 22, 2 (2007), pp.1–3.

Bolger, Dermot. 'Foreword', in Dermot Bolger (ed.), *Ireland in Exile: Irish Writers Abroad* (Dublin: New Island Books, 1993), pp.7–10.

———— 'Introduction', in Dermot Bolger (ed.), *The New Picador Book of Contemporary Irish Fiction* (London: Picador, 2000), pp.xi–xxxi.

Borradori, Giovanna. *A Philosophy in a Time of Terror: Dialogues with Jürgen Haber-mas and Jacques Derrida* (London and Chicago: University of Chicago Press, 2003).

Boscaljon, Daniel. 'Possibilities of Redemption through the Novel', in Andrew Hass, David Jasper and Elisabeth Jay (eds), *The Oxford Handbook of English Literature and Theology* (Oxford: Oxford University Press, 2007), pp.760–75.

Bourke, Angela. 'The Baby and the Bathwater: Cultural Loss in Nineteenth-Century Ireland', in Tadhg Foley and Seán Ryder (eds), *Ideology and Ireland in the Nine-teenth Century* (Dublin: Four Courts Press, 1998), pp.79–92.

Brewster, Scott. 'Rites of Defilement: Abjection and the Body Politic in Northern Irish Poetry', *Irish University Review*, 35, 2 (2005), pp.304–19.

Brown, Terence. *Ireland: A Social and Cultural History, 1922–2002* (London: Harper-Collins, 2002).

Buck-Morss, Susan. *Thinking Past Terror: Islamism and Cultural Theory on the Left* (London: Verso, 2003).

Burke, Mary. *Tinkers: Synge and the Cultural History of the Irish Traveller* (Oxford: Ox-ford University Press, 2009).

Carter, Paul. *The Road to Botany Bay* (London: Faber, 1987).

Carver, Raymond. *Fires: Essays, Poems, Stories* (New York: Vintage Books, 1984).

Castle, Gregory. *Reading the Modernist Bildungsroman* (Gainesville, FL: University Press of Florida, 2006).

Chakrabarty, Dipesh. 'Minority Histories, Subaltern Pasts', *Postcolonial Studies*, 1, 1 (1998), pp.15–29.

Cleary, Joe. *Literature, Partition and the Nation State: Culture and Conflict in Ireland, Israel and Palestine* (Cambridge: Cambridge University Press, 2002).

———— *Outrageous Fortune: Capital and Culture in Modern Ireland* (Dublin: Field Day Books, 2006).

Cohen Bull, C.J. 'Sense, Meaning, and Perception in Three Dance Cultures', in J.C. Desmond (ed.), *Meaning in Motion: New Cultural Studies of Dance* (Durham, NC and London: Duke University Press, 1997), pp.269–88.

Corcoran, Mary P. 'The Process of Migration and the Reinvention of Self: The Expe-riences of Returning Irish Emigrants', *Éire-Ireland*, 37, 1 and 2 (2002), pp.175–91.

Cronin, Michael. 'Inside Out: Time and Place in Global Ireland', in Eamon Maher (ed.), *Cultural Perspectives on Globalisation and Ireland* (Bern: Peter Lang, 2009), pp.11–30.

Deleuze, Gilles and Guattari, Felix. *Kafka: Towards a Minor Literature* (Minneapolis, MN and London: University of Minnesota Press, 1986).

Dempster, Elizabeth. 'Women Writing the Body: Let's Watch a Little How She Dances', in Susan Sheridan (ed.), *Grafts: Feminist Cultural Criticism* (London: Verso, 1988), pp.35–54.

Derrida, Jacques. 'Choreographies', *Points: Interviews, 1974–1994* (Stanford, CA: Stanford University Press, 1995), pp.89–108.

———— 'Autoimmunity: Real and Symbolic Suicides – A Dialogue with Jacques Derrida', in Giovanna Borradori (ed.), *Philosophy in a Time of Terror* (London and Chicago: University of Chicago Press, 2003), pp.85–136.

Doloughan, Fiona. 'The Myth of the Great Return: Memory, Longing and Forgetting in Milan Kundera's *Ignorance*', in Michael Hanne (ed.), *Creativity in Exile* (New York and Amsterdam: Rodopi, 2004), pp.141–50.

Dow Adams, Timothy, 'Introduction: Life Writing and Light Writing: Autobiography and Photography', *Modern Fiction Studies*, 40, 3 (1994), pp.459–92.

Fabian, Johannes. *Time and the Other: How Anthropology Makes its Object* (New York: Columbia University Press, 1983).

Feldman, Allen. *Formations of Violence: The Narrative of the Body and Political Terror in Northern Ireland* (Chicago and London: University of Chicago Press, 1991).

Fennell, Desmond. *The State of the Nation: Ireland since the Sixties* (Dublin: Ward River Press, 1983).

Fonseca, Isabel. *Bury Me Standing: The Gypsies and their Journey*, (London: Vintage, 1995).

Forkner, Ben. 'The Irish Short Story (1980–2000): Ireland Anthologized', *Etudes Anglaises*, 54, 2 (2001), pp.151–66.

Fournier, Valerie. 'Utopianism and the Cultivation of Possibilities: Grassroots Movements of Hope', in Martin Parker (ed.), *Utopia and Organization* (Oxford: Blackwell, 2002), pp.189–216.

Geoghegan, Vincent. *Ernst Bloch* (London: Routledge, 1996).

Habermas, Jürgen. 'Fundamentalism and Terror: A Dialogue with Jürgen Habermas', in Giovanna Borradori (ed.), *Philosophy in a Time of Terror* (London and Chicago: University of Chicago Press, 2003), pp.25–43.

Hagan, Edward A. *Goodbye Yeats and O'Neill: Farce in Contemporary Irish and Irish-American Narratives* (New York and Amsterdam: Rodopi, 2010).

Hancock, Ian. 'The Struggle for the Control of Identity', in Michael Hayes (ed.), *Road Memories: Aspects of Migration History* (Newcastle: Cambridge Scholars Publishing, 2007), pp.1–19.

Hand, Derek. *Irish University Review – Special Issue – John Banville*, 36, 1 (Spring/Summer 2006), pp.viii–xii.

Harte, Liam and Parker, Michael (eds), *Contemporary Irish Fiction: Themes, Tropes, Theories* (Basingstoke: Palgrave, 2000).

Heaney, Carmel (ed.), *Ireland Worldwide: The Newsletter of The Irish Diaspora* (November 1993), volume 1, pp.1–8.

Heaney, Seamus. *The Spirit Level* (London: Faber & Faber, 1996).
——————— *Finders Keepers: Selected Prose 1971–2001* (London: Faber & Faber, 2002).
——————— *District and Circle* (London: Faber & Faber, 2006).

Hepburn, Allan. 'Noise, Music, Voice, *Dubliners*', in Sebastian Knowles (ed.), *Bronze by Gold: The Music of Joyce* (New York and London: Garland Publishing, 1999), pp.189–212.

Herron, Tom. 'The Body's in the Post: Contemporary Irish Poetry and the Dispersed Body', in Colin Graham and Richard Kirkland (eds), *Ireland and Cultural Theory: The Mechanics of Authenticity* (Basingstoke: Macmillan, 1999), pp.193–209.

Hillan, Sophia. 'Wintered Into Wisdom: Michael McLaverty and Seamus Heaney, and the Northern Word-Hoard', *New Hibernia Review*, 9, 3 (2005), pp.86–106.

Hutcheon, Linda. *The Politics of Postmodernism* (London and New York: Routledge, 1989).

Huyssen, Andreas. 'Introduction: World Cultures, World Cities', in Andreas Huyssen (ed.), *Other Cities, Other Worlds: Urban Imaginaries in a Globalizing Age* (Durham, NC and London: Duke University Press, 2008), pp.1–23.

Imhof, Rudiger. *The Modern Irish Novel: Irish Novelists after 1945* (Dublin: Wolfhound Press, 2002).

Ingman, Heather. *A History of the Irish Short Story* (Cambridge: Cambridge University Press, 2009).

Jeffers, Jennifer M. *The Irish Novel at the End of the Twentieth Century: Gender, Bodies, and Power* (Basingstoke: Palgrave, 2002).

Jenkins, Richard. *Refiguring History: New Thoughts on an Old Discipline* (London and New York: Routledge, 2003).

Kearney, Richard. *On Stories* (London: Routledge, 2002).

———— *Strangers, Gods and Monsters: Interpreting Otherness* (London: Routledge, 2003).

Kelly, Aaron. *The Thriller and Northern Ireland since 1969: Utterly Resigned Terror* (Aldershot: Ashgate, 2005).

Keniston, Ann and Follansbee Quinn, Jeanne (eds), *Literature after 9/11* (New York and London: Routledge, 2008).

Kennedy-Andrews, Elmer. *Fiction and the Northern Ireland Troubles since 1969: (De-) constructing the North* (Dublin: Four Courts Press, 2003).

———— 'The Novel and the Northern Troubles', in John Wilson Foster (ed.), *The Cambridge Companion to the Irish Novel* (Cambridge: Cambridge University Press, 2006), pp.238–58.

Kiberd, Declan. 'White Skins, Black Masks? Celticism and *Négritude*', *Éire-Ireland*, 31, 1 and 31, 2 (1996), pp.163–75.

Kundera, Milan. *The Curtain* (London: Faber, 2007).

Lea, Daniel. 'Aesthetics and Anaesthetics: Anglo-American Writers' Responses to September 11', *Symbiosis: A Journal of Anglo-American Literary Relations*, 11, 2 (2007), pp.3–26.

Lee, Hermione. *Virginia Woolf's Nose: Essays on Biography* (Princeton, NJ and Oxford: Princeton University Press, 2005).

Leigh Foster, Susan. 'Dancing Bodies', in Jonathan Cary and Sandford Kwinter (eds), *Incorporations* (New York: Urzone, 1992), pp.480–95.

Lepecki, Andre. *Exhausting Dance: Performance and the Politics of Movement* (New York and Abingdon: Routledge, 2006).

Levitas, Ruth. *The Concept of Utopia* (Bern: Peter Lang, 2010).

Levitas, Ruth and Moylan, Tom. 'Introduction: The Once and Future Orpheus', *Utopian Studies – Special Issue: Music and Utopia*, 21, 2 (2010), pp.204–14.

Liegois, Jean-Pierre. *Gypsies: An Illustrated History* (London, 1985).

Lingard, Joan. *Across the Barricades* (London: Hamish Hamilton, 1972).

Louvel, Lilian, Menegaldo, Gilles and Fortin, Anne-Laure. 'An Interview with Ian McEwan', *Études Britanniques Contemporaines*, vol.8, (1995), pp.1–12.

McCabe, Eugene. *Christ in the Fields* (London: Minerva, 1993).

McCabe, Patrick. *The Butcher Boy* (London: Picador, 1992).

McDonald, Ronan. 'Strategies of Silence: Colonial Strains in Short Stories of the Troubles', *The Yearbook of English Studies*, 35, 1(January 2005), pp.249–63.

McEwan, Ian. 'Only Love and then Oblivion,' *Guardian* (15 September 2001).

McVeigh, Robbie. 'Theorising Sedentarism: The Roots of Anti-Nomadism', in Thomas Acton (ed.), *Gypsy Politics and Traveller Identity* (Hatfield: University of Hertfordshire Press, 1997), pp.7–25.

Mohr, Dunja M. and Mayer Sylvia (eds), *Zeitschrift fur Anglistik und Americanistik – A Quarterly of Language, Literature and Culture – Special Issue: 9/11 as Catalyst: American and British Responses*, vol. LVIII (2010).

Moretti, Franco. *The Way of the World: The Bildungsroman in European Culture* (London: Verso, 2000 [1987]).

Morgan-Tamosounas, Rikki and Rings, Guido. 'Images of the Self and the Other in Postcolonial European Film', in Rikki Morgan-Tamosounas and Guido Rings (eds), *European Cinema: Inside Out* (Heidelberg: Heidelberg Universistatsverlag, 2003), pp.11–23.

Morley, Catherine. 'The End of Innocence – Tales of Terror After 9/11', *Review of International American Studies*, 3, 3 and 4, 1 (2008/2009), pp.82–93.

Nussbaum, Martha. *Love's Knowledge: Essays on Philosophy and Literature* (Oxford and New York: Oxford University Press, 1990).

———— 'The Literary Imagination in Public Life', in Jane Adamson, Richard Freadman and David Parker (eds), *Renegotiating Ethics in Literature, Philosophy and Theory* (Cambridge: Cambridge University Press, 1998), pp.222–46.

O'Connor, Frank. *The Lonely Voice: A Study of the Short Story* (Cleveland, OH: World Publishing, 1963).

O'Connor, Joseph. 'Introduction', in Dermot Bolger (ed.), *Ireland in Exile: Irish Writers Abroad* (Dublin: New Island Books, 1993), pp.11–18.

O'Faoláin, Seán. *The Short Story* (Cork: Mercier Press, 1948).

O'Toole, Fintan. *The Lie of the Land: Irish Identities* (Dublin: New Island Books, 1998).

Patten, Eve. 'Contemporary Irish Fiction', in John Wilson Foster (ed.), *The Cambridge Companion to the Irish Novel* (Cambridge: Cambridge University Press, 2006), pp.259–75.

Peach, Linden. *The Contemporary Irish Novel: Critical Readings* (Basingstoke: Palgrave, 2004).

Perez Firmat, Gustavo, *Literature and Liminality: Festive Readings in the Hispanic Tradition* (Durham, NC: Duke University Press, 1986).

Phelan, Peggy. *Unmarked: The Politics of Performance* (New York and London: Routledge, 1993).

Phillips, Adam. *On Flirtation* (London: Faber & Faber, 1994).

Pichova, Hana. *The Art of Memory in Exile: Vladimir Nabokov and Milan Kundera* (Carbondale and Edwardsville, IL: Southern Illinois University Press, 2002).

Rothberg, Michael. 'Seeing Terror, Feeling Art: Public and Private in Post-9/11 Literature', in Ann Keniston and Jeanne Follansbee Quinn (eds), *Literature after 9/11* (London: Routledge, 2008), pp.123–42.

Russell, Sharman Apt. *Hunger: An Unnatural History* (New York: Basic Books, 2005).

Said, Edward W. *Orientalism* (London: Vintage, 1978).

———— *Culture and Imperialism* (London: Vintage, 1993).

———— *Representations of the Intellectual: The 1993 Reith Lectures* (New York: Pantheon Books, 1994).

Simpson, David. *9/11: The Culture of Commemoration* (London and Chicago: University of Chicago Press, 2006).

Sontag, Susan. *At the Same Time: Essays and Speeches* (London: Hamish Hamilton, 2007).

Soja, Edward. 'The Spatiality of Social Life: Towards a Transformative Retheorisation', in Derek Gregory and John Urry (eds), *Social Relations and Spatial Structures* (Basingstoke: Macmillan, 1985), pp.90–127.

Soyinka, Wole. *The Climate of Fear* (London: Profile Books, 2004).

Stewart, Michael. *The Time of the Gypsies* (Boulder, CO: Westview Press, 1997).

Storey, Michael. *Representing the Troubles in Irish Short Fiction* (Washington: Catholic University of America Press, 2004).

Thomas, Helen. *The Body, Dance and Cultural Theory* (Basingstoke: Palgrave, 2003).

Turner, Edith L.B. *On the Edge of the Bush: Anthropology as Experience* (Tucson, AZ: University of Arizona Press, 1985).

Turner, Victor W. *Drama, Fields, and Metaphors: Symbolic Action in Human Society* (Ithaca, NY: Cornell University Press, 1974).

———— 'Dewey, Dilthey, and Drama: An Essay in the Anthropology of Experience', in Victor W. Turner and Edward M. Bruner (eds), *The Anthropology of Experience* (Chicago: University of Illinois Press, 1986), pp.33–44.

————— 'Liminality and Community', in Jeffrey C. Alexander and Steven Seidman (eds), *Culture and Society: Contemporary Debates* (Cambridge: Cambridge University Press, 1990), pp.147–54.

Vansina, Jan. 'Memory and Oral Tradition', in Joseph C. Miller (ed.), *The African Past Speaks: Essays on Oral Tradition and History* (Folkestone: Dawson, 1980), pp.262–79.

Vàzquez, José Santiago Fernàndez. 'Recharting the Geography of Genre: Ben Okri's *The Famished Road* as a Postcolonial Bildungsroman', *The Journal of Commonwealth Literature*, 37, 2 (2002), pp.85–106.

Vendler, Helen. *Seamus Heaney* (London: HarperCollins, 1998).

Versluys, Kristiaan. *Out of the Blue: September 11 and the Novel* (New York: Columbia University Press, 2009).

Vieira, Fatima. 'The Concept of Utopia', in Gregory Claeys (ed.), *The Cambridge Companion to Utopian Literature* (Cambridge: Cambridge University Press, 2010), pp.3–27.

Werbner, Pnina. 'Introduction: The Materiality of Diaspora – Between Aesthetic and "Real" Politics', *Diaspora*, 9, 1 (2000), pp.5–20.

Witkin, Robert W. *Adorno on Music* (London: Routledge, 1998).

ŽiŽek, Slavoj. *Welcome to the Desert of the Real* (London: Verso, 2002).

Index